COMPARATIVE
ISSUES IN
PARTY AND
ELECTION
FINANCE

*This is Volume 4 in a series of studies
commissioned as part of the research program
of the Royal Commission on Electoral Reform
and Party Financing*

COMPARATIVE ISSUES IN PARTY AND ELECTION FINANCE

~

F. Leslie Seidle
Editor

Volume 4 of the Research Studies

ROYAL COMMISSION ON ELECTORAL REFORM
AND PARTY FINANCING
AND CANADA COMMUNICATION GROUP –
PUBLISHING, SUPPLY AND SERVICES CANADA

DUNDURN PRESS
TORONTO AND OXFORD

© Minister of Supply and Services Canada, 1991
Printed and bound in Canada
ISBN 1-55002-100-1
ISSN 1188-2743
Catalogue No. Z1-1989/2-41-4E

Published by Dundurn Press Limited in cooperation with the Royal
Commission on Electoral Reform and Party Financing and Canada
Communication Group – Publishing, Supply and Services Canada.

Canadian Cataloguing in Publication Data

Main entry under title:
Comparative issues in party and election finance

(Research studies ; 4)
Issued also in French under title: Le Financement des partis et des élections.
ISBN 1-55002-100-1

    1. Campaign funds – Canada. 2. Elections – Canada. 3. Political parties –
Canada. I. Seidle, F. Leslie. II. Canada. Royal Commission on Electoral
Reform and Party Financing. III. Series: Research studies (Canada. Royal
Commission on Electoral Reform and Party Financing) ; 4.

JL195.C64 1991   324.271   C91-090516-9

Dundurn Press Limited   Dundurn Distribution
2181 Queen Street East   73 Lime Walk
Suite 301   Headington
Toronto, Canada   Oxford, England
M4E 1E5   OX3 7AD

CONTENTS

TABLES

FOREWORD

The ROYAL COMMISSION on Electoral Reform and Party Financing was established in November 1989. Our mandate was to inquire into and report on the appropriate principles and process that should govern the election of members of the House of Commons and the financing of political parties and candidates' campaigns. To conduct such a comprehensive examination of Canada's electoral system, we held extensive public consultations and developed a research program designed to ensure that our recommendations would be guided by an independent foundation of empirical inquiry and analysis.

The Commission's in-depth review of the electoral system was the first of its kind in Canada's history of electoral democracy. It was dictated largely by the major constitutional, social and technological changes of the past several decades, which have transformed Canadian society, and their concomitant influence on Canadians' expectations of the political process itself. In particular, the adoption in 1982 of the *Canadian Charter of Rights and Freedoms* has heightened Canadians' awareness of their democratic and political rights and of the way they are served by the electoral system.

The importance of electoral reform cannot be overemphasized. As the Commission's work proceeded, Canadians became increasingly preoccupied with constitutional issues that have the potential to change the nature of Confederation. No matter what their beliefs or political allegiances in this continuing debate, Canadians agree that constitutional change must be achieved in the context of fair and democratic processes. We cannot complacently assume that our current electoral process will always meet this standard or that it leaves no room for improvement. Parliament and the national government must be seen as legitimate; electoral reform can both enhance the stature of national political institutions and reinforce their ability to define the future of our country in ways that command Canadians' respect and confidence and promote the national interest.

In carrying out our mandate, we remained mindful of the importance of protecting our democratic heritage, while at the same time balancing it against the emerging values that are injecting a new dynamic into the electoral system. If our system is to reflect the realities of Canadian political life, then reform requires more than mere tinkering with electoral laws and practices.

Our broad mandate challenged us to explore a full range of options. We commissioned more than 100 research studies, to be published in a 23-volume collection. In the belief that our electoral laws must measure up to the very best contemporary practice, we examined election-related laws and processes in all of our provinces and territories and studied comparable legislation and processes in established democracies around the world. This unprecedented array of empirical study and expert opinion made a vital contribution to our deliberations. We made every effort to ensure that the research was both intellectually rigorous and of practical value. All studies were subjected to peer review, and many of the authors discussed their preliminary findings with members of the political and academic communities at national symposiums on major aspects of the electoral system.

The Commission placed the research program under the able and inspired direction of Dr. Peter Aucoin, Professor of Political Science and Public Administration at Dalhousie University. We are confident that the efforts of Dr. Aucoin, together with those of the research coordinators and scholars whose work appears in this and other volumes, will continue to be of value to historians, political scientists, parliamentarians and policy makers, as well as to thoughtful Canadians and the international community.

Along with the other Commissioners, I extend my sincere gratitude to the entire Commission staff for their dedication and commitment. I also wish to thank the many people who participated in our symposiums for their valuable contributions, as well as the members of the research and practitioners' advisory groups whose counsel significantly aided our undertaking.

Pierre Lortie
Chairman

INTRODUCTION

THE ROYAL COMMISSION's research program constituted a comprehensive and detailed examination of the Canadian electoral process. The scope of the research, undertaken to assist Commissioners in their deliberations, was dictated by the broad mandate given to the Commission.

The objective of the research program was to provide Commissioners with a full account of the factors that have shaped our electoral democracy. This dictated, first and foremost, a focus on federal electoral law, but our inquiries also extended to the Canadian constitution, including the institutions of parliamentary government, the practices of political parties, the mass media and nonpartisan political organizations, as well as the decision-making role of the courts with respect to the constitutional rights of citizens. Throughout, our research sought to introduce a historical perspective in order to place the contemporary experience within the Canadian political tradition.

We recognized that neither our consideration of the factors shaping Canadian electoral democracy nor our assessment of reform proposals would be as complete as necessary if we failed to examine the experiences of Canadian provinces and territories and of other democracies. Our research program thus emphasized comparative dimensions in relation to the major subjects of inquiry.

Our research program involved, in addition to the work of the Commission's research coordinators, analysts and support staff, over 200 specialists from 28 universities in Canada, from the private sector and, in a number of cases, from abroad. Specialists in political science constituted the majority of our researchers, but specialists in law, economics, management, computer sciences, ethics, sociology and communications, among other disciplines, were also involved.

In addition to the preparation of research studies for the Commission, our research program included a series of research seminars, symposiums and workshops. These meetings brought together the Commissioners, researchers, representatives from the political parties, media personnel and others with practical experience in political parties, electoral politics and public affairs. These meetings provided not only a forum for discussion of the various subjects of the Commission's mandate, but also an opportunity for our research to be assessed by those with an intimate knowledge of the world of political practice.

These public reviews of our research were complemented by internal and external assessments of each research report by persons qualified in the area; such assessments were completed prior to our decision to publish any study in the series of research volumes.

The Research Branch of the Commission was divided into several areas, with the individual research projects in each area assigned to the research coordinators as follows:

F. Leslie Seidle	Political Party and Election Finance
Herman Bakvis	Political Parties
Kathy Megyery	Women, Ethno-Cultural Groups and Youth
David Small	Redistribution; Electoral Boundaries; Voter Registration
Janet Hiebert	Party Ethics
Michael Cassidy	Democratic Rights; Election Administration
Robert A. Milen	Aboriginal Electoral Participation and Representation
Frederick J. Fletcher	Mass Media and Broadcasting in Elections
David Mac Donald (Assistant Research Coordinator)	Direct Democracy

These coordinators identified appropriate specialists to undertake research, managed the projects and prepared them for publication. They also organized the seminars, symposiums and workshops in their research areas and were responsible for preparing presentations and briefings to help the Commission in its deliberations and decision making. Finally, they participated in drafting the Final Report of the Commission.

On behalf of the Commission, I welcome the opportunity to thank the following for their generous assistance in producing these research studies – a project that required the talents of many individuals.

In performing their duties, the research coordinators made a notable contribution to the work of the Commission. Despite the pressures of tight deadlines, they worked with unfailing good humour and the utmost congeniality. I thank all of them for their consistent support and cooperation.

In particular, I wish to express my gratitude to Leslie Seidle, senior research coordinator, who supervised our research analysts and support staff in Ottawa. His diligence, commitment and professionalism not only set high standards, but also proved contagious. I am grateful to Kathy Megyery, who performed a similar function in Montreal with equal aplomb and skill. Her enthusiasm and dedication inspired us all.

On behalf of the research coordinators and myself, I wish to thank our research analysts: Daniel Arsenault, Eric Bertram, Cécile Boucher, Peter Constantinou, Yves Denoncourt, David Docherty, Luc Dumont, Jane Dunlop, Scott Evans, Véronique Garneau, Keith Heintzman, Paul Holmes, Hugh Mellon, Cheryl D. Mitchell, Donald Padget, Alain Pelletier, Dominique Tremblay and Lisa Young. The Research Branch was strengthened by their ability to carry out research in a wide variety of areas, their intellectual curiosity and their team spirit.

The work of the research coordinators and analysts was greatly facilitated by the professional skills and invaluable cooperation of Research Branch staff members: Paulette LeBlanc, who, as administrative assistant, managed the flow of research projects; Hélène Leroux, secretary to the research coordinators, who produced briefing material for the Commissioners and who, with Lori Nazar, assumed responsibility for monitoring the progress of research projects in the latter stages of our work; Kathleen McBride and her assistant Natalie Brose, who created and maintained the database of briefs and hearings transcripts; and Richard Herold and his assistant Susan Dancause, who were responsible for our research library. Jacinthe Séguin and Cathy Tucker also deserve thanks – in addition to their duties as receptionists, they assisted in a variety of ways to help us meet deadlines.

We were extremely fortunate to obtain the research services of first-class specialists from the academic and private sectors. Their contributions are found in this and the other 22 published research volumes. We thank them for the quality of their work and for their willingness to contribute and to meet our tight deadlines.

Our research program also benefited from the counsel of Jean-Marc Hamel, Special Adviser to the Chairman of the Commission and former

Chief Electoral Officer of Canada, whose knowledge and experience proved invaluable.

In addition, numerous specialists assessed our research studies. Their assessments not only improved the quality of our published studies, but also provided us with much-needed advice on many issues. In particular, we wish to single out professors Donald Blake, Janine Brodie, Alan Cairns, Kenneth Carty, John Courtney, Peter Desbarats, Jane Jenson, Richard Johnston, Vincent Lemieux, Terry Morley and Joseph Wearing, as well as Ms. Beth Symes.

Producing such a large number of studies in less than a year requires a mastery of the skills and logistics of publishing. We were fortunate to be able to count on the Commission's Director of Communications, Richard Rochefort, and Assistant Director, Hélène Papineau. They were ably supported by the Communications staff: Patricia Burden, Louise Dagenais, Caroline Field, Claudine Labelle, France Langlois, Lorraine Maheux, Ruth McVeigh, Chantal Morissette, Sylvie Patry, Jacques Poitras and Claudette Rouleau-O'Toole.

To bring the project to fruition, the Commission also called on specialized contractors. We are deeply grateful for the services of Ann McCoomb (references and fact checking); Marthe Lemery, Pierre Chagnon and the staff of Communications Com'ça (French quality control); Norman Bloom, Pamela Riseborough and associates of B&B Editorial Consulting (English adaptation and quality control); and Mado Reid (French production). Al Albania and his staff at Acart Graphics designed the studies and produced some 2 400 tables and figures.

The Commission's research reports constitute Canada's largest publishing project of 1991. Successful completion of the project required close cooperation between the public and private sectors. In the public sector, we especially acknowledge the excellent service of the Privy Council unit of the Translation Bureau, Department of the Secretary of State of Canada, under the direction of Michel Parent, and our contacts Ruth Steele and Terry Denovan of the Canada Communication Group, Department of Supply and Services.

The Commission's co-publisher for the research studies was Dundurn Press of Toronto, whose exceptional service is gratefully acknowledged. Wilson & Lafleur of Montreal, working with the Centre de Documentation Juridique du Québec, did equally admirable work in preparing the French version of the studies.

Teams of editors, copy editors and proofreaders worked diligently under stringent deadlines with the Commission and the publishers to prepare some 20 000 pages of manuscript for design, typesetting and printing. The work of these individuals, whose names are listed elsewhere in this volume, was greatly appreciated.

Our acknowledgements extend to the contributions of the Commission's Executive Director, Guy Goulard, and the administration and executive support teams: Maurice Lacasse, Denis Lafrance and Steve Tremblay (finance); Thérèse Lacasse and Mary Guy-Shea (personnel); Cécile Desforges (assistant to the Executive Director); Marie Dionne (administration); Anna Bevilacqua (records); and support staff members Michelle Bélanger, Roch Langlois, Michel Lauzon, Jean Mathieu, David McKay and Pierrette McMurtie, as well as Denise Miquelon and Christiane Séguin of the Montreal office.

A special debt of gratitude is owed to Marlène Girard, assistant to the Chairman. Her ability to supervise the logistics of the Commission's work amid the tight schedules of the Chairman and Commissioners contributed greatly to the completion of our task.

I also wish to express my deep gratitude to my own secretary, Liette Simard. Her superb administrative skills and great patience brought much-appreciated order to my penchant for the chaotic workstyle of academe. She also assumed responsibility for the administrative coordination of revisions to the final drafts of volumes 1 and 2 of the Commission's Final Report. I owe much to her efforts and assistance.

Finally, on behalf of the research coordinators and myself, I wish to thank the Chairman, Pierre Lortie, the members of the Commission, Pierre Fortier, Robert Gabor, William Knight and Lucie Pépin, and former members Elwood Cowley and Senator Donald Oliver. We are honoured to have worked with such an eminent and thoughtful group of Canadians, and we have benefited immensely from their knowledge and experience. In particular, we wish to acknowledge the creativity, intellectual rigour and energy our Chairman brought to our task. His unparalleled capacity to challenge, to bring out the best in us, was indeed inspiring.

Peter Aucoin
Director of Research

PREFACE

TWENTY-FIVE YEARS ago, following a review of the costs of election campaigns, the pattern of party finance and related issues, the Committee on Election Expenses (Barbeau Committee) issued its report. The Committee's conclusions provided the basis for the 1974 *Election Expenses Act*, which led to what was then considered Canada's most comprehensive regulatory framework for party and election finance. The main elements of the 1974 reforms were: limits on the election expenses of registered political parties and candidates; disclosure of parties' and candidates' revenue and spending; and public funding through post-election reimbursements to parties and candidates, as well as an income tax credit for contributions to either.

While amendments in 1977 and 1983 did not alter the main lines of the federal regulatory framework, developments during the past 15 years or so have led to calls for an assessment of its operation and effects. Some have asked whether the objectives on which the 1974 legislation was based are still being met – or, indeed, remain valid. A number of factors account for this, among them changes in party and campaign management techniques, the implications of the adoption of the *Canadian Charter of Rights and Freedoms* in 1982, the role of interest groups in elections and developments in the regulation of political finance at the provincial level.

The Royal Commission on Electoral Reform and Party Financing was mandated to consider, among other issues, "the appropriate principles and process that should govern ... the financing of political parties and of candidates' campaigns, including ... the means by which political parties should be funded, the provision of funds to political parties from any source, the limits on such funding and the uses to which such funds ought, or ought not, to be put." To assist it in carrying out these aspects of its mandate, an extensive series of research studies on party and election finance was undertaken by members of the academic profession, consultants and research analysts employed by the Commission. The principal studies are published in this volume and the four others in this research area.

The research projects in the party and election finance area were intended to assist the Commission in taking decisions on a number of issues at the heart of its mandate. In this regard, the studies in these five volumes are relevant to three of the six objectives of electoral reform referred to in Volume 1, chapter 1 of the Final Report: promoting fairness in the electoral process; strengthening the parties as primary political organizations; and enhancing public confidence in the integrity of the electoral process. These studies canvass issues relevant to these objectives, draw on comparative experience (both within Canada and elsewhere) and discuss possible reforms. In so doing, they address fundamental questions such as how to circumscribe the influence of money in politics; how to encourage greater participation in the financing of parties and candidates and in the electoral process, including the nomination stage; how to ensure a high degree of transparency in relation to political finance; and whether and in what ways public funding should be part of the system.

In considering possible reforms, the Commission looked at developments in this area at the provincial level (see Volume 3 of the Research Studies) and in other democracies. This volume includes four research studies on political finance and its regulation in the United States and Western Europe. Additional comparative work was carried out by Commission analysts; four research notes (on Great Britain, France, the Federal Republic of Germany and Australia) are to be published as part of the Commission's Working Papers.

The first study in this volume, "The Regulation of Election Finance in the United States and Proposals for Reform" by Herbert Alexander, traces the evolution of the American federal regulatory framework since the early 1970s. He describes the framework as a hybrid: the highly regulated presidential campaign structure (with spending limits and public funding) contrasts with the congressional regimen (where, apart from disclosure and contribution limits, in Professor Alexander's words, "the political equivalent of the free market reigns"). The study surveys major issues in debate in the United States and recent legislative proposals. There is also a discussion of the relatively comprehensive regulatory approach adopted by New Jersey, Minnesota and New York City.

Robert Mutch, in his study "The Evolution of Campaign Finance Regulation in the United States and Canada," charts the development of federal legislation in the two countries, starting early this century. He concludes that scandal has been the most important factor in prompting reform in this area and discusses how scandals in the United States have influenced Canadian lawmakers. The concluding section of Dr. Mutch's study analyses the impact of judicial review in the two countries, particularly the *Buckley* and *National Citizens' Coalition* decisions.

In "Innovation and Equity: The Impact of Public Funding," Jane Jenson draws on Western European experience as a basis for her critique of public funding for Canadian federal parties and candidates. In her view, the Canadian system discourages pluralism and access because of the procedures for party registration and the thresholds for access to public funding; rewards fund-raising and spending more than the ability to gain votes; and is unduly focused on "the electoral moment." She proposes several options intended to foster greater fairness and strengthen political parties as "a crucial bridge between the citizen and the state."

Michael Pinto-Duschinsky's study, "The Party Foundations and Political Finance in Germany," describes the origins and activities of the *Stiftungen*, each of which is legally independent but linked in practice with one of the political parties represented in the Bundestag. As a major element of public funding of the political process, government funding of the foundations currently accounts for some 97 percent of their income. The study indicates that the foundations have been relatively successful in promoting participation and party membership, fostering effective party research and organization, and securing fairness. At the same time, as Dr. Pinto-Duschinsky notes, the role of the foundations within the broader system of German political finance is sometimes criticized.

The Commission owes a considerable debt of gratitude to the researchers who agreed to undertake the studies in this area. Through their dedication and professionalism, their responsiveness to the Commission's priorities and their cooperation in meeting deadlines, all those whose work appears in these volumes have contributed greatly to the research program. A number of the researchers presented their findings at Commission seminars and/or meetings. We valued their participation on these occasions, as well as their willingness to respond to a range of questions and requests for information, particularly during the period when the Commission's Final Report was being prepared. I would also like to express my personal gratitude to Peter Aucoin, whose suggestions and counsel helped in so many ways as these research studies were planned, discussed and carried forward for publication.

The Commission's publication program reflects the central role research played in the work of the Royal Commission on Electoral Reform and Party Financing. It is hoped these studies will illuminate debate on the Commission's recommendations and, in so doing, help chart the way to a modern and responsive regulatory framework for party and election finance that will bolster electoral democracy in Canada.

F. Leslie Seidle
Senior Research Coordinator

COMPARATIVE
ISSUES IN
PARTY AND
ELECTION
FINANCE

1

THE REGULATION OF ELECTION FINANCE IN THE UNITED STATES AND PROPOSALS FOR REFORM

Herbert E. Alexander

THROUGHOUT THE PAST generation, the integrity of the electoral process has been an issue in both the United States and Canada. The result has been simultaneous efforts to regulate the financing of the electoral systems of the two countries.

In both nations, efforts to reform have been closely connected with scandals but also associated with a fear that the increasingly television-oriented nature of campaigns was pricing candidates or parties out of the political arena. These issues, in turn, led directly to major campaign finance legislation in the United States and Canada during the 1970s: The U.S. Congress enacted no fewer than five significant campaign laws during that decade, while the Canadian Parliament in 1974 approved the sweeping *Election Expenses Act*.

And today, both the U.S. and Canadian legislatures are contemplating major overhauls of their respective campaign laws amid the realization that existing statutes have produced some unforeseen and unintended consequences in their respective electoral systems.

Despite such parallels, however, it must be emphasized that the U.S. and Canadian experiences with campaign reform are not interchangeable. Foremost among the reasons is that the United States lacks a Canadian-style, party-oriented type of politics. In fact, the U.S. reforms of the 1970s tended to weaken the power of the political parties – so much so that some critics blame those laws for the brand of interest-group politics now omnipresent at both the federal and state levels.

As in Great Britain, Canada's parliamentary system features a highly centralized party structure, and the important functions of fiscal coordination and distribution of money during elections rest largely with party committees. U.S. politics, on the other hand, centres on candidates, not parties. Money is most often contributed to candidates and their personal campaign committees, and political parties must compete with candidates for the available dollars. Campaign strategies and tactics, particularly since the advent of radio and television, tend to project a candidate's personality; in many instances, party identification is downplayed or even totally ignored.

Any preface to a study of the federal political finance system in the United States also must underscore the fact that the Congress has been merely one of several players in determining how the system works. While Congress has drafted the laws and presidents have signed them, their actual implementation has been shaped by the interpretations of regulatory agencies and the courts, to say nothing of savvy election lawyers and political operatives constantly looking for innovative ways to avoid the law or to interpret it favourably.

For example, while Congress in 1974 loosened restrictions on the formation of political action committees, or PACs, it was an opinion handed down by the Federal Election Commission (FEC) in 1975 that prompted a dramatic increase in the number of corporate PACs. And the growth of these controversial groups was further accelerated in 1976, when the U.S. Supreme Court ruled that mandatory ceilings on spending in congressional campaigns violated the First Amendment to the U.S. Constitution.[1] The result is that, today, reform efforts are being fueled in large part by concern over the increasing dependence on PACs to fund congressional campaigns.

The constant testing of the legal parameters of U.S. campaign finance law has produced a regulatory system that can best be described as a hybrid. On one hand, there is the presidential campaign structure, a highly regulated system in which candidates receive significant amounts of public funding in return for agreeing voluntarily to expenditure ceilings and limits on the use of their personal wealth. On the other hand, there is the congressional regimen, where – like the presidential system – candidates must disclose receipts and expenditures and abide by limits on contributions from individuals, PACs and political parties. Other than that, however, the political equivalent of the free market reigns in congressional races as a result of the 1976 Supreme Court ruling coupled with the unwillingness of the Congress to enact public financing and spending limits for campaigns for the Senate and the House.

The difference in the regulatory structures of presidential and congressional campaigns naturally has produced substantial variation in the issues confronting each system. It also has prompted reformers and their legislative allies to push to narrow those differences – by seeking to enact public financing and to impose constitutionally acceptable restrictions on congressional campaigns. The problems bedevilling the operation of U.S. campaign finance laws and the proposals to resolve them are a central focus of this study.

First, however, a short history is necessary to show how the current situation evolved.

HISTORY

The decade of the 1970s saw the most sweeping changes in federal election statutes since the Progressive Era more than 60 years earlier. As mentioned, five major campaign finance laws were passed by Congress before the decade was out: the *Federal Election Campaign Act of 1971* and the *FECA Amendments of 1974, 1976* and *1979* as well as the *Revenue Act of 1971*. While this surge of activity is often associated with the Watergate scandal of the early 1970s, it should be noted that two of these laws – the basic *Federal Election Campaign Act* and the *Revenue Act* – were enacted by Congress almost six months prior to the genesis of that scandal in mid-1972.

Prologue: 1925–71

The *Federal Election Campaign Act* replaced a statute that had been on the books more than 45 years: the *Federal Corrupt Practices Act of 1925*. That law, passed in response to the "Teapot Dome" scandal of the early 1920s, was, in turn, a codification of several campaign reform laws enacted in the 1907–11 period at the height of the Progressive Era.

Whatever the intentions of its framers, the *Federal Corrupt Practices Act* was notable mainly for its ineffectiveness during the years following its enactment. The law contained limits on spending in congressional races that were so unrealistically low that they were simply ignored by federal regulators as well as by candidates. The statute also required disclosure of campaign spending by candidates for Congress (presidential aspirants were not covered). However, it was so imprecisely worded that many candidates chose to interpret it as requiring disclosure of only their personal expenditures and thereby reported only a fraction of their actual campaign costs.

In 1940, Congress supplemented the *Federal Corrupt Practices Act* with a provision in the so-called Hatch Act limiting to $5 000 per year contributions by individuals to a federal candidate or campaign committee. This had little effect on restraining large contributors: a candidate would simply set up numerous campaign committees, and a well-endowed contributor could give $5 000 to each.

The pressure for changing this loophole-ridden system began building after the Second World War and received a major boost when John F. Kennedy appointed the President's Commission on Campaign Costs in late 1961 (President's Commission 1962). In May 1966, Kennedy's successor, Lyndon B. Johnson, called upon Congress to pass comprehensive campaign finance reform – partly, he said, to deflect congressional criticism that Democratic Party donors were benefiting from lucrative federal contracts. "Despite the soaring expense of political campaigns, we have done nothing to insure that able men of modest means can undertake elective service unencumbered by debts of loyalty to wealthy supporters. We have laws dealing with campaign financing. But they have failed ... They are more loophole than law. They invite evasion and circumvention. They must be revised."[2]

But it was five more years before campaign finance reform was enacted into law. While reform legislation – belatedly backed by Johnson – was approved by Congress in 1966, it was suspended by the Senate a year later amid disagreements over how or whether it should be implemented.

Federal Election Campaign Act of 1971
Throughout both Canadian and U.S. history, campaign reform laws almost always have owed their enactment to scandal. "Response to scandal has been the usual impetus for electoral reform in Canada, whether it was the Pacific Scandal, the Winnipeg General Strike, or the FLQ crisis," Patrick Boyer, a member of the Canadian Parliament, recently remarked (Canadian Study of Parliament Group 1990, 2). Likewise, the U.S. reform statutes adopted during the early part of the 20th century were a direct response to the excesses of the Gilded Age and the Teapot Dome affair; the Federal Election Campaign Act amendments of the mid-1970s were Watergate induced.

One of the few exceptions to this historical pattern was the passage of the original Federal Election Campaign Act of 1971, commonly known as FECA. Instead of scandal, the legislative impetus was a concern that rapidly rising campaign costs were pricing many candidates out of the market. According to figures compiled by the Federal Communications Commission, the amount spent on television and radio by U.S. political candidates had increased 150 percent between 1956 and 1964. In 1970, the year before the passage of FECA, a study by the National Committee for an Effective Congress found that in the seven largest states where Senate elections were held, 11 of 15 candidates were millionaires.[3]

Ironically, FECA was destined to have little or no effect in controlling campaign costs. A provision was included that limited candidates for federal office to 10 cents per voter on "communications media." This was replaced by a more comprehensive series of limits in 1974, which, in turn, were declared unconstitutional by the U.S. Supreme Court in 1976 (see section below on the *Buckley v. Valeo* decision).

However, other provisions of the FECA have, over the past two decades, shed a great deal of light on the ways in which American campaigns are conducted. The Act established a framework for comprehensive campaign disclosure for presidential and congressional candidates, and set an example that state legislatures across the country were to look to as a model. Today, all 50 states require some form of campaign finance disclosure for statewide and state legislative candidates – and often for local campaigns as well.

Under the provisions of FECA, political committees with $1 000 or more in receipts or expenditures are required to file regular reports. This monetary test closed the long-standing loophole in the *Federal Corrupt Practices Act* that had required reporting only by those committees operating in two or more states; this had long allowed committees operating in just one state to avoid disclosing their receipts and expenditures.

FECA also required that expenditures and donations of more than $100 by and to federal candidates and political committees be itemized and listed for disclosure, including the contributor's name, address, occupation, place of business and the date and amount of the contribution. (The 1979 FECA amendments raised the threshold for itemization to in excess of $200.) And, in another contrast to the *Federal Corrupt Practices Act*, the new law's disclosure requirements covered primaries as well as general elections.

Finally, FECA firmly established the principle of both pre- and post-election disclosure in federal campaign finance. The current FECA filing schedule (the 1979 FECA amendments made some relatively minor adjustments to the 1971 law) calls for congressional candidates to file quarterly reports during an election year and semi-annual reports in the "off years."

In addition, office seekers must file reports 12 days before primary and general elections, and thereafter report last-minute contributions of $1 000 or more in writing within 48 hours. Like congressional hopefuls, presidential aspirants file semi-annually except for a year in which the presidency is at stake; they then must file monthly if they have raised more than $100 000. (This, of course, differs markedly from the Canadian parliamentary system, in which the uncertain scheduling of elections and the short duration of campaigns provide obstacles to disclosure once the election has been called.)

To collect and monitor the required financial information, the Senate-passed version of the 1971 law proposed the creation of an independent commission to administer and enforce the law. But this proposal was killed by the House of Representatives, and it would be another three years before Congress would create such an independent agency.

The episode illustrates the dichotomy between the Senate and the House on campaign finance reform that persists to this day. It is a split that transcends partisan affiliations. Many House members represent relatively homogeneous districts that provide them with "safe seats"; they are consequently leery of anything that disturbs the electoral status quo. On the other hand, members of the Senate – many of whom represent large, diverse states – are more accustomed to competitive elections and generally are less fearful of enhancing opportunities for political challengers.

President Richard M. Nixon signed FECA on 7 February 1972, and it took effect on 7 April 1972. Ironically, the law was to play a key role in the Watergate affair that led to Nixon's resignation two and a half years later.

Revenue Act of 1971

President Nixon also signed the *Revenue Act of 1971* after exacting a concession from Congress that public financing of presidential elections would be postponed until after the 1972 election. This saved Nixon, then seeking his second term, from having to compete under a system of public financing.

The *Revenue Act of 1971* had its origins in the 1966 *Long Act* (named for Sen. Russell B. Long, D–Louisiana). The Senate thwarted the implementation of that Act in 1967. The 1971 law reflected the *Long Act* in that it created a Presidential Election Campaign Fund supplied by a $1 "checkoff" on federal income tax returns. But the *Revenue Act* revised Long's original proposal so that the funding would go directly to presidential candidates rather than being funnelled through political parties. The latter proposal had engendered criticism from several legislators who feared it would place excessive power in the hands of party chairpersons.[4]

The income tax checkoff has been a fixture on federal income tax returns since 1972. Anyone with at least $1 in income tax liability is permitted to designate that amount ($2 on joint returns) to the

Presidential Election Campaign Fund. (See "Presidential Campaigns" section of "Issues for the 1980s" for a discussion of declining taxpayer participation in the checkoff.)

The *Revenue Act of 1971* also provided for a tax credit and tax deduction to encourage political contributions. However, these incentives turned out to be short lived. The deduction was raised in 1974 from $50 to $100 ($200 on a joint return) but was then repealed by the *Revenue Act of 1978*. Meanwhile, the tax credit for one-half the amount of contributions up to a limit of $12.50 was raised to $25 ($50 on a joint return) in 1974 and then to $50 ($100 on a joint return) in 1978 to counterbalance the repeal of the deduction. But the credit was repealed when Congress overhauled the federal income tax system in 1986. There have since been numerous calls to reinstate the credit as a means of encouraging small donations from individual contributors, much as the Canadian system seeks to accomplish this by providing tax deductions for donations of less than $500 Canadian.

FECA Amendments of 1974

The Watergate scandal brought passage of the *Federal Election Campaign Act Amendments of 1974*, which represented the most sweeping change imposed on the interaction between money and politics since the creation of the American Republic almost 200 years earlier. The 1974 law continues to have a profound impact on the ways in which today's federal election campaigns are conducted.

In July 1973, the Senate passed a bill that put a ceiling on campaign spending, limited individual contributions and created an independent election commission. But, once again, the measure stalled in the House.

In the spring of 1974, after shutting off a filibuster by southern Democrats and conservative Republicans, the Senate passed a second reform bill that combined its 1973 measure with a call for public funding of congressional as well as presidential elections. Finally, just hours before Nixon announced his resignation from the presidency on 8 August 1974, the House overwhelmingly passed campaign reform legislation. But it differed markedly from the Senate bill in that it provided public financing only for presidential elections. After an often bitter standoff between House and Senate negotiators that lasted for weeks, the Senate conceded, and the final bill, signed by President Gerald R. Ford on 15 October 1974, contained public funding only for presidential elections.

However, the FECA *Amendments of 1974* greatly expanded upon the *Revenue Act of 1971*, which had provided grants to presidential candidates for the general election only. Included were public matching funds for small private donations raised during the prenomination period, flat grants to political parties for their national nominating conventions, and large grants to major party presidential nominees to provide full public financing of general election campaigns. This structure also contained spending limits on presidential candidates in both the pre- and post-nomination periods. Coincidentally, the Canadian system of spending ceilings and public funding for political parties was enacted the same year. (See "Presidential Campaigns" in the next section for a description of the U.S. public funding structure.)

The presidential financing system, which has operated in the last four presidential elections beginning in 1976, is one of three major provisions of the FECA *Amendments of 1974* still in force today. An independent regulatory agency, the Federal Election Commission (FEC), was formed to collect disclosure reports, administer public financing and enforce election statutes. But from the outset, some members of Congress clearly did not want the commission to exercise much independence when it came to regulating congressional elections. The FEC was structured originally so that four of its six members were appointees of the House and Senate. When this scheme was rejected by the Supreme Court (see the following section on *Buckley v. Valeo*), Congress responded by further circumscribing the FEC's power.

The other major part of the 1974 law still in effect sharply curtailed the role of that long-time fixture of American politics – the large contributor. In contrast to the millions of dollars contributed by men such as insurance magnate Clement Stone and the hundreds of thousands by General Motors heir Stewart Mott during the 1972 campaign, individuals were barred from giving a presidential or congressional candidate more than $1 000 per election. They also were not permitted to exceed an annual aggregate ceiling of $25 000 for contributions to all federal candidates and committees (see table 1.1).

If the FECA *Amendments of 1974* shut off one major source of campaign cash, they spurred the growth of another: the political action committee, or PAC. In that respect, the 1974 law provides an example of campaign reform's law of unforeseen consequences: Given the pluralistic and dynamic nature of the U.S. political system, efforts to solve one set of problems plaguing the system almost invariably give rise to another set of problems. As noted earlier, PACs have served to increase the role of special interests in the political process and have become as controversial as the individual "fat cats" of yesteryear; however, the institutionalization of contributions raised through PAC solicitation systems and PAC special interest pleading linked to lobbying causes more concern than did the individualistic large contributor of earlier years.

Table 1.1
Contribution limits
(in dollars)

Contributions from:	To candidate or his/her authorized committee	To national party committee[a] per calendar year	To any other committee per calendar year	Total contributions per calendar year[b]
Individual	1 000 per election[c]	20 000	5 000	25 000
Multicandidate committee[d]	5 000 per election	15 000	5 000	no limit
Party committee	1 000 or 5 000[e] per election	no limit	5 000	no limit
Republican or Democratic Senatorial Campaign committee,[f] or the national party committee, or a combination of both	17 500 to Senate candidate per calendar year in which candidate seeks election	N/A	N/A	N/A
Any other committee or group[g]	1 000 per election	20 000	5 000	no limit

Source: Federal Election Commission.

[a]For purposes of this limit, each of the following is considered a national party committee: a party's national committee, the Senate Campaign committees and the National Congressional committees, provided they are not authorized by any candidate.

[b]Calendar year extends from January 1 through December 31. Individual contributions made or earmarked to influence a specific election of a clearly identified candidate are counted as if made during the year in which the election is held.

[c]Each of the following elections is considered a separate election: primary election, general election, run-off election, special election and party caucus or convention which has authority to select the nominee.

[d]A multicandidate committee is any committee with more than 50 contributors which has been registered for at least six months and, with the exception of state party committees, has made contributions to five or more federal candidates.

[e]Limit depends on whether or not party committee is a multicandidate committee.

[f]Republican and Democratic Senatorial Campaign committees are subject to all other limits applicable to a multicandidate committee.

[g]Group includes an organization, partnership or group of persons.

N/A = not applicable.

PACs were legal prior to the passage of the 1974 law. But, traditionally, they were utilized primarily by labour unions, which collected voluntary political contributions from members and funnelled them to favoured candidates. While the FECA of 1971 legitimized PACs, the blossoming of the corporate PAC can be traced to the 1974 FECA amendments, in which Congress repealed the provision of the 1939–40 *Hatch Act* barring corporations and unions that held federal contracts from forming PACs.

Ironically, it was organized labour that took the lead in lobbying for the repeal: unions with government contracts to train workers were concerned that they would have to abolish their PACs unless the law was changed. But the far more significant impact was to allow many large corporations with defence contracts to establish PACs. Many of the largest companies in the United States have since done so.

At the time of the *FECA Amendments of 1974*, the PAC issue received far less attention than the series of mandatory spending limits placed on congressional races. These limits never took effect. They were to be wiped out little more than a year later by a landmark Supreme Court ruling.

Buckley v. Valeo: Campaign Reform and the Constitution

In January 1975, a few days after the 1974 law became effective, a suit was brought contending that the new law violated several rights guaranteed by the First Amendment to the U.S. Constitution.[5] On 30 January 1976, a little more than a year after the case was filed, the Supreme Court reversed a U.S. Court of Appeals ruling and found several major sections of the *FECA Amendments of 1974* to be unconstitutional (*Buckley v. Valeo* 1976). The decision was to have a significant impact on the regulation not only of federal elections but also of state and local elections.

In *Buckley v. Valeo*, the court faced a difficult judicial task: to balance the First Amendment rights of free speech and free association against the clear power of the legislature to enact laws to protect the integrity of the electoral system. The central question was posed by Justice Potter Stewart during oral arguments: Is money speech and speech money? Or, stated differently, is an expenditure for speech the same thing as speech itself, given the expenditures necessary to buy broadcast time or newspaper space to reach large audiences?

A majority of the court answered the question in the affirmative, ruling expenditure limits to be a "substantial" restraint on free speech that could prevent a candidate from making "significant use of the most effective modes of communication." Consequently, the Supreme Court rejected as unconstitutional the mandatory spending limits placed on presidential and congressional campaigns by the 1974 law. Also thrown out were restrictions on the amount a candidate could spend using his or her personal resources. (The 1971 FECA law had limited presidential and vice-presidential candidates to contributing $50 000 of their own money or that of their immediate family; for Senate and House candidates, the thresholds were $35 000 and $25 000, respectively.)

However, the court made a significant exception to this finding: If a candidate voluntarily accepted public financing, the government could require him or her to abide by campaign expenditure limits and other restrictions as a condition of that acceptance. The impact of this was to preserve the presidential financing structure outlined in the 1974 FECA amendments; during the last four presidential elections, all but one of the major candidates have taken public funding and abided by the prescribed limits. But the *Buckley* decision invalidated the spending ceilings in congressional races because the 1974 law did not provide public financing as a means of enticing legislative candidates to comply voluntarily with the limits.

While eliminating mandatory spending limits, the justices ruled the other major underpinning of the 1974 FECA amendments – contribution limits – to be constitutional. The court asserted that these represented only a marginal restriction on a contributor's First Amendment rights because "the quantity of communication by the contributor does not increase perceptibly with the size of his contribution." In this instance, the court said that First Amendment considerations were outweighed by the possible influence of large contributors on a candidate's positions, which, in turn, could lead to real or perceived corruption once the candidate took office.

Finally, the Supreme Court, while upholding the concept of a bipartisan regulatory commission to administer campaign finance laws, ruled the nomination procedure of the new Federal Election Commission to be unconstitutional. The court said that the requirement in the 1974 FECA amendments that four of the six commission members be appointed by Congress represented an attempt by the legislative branch to assume powers reserved for the President. The need for Congress to reconstitute the FEC to meet the court's objections opened the way for the third debate over federal campaign finance law within five years.

FECA Amendments of 1976

The 1976 FECA amendments were designed to conform the law to the *Buckley* decision. That decision, in fact, gave Congress 30 days to transform the Federal Election Commission into a body entirely appointed by the president. President Ford wanted legislation that would simply remedy the FEC's constitutional flaws, and he argued against Congress reopening the entire campaign finance reform debate. He did not get his wish, as Congress undertook significant revisions dealing with the FEC's powers. A highly partisan clash over PACs ensued as labour, alarmed at a FEC decision favourable to the growth of corporate PACs, sought to limit the fund-raising ability of such committees.

The FEC, formally organized in April 1975, was created to centralize the administrative and enforcement functions that had been divided between three different congressional offices in the FECA legislation in 1971. From the outset, there was apparent potential for conflict between the new commissioners' ties to Capitol Hill and their responsibility for impartial handling of campaign finance issues involving Congress: under the procedure ultimately ruled unconstitutional by the Supreme Court in 1976, four of the first six appointments to the commission were former U.S. House members.

Nonetheless, conflict soon erupted between some powerful members of Congress and their ex-colleagues on the Commission. In fact, Congress rejected the first two regulations proposed by the FEC.[6]

Meanwhile, in November 1975, barely two months before the *Buckley* decision, the FEC issued advisory opinion (AO) 1975–23 in the so-called SunPAC case. In a 4–2 decision, the FEC ruled that SunPAC, the Sun Oil Co.'s political action committee, could use corporate funds to solicit voluntary political contributions from employees and stockholders. Reassured by the FEC about the legal validity of corporate PACs, the business community soon recognized their potential as a means of competing with labour unions for political influence. Consequently, in the six months following the SunPAC decision, the number of corporate PACs more than doubled.

Labour, which had badly miscalculated how much the *FECA Amendments of 1974* would benefit corporate PACs, counter-attacked when the *FECA Amendments of 1976* reached the floor of Congress. Angered by FEC's SunPAC opinion, labour lined up behind a Democratic Party proposal under which companies would be allowed to solicit PAC contributions only from stockholders and "executive or administrative personnel."

But the Republicans, who saw in corporate PACs a major new ideological and financial ally, rushed to their defence, arguing that the Democrats' proposal would tip the "partisan advantage" towards labour. President Ford hinted at a veto if the restrictions on corporate PACs remained in the Bill. Ultimately, a compromise was reached under which corporate PACs were permitted to seek contributions from all company employees, by mail, twice a year. Although the restrictions hardly pleased business interests, they did little to impede the continuing growth of corporate and trade association PACs during the decade that followed.

The 1976 PAC debate also provided another lesson in campaign finance reform's law of unforeseen consequences. While the Republicans viewed corporate and trade association PACs as their natural allies, many of these PACs turned out to be far more pragmatic than ideological in their choice of candidates: a substantial portion of their donations were directed to Democrats in the years to come. This increasingly angered the Republicans as time went on, and, little more than a decade after the 1976 FECA amendments, a Republican president and Grand Old Party (GOP) congressional leaders were advocating an outright abolition of PACs. (See "Congressional Campaigns" in the next section for discussion of the PAC issue.)

To meet the constitutional objections raised by the Supreme Court, the 1976 FECA amendments also reconstituted the FEC as a six-member body appointed by the president and subject to confirmation by the Senate. Having lost the ability to directly appoint commissioners, Congress moved aggressively to make its own partisan recommendations to the President when seats on the Commission came open. (See "The FEC under Fire" in the following section.)

Congress also sought other means to keep the FEC on a tight leash. For example, it mandated that a vote of four Commission members would be necessary to issue regulations and advisory opinions, as well as to initiate civil actions and investigations. On a Commission that, under law, could contain no more than three members of the same political party, the effect of this was to give both the Democrats and the Republicans veto power over Commission actions. During the 1980s, this requirement has produced 3–3 stalemates on some of the most controversial questions facing the FEC; in two major instances, the Commission acted only after being faced with federal court orders.

FECA Amendments of 1979

By the time the *FECA Amendments of 1976* were signed into law in May of that year, it was clear that the initiative in campaign finance regulation had passed from reformers and their allies in the media to those directly affected by the new rules of the game: incumbent legislators, political parties and major interest groups. President Jimmy Carter, who took office in January 1977, sought to make public financing of congressional elections a major legislative priority. But the proposal did not succeed in gaining a majority in either house of Congress during Carter's term.

The one major piece of campaign-related legislation that did pass was the *FECA Amendments of 1979*, which were far more a response to the complaints of political candidates and operatives than to the visions of reformers. The 1979 FECA amendments were designed largely to reduce the paperwork burden on campaigns by easing the reporting requirements imposed on candidates and political committees. They thus represented a relaxation of some of the constraints that earlier reforms had placed on those in the political process.

During the late 1970s, there was considerable discussion regarding the impact of the FECA among those regulated by federal campaign law. In response, the House Administration Committee in August 1978 commissioned a study by Harvard University's Institute of Politics. The assessment singled out three problems: it found that the law set individual contribution limits too low, it imposed burdensome reporting requirements on campaigns, and it weakened the role of political parties (Harvard University 1979). Several of the recommendations in the report were influential when possible revisions to FECA were taken up by the Senate Rules Committee in mid-1979.

Perhaps the greatest controversy during the debate over the 1979 FECA amendments centred around the conversion of excess campaign funds to personal use. The Senate wanted to ban such a practice; the House did not. In a compromise, the final legislation barred the conversion of campaign funds to personal use but exempted all House members in office at the time of the law's enactment: 8 January 1980. They were given the prerogative of converting the campaign funds upon retirement.

This provision, which became known as the "grandfather clause," did not end the controversy. Throughout the 1980s, there were calls to do away with that clause, as media stories focused on retiring House members who, in some cases, converted hundreds of thousands in campaign dollars to personal use. Finally, in a November 1989 pay-raise package, Congress repealed the grandfather clause as of January 1993, thereby giving senior House members several years to decide whether to retire and take personal advantage of campaign treasuries that in some cases exceeded half a million dollars.

Virtually overlooked amidst the grandfather clause debate were provisions in the *FECA Amendments of 1979* that were to have far-reaching and often controversial effects during the 1980s.

In response to complaints that some of the law's restrictions had eliminated the role of state and local parties in presidential contests, the 1979 law allowed state and local parties to underwrite voter registration and get-out-the-vote drives on behalf of presidential tickets without regard to financial limits. This provision also applied to campaign material used in volunteer activities, such as slate cards, sample ballots, palm cards, and certain buttons, bumper stickers, and brochures. In addition, the law permitted certain of these party- or ticket-oriented materials to make passing reference to a presidential candidate without it counting against the spending limits of the presidential contest.

The growth of these activities fuelled the "soft money" debate of the 1980s as presidential campaigns took full advantage of the 1979 amendments to exceed the official spending ceiling imposed by law.

Reform Takes a Pause

By the beginning of the 1980s, the United States had in place a system of election regulation that had taken most of the previous decade to enact and fine-tune. Federal elections were subject to strict rules for disclosure of spending and receipts, and the role of the wealthy donor was greatly diminished by the availability of public funding in presidential races and the presence of contribution limits in both presidential and congressional contests. Unlike the negative reforms of prior decades, which attempted to prevent abuses by a series of restrictions, limitations and prohibitions, public financing represented a step forward in that it provided an alternative – public funding in presidential campaigns – to less desirable forms of private money.

In 1980, Ronald Reagan's landslide victory returned the Senate to Republican control for the first time in a quarter of a century. The House remained in Democratic hands, but reform elements there saw little opportunity for change during Reagan's first term, and campaign finance proposals languished.

It was not until late 1986, when the Democrats recaptured control of the Senate, that campaign finance reform was to move once again to the top of the legislative agenda. By that time, the Republicans, too, had begun to see that certain types of reform might be in their interest. While far apart on solutions, leading legislators in both major U.S. political parties had become increasingly concerned as problems with the federal campaign finance system became more and more apparent.

ISSUES FOR THE 1980s

The failure of Congress to act on campaign finance reform throughout the 1980s can be attributed to the convergence of several political realities. The decade produced no scandal that sparked great public outrage. Numerous legislators in both major political parties did not see reform as being in their electoral self-interest, and the lack of public attention made it easy for them to ignore the issue. Finally, as pressure for change began to grow toward the end of the 1980s, sharp partisan differences between Democrats and Republicans emerged, making compromise elusive.

As Mitch McConnell of Kentucky, the Senate Republicans' point man on the issue, candidly observed: "Campaign finance is the rules of the game in our democracy, and either side would love to write the rules in a way that benefits them to the detriment of the other side" (Peck 1990, 3).

The following section focuses on the issues that arose in the presidential and congressional systems of political finance during the 1980s, as well as the problems experienced by the Federal Election Commission. It also outlines some proposed legislative solutions.

Presidential Campaigns

Whatever its shortcomings, the U.S. system of public funding of presidential campaigns can claim some degree of success since first being implemented in 1976. During the pre-nomination period (the primary and caucus election process) it has enhanced access to voters by supplementing the treasuries of those candidates with limited name recognition and inadequate financial resources. For example, in 1976, a long-shot aspirant named Jimmy Carter captured both the Democratic presidential nomination and the election. In 1980, Republican George Bush, then relatively unknown to rank-and-file voters despite having held several appointed government positions, mounted an unexpectedly strong challenge to Ronald Reagan. It landed Bush the vice-presidential nomination and put him on the road to the White House.

In addition, the combination of contribution limits and extensive disclosure and compliance requirements has prevented a recurrence of the free-wheeling atmosphere that pervaded the 1972 Nixon campaign. This suggests that the laws of the early 1970s have succeeded in altering the behaviour of candidates, committees and contributors so as to achieve some of the goals of campaign reform.

However, if one views the reforms of the 1970s as an effort to regulate the flow of money into presidential campaigns, it is a regulatory structure in some jeopardy. While the structure worked well when first put into place in 1976, it began to spring leaks during the campaigns of 1980 and 1984; in 1988, major cracks appeared. The problems are attributable less to deficiencies in the law itself than to the inventiveness of political actors in circumventing the statutes and the difficulty of strictly regulating political money in a pluralistic society.

At the outset, it is important to note that the laws governing presidential campaigns have changed little since the adoption of the *FECA Amendments of 1974*. In the pre-nomination period, a presidential aspirant is limited in how much he or she may receive from any individual contributor ($1 000) or a political action committee ($5 000). PAC donations are not "matchable." But a candidate may receive public

Table 1.2
Major-party presidential campaign expenditure limits and public funding, 1976–88
(in millions of dollars)

Year	Pre-nomination campaign						Nominating convention	General election campaign					
	National spending limit[a]		Exempt fund-raising[b]		Overall spending limit[c]			National Public treasury grant[d]		Party spending limit[e]		Overall spending limit[f]
1976	10.9	+	2.2	=	13.1		2.2[g]	21.8	+	3.2	=	25.0
1980	14.7	+	2.9	=	17.7		4.4	29.4	+	4.6	=	34.0
1984	20.2	+	4.0	=	24.2		8.1	40.4	+	6.9	=	47.3
1988	23.1	+	4.6	=	27.7		9.2	46.1	+	8.3	=	54.4

Source: Citizens' Research Foundation based on FEC data.

Note: Totals may not be exact due to rounding.

[a]Based on $10 million plus cost-of-living allowance (COLA) increases using 1974 as the base year. Eligible candidates may receive no more than one-half the national spending limit in public matching funds. To become eligible candidates must raise $5 000 in private contributions of $250 or less in each of 20 states. The federal government matches each contribution to qualified candidates up to $250. Publicly funded candidates also must observe spending limits in the individual states equal to the greater of $200 000 + COLA (base year 1974), or $0.16 x the voting-age population (VAP) of the state + COLA.

[b]Candidates may spend up to 20 percent of the national spending limit for fund-raising.

[c]Legal and accounting expenses to insure compliance with the law are exempt from the spending limit.

[d]Based on $20 million + COLA (base year 1974).

[e]Based on $0.02 x VAP of the United States + COLA.

[f]Compliance costs are exempt from the spending limit.

[g]Based on $2 million + COLA (base year 1974). Under the 1979 FECA amendments, the basic grant was raised to $3 million. In 1984, Congress raised the basic grant to $4 million.

matching funds for each contribution from an individual up to $250. First, the candidate must demonstrate the viability of his or her campaign by collecting $5 000 (in up to $250 amounts) in each of 20 states, for a nationwide total of $100 000. There is a cap on the total amount of public funds available to a candidate during the pre-nomination period; it increases every four years based on the consumer price index (see table 1.2).

During the general election, the presidential nominee of each major political party receives full public financing. Each candidate receives a flat grant, which may be supplemented by a limited amount of funds spent on his or her behalf by each national political party. With that exception, the two presidential nominees are theoretically barred from raising private funds for their campaigns during the general election. As will be discussed later, these restrictions bear little resemblance to current reality.

Some $500 million was spent on the 1988 presidential campaign, including the pre-nomination period, national conventions and the general election (Alexander and Bauer 1991, 11).[7] More than a third of this represents funds provided by U.S. taxpayers (ibid., table 2.6). In return for this public subsidy, presidential candidates agreed to abide by expenditure limitations in the pre-nomination and general election periods and to limit use of their personal assets (as noted in *Buckley v. Valeo* in the last section). The expenditure ceilings also are indexed to inflation; consequently, the spending limits, as noted in table 1.1, more than doubled between 1976 and 1988.

This, however, has not discouraged candidates and their operatives from devising increasingly imaginative means to get around these ceilings – so much so that they have become largely meaningless. There is no better example than the 1988 presidential campaigns, when Democrat Michael Dukakis and Republican George Bush each helped to raise half again as much money as the general election limit defined by law (Alexander and Bauer 1991, table 3.4, 41).

To some extent, the problem of compliance with expenditure ceilings in U.S. presidential elections mirrors the 1988 Canadian campaign, when the expenditure limits on political parties were undermined by the so-called political interest groups – which spent freely in connection with the debate over the U.S.-Canada Free Trade Agreement. In the United States, the first major holes in the spending limit dike appeared during the 1980 presidential election, the second such contest featuring public financing and expenditure ceilings.

The 1980 Campaign

Yet another major element of the *Buckley* decision involved "independent expenditures." The decision made clear that such activity by individuals or groups was a constitutionally protected form of free speech as long as the spending was truly independent. Consequently, independent expenditures could not be coordinated with candidates or their organizations or consented to by candidates or their agents, but they could be spent on behalf of or against a non-cooperating candidate.

The result was the creation of several independent expenditure groups in the late 1970s, the most prominent of which were strongly conservative and pro-Republican. In 1980, most of their efforts were devoted to electing Ronald Reagan. To illustrate the degree to which this device undercut spending limits, Reagan was limited to a total of $51.7 million during the pre-nomination and general election that year. However, according to Federal Election Commission data, independent expenditure campaigns spent another $12.5 million promoting Republican presidential candidates that year, most of it on Reagan's behalf.[8] One aspect of independent spending totals requires explanation. Not all such spending is for direct campaigning by means of communicating with voters; totals also include fund-raising and administrative costs of the political committee undertaking the independent expenditures.

Meanwhile, Reagan's own advisers came up with another way around the expenditure limits: the "presidential PAC." After losing his bid for the Republican presidential nomination to Gerald Ford in 1976, Reagan started a PAC ostensibly to contribute money to conservative candidates at the state and local levels. However, its true purpose was to promote Reagan himself as he prepared for another run for the presidency in 1980. As Anthony Corrado has said, "most of the PAC's funds were used to hire staff and consultants, develop fund-raising programs, recruit volunteers, subsidize Reagan's travel and host receptions on his behalf" (Corrado 1990).

The object of the PAC was to get around provisions of the *Federal Election Campaign Act* dictating that once a person declares his or her intention to run for president and registers a principal campaign committee with the FEC, the meter begins running on the pre-nomination expenditure ceiling. There is another advantage to the presidential PAC, since used by many other candidates: an individual donor is permitted to contribute five times as much money to a PAC ($5 000 maximum) as to a presidential or congressional candidate's campaign committee ($1 000 limit).

The 1984 Campaign

Just as Reagan found ways around the spending limits during the 1980 pre-nomination process, so did former Vice-President Walter Mondale in winning the Democratic Party nomination four years later.

Besides agreeing to overall expenditure ceilings in the pre-nomination process, candidates receiving public funding must abide by a complex series of state-by-state limits, based on population size. These have proved to be highly constraining in an era in which several state primary elections are often held on the same day, and candidates for a party's nomination must depend on high-cost television rather than personal campaigning in many states. The limits also have proved troublesome for candidates in small states that hold high-stakes contests early in the pre-nomination process.

The result has been a continuing series of subterfuges to evade a particular state's spending limit. For example, candidates have felt compelled to throw tremendous resources into New Hampshire, which traditionally has been the site of the first presidential primary election. Given the state's relatively small population and its correspondingly low spending limit, candidates have used such strategies as buying time on Boston TV stations – which reach more than three-quarters of New Hampshire's population – and charging the cost partially to the Massachusetts limit rather than wholly to the New Hampshire limit. Candidates campaigning in western New Hampshire have been known to spend the night in Vermont, allowing them to charge lodging costs for themselves and their staffs against the Vermont limit.

In 1984, the Mondale campaign sought to escalate this creative accounting through a device known as the "delegate committee." A study of existing law by Mondale's legal staff uncovered a 1980 FEC decision permitting those seeking to become national convention delegates to raise and spend money on their own behalf for such grassroots activities as brochures, buttons and bumper stickers (Germond and Witcover 1985, 226). These delegate committees had to operate independently of a national presidential campaign effort.

At the time, the Mondale campaign was fast approaching the prenomination spending ceiling. Compounding the problem was the fact that many of Mondale's most reliable supporters had "maxed out" by giving the campaign the $1 000 limit on individual contributions. High-ranking Mondale campaign officials saw the delegate committees as a way around both the contribution and spending limits.

There was a second major factor behind creation of the delegate committees. Mondale, in an effort to free himself from criticism that he was too close to many of the Democratic Party's "special interest" groups, had declared that he would not accept PAC donations. However, a top Mondale campaign official quietly informed the delegate committees by memo that because they were theoretically independent of the Mondale campaign, they could accept PAC money (Germond and Witcover 1985, 229). Organized labour, which had endorsed Mondale, proceeded to contribute substantial amounts of PAC dollars to the delegate committees.

When stories about these committees surfaced in the media, they unsurprisingly prompted criticism that Mondale was flouting the spending limits. The controversy became so intense that Mondale ordered the delegate committees shut down in late April 1984. By then, however, he was well on his way to becoming the Democratic Party nominee.

In May 1984, the FEC found "reason to believe" that the Mondale campaign was in violation of the law because the delegate committees were not functioning in a truly independent fashion (Germond and Witcover 1985, 273). The Commission's decision was not disclosed until 27 November, after the general election. At that time, it also was announced that negotiations between the FEC and the Mondale campaign had produced an agreement in which the latter paid the federal government almost $400 000 to resolve the matter.[9]

The 1988 Campaign

The fourth presidential campaign held since the passage of the 1974 amendments witnessed an escalation of the efforts to skirt the spending limits. Because 1988 was the first election since the reforms in which an incumbent president was not running, there were hotly contested battles for the nominations of both major political parties, and this was reflected in the increase in spending. Although the rate of inflation between 1984 and 1988 was only 13.5 percent, total presidential campaign costs rose by 54 percent during that period (Alexander and Bauer 1991, 11).

Use of the presidential PAC reached new highs. In fact, presidential PAC spending for 1988 was more than twice the combined amounts expended in advance of the 1980 and 1984 elections (Alexander and Bauer 1991, 15). Another well-worn way around the presidential limits – independent expenditures – declined somewhat between 1984 and 1988. Nonetheless, they still played a crucial role in the general election campaign. Michael Dukakis' campaign was hurt by explosive ads highlighting a felon named Willie Horton, who, while on a prison furlough program in Massachusetts, had escaped and brutally raped a Maryland woman. These commercials, designed to question Dukakis' record on crime, were produced and aired not by the Bush campaign, but by two independent expenditure groups, and were widely shown on television news programs (ibid., 86–87).

But the most controversial element in the financing of the 1988 presidential campaign was a device that has come to be known in the American political vocabulary as "soft money." In contrast to "hard money" regulated by the FECA, soft money was subject to neither the limits nor the disclosure requirements of federal law. In the context of major political parties, soft money refers to funds channelled to state and local party organizations for voter registration and get-out-the-vote efforts. These state and local party affiliates are outside the reach of federal law.

Because soft money has been raised primarily by officials of presidential campaigns, critics charge that it is benefiting presidential candidates while undermining the spending limits imposed on them. Because presidential candidates themselves have helped to raise this money, it raises questions about whether they are violating the legal provisions by which – in return for public subsidies – they agree to strict limits on private fund-raising during the general election. Finally, because soft money permits the collection of unlimited donations from individuals, critics say it is a throwback to the days of the very large contributor.

Soft money has been present in presidential campaigns throughout the 1980s. What distinguished 1988 from past elections was its quantity. During the 1988 general election, more than twice as much soft money was expended as during the 1980 and 1984 general elections combined.

In 1980 and 1984, the Republicans had far outstripped the Democrats in raising soft money. The Republicans raised $15 million in both elections while the Democrats were only able to raise $4 million in 1980 and $6 million in 1984 (Citizens' Research Foundation). That changed dramatically in 1988 when the Dukakis campaign raised $23 million, and a Republican response produced $22 million in soft money for the Bush campaign.

This money was raised frantically, as if no public funding or expenditure limits existed, and it was raised in large individual donations far in excess of federal contribution limits. The Republicans claimed 267 contributors of $100 000 or more; the Democrats counted 130 individuals who donated or raised amounts in six figures (Houston 1988).[10] This return of the very large contributor seriously eroded the concept behind the presidential funding structure embodied in the *FECA Amendments of 1974*. Public funds were intended to provide most or all of the money serious candidates needed to present themselves to the electorate, yet soft money offers a pathway into presidential politics for direct corporate and labour donations; the former was barred at the federal level in 1907 and the latter in 1943. But 30 states permit direct corporate contributions, and 41 allow direct labour contributions. Therefore, a donation can be directed by a party's national committee from, say, a corporation in a state that bars corporate contributions to a state party committee in a state that allows corporate donations.

Soft money is not the only form of disbursement in presidential campaigns that is spent outside the general election limits. As table 1.3 illustrates, while the spending limit was $54.4 million (federal grants of $46.1 plus national party spending of $8.3 million), the amounts actually spent by or on behalf of the major-party candidates totalled $93.7 million for Bush and $106.5 million for Dukakis. In addition to state

Table 1.3

Sources of funds, major-party presidential candidates, 1988 general election
(in millions of dollars)

	Sources of funds	Bush	Dukakis
Limited campaign			
Candidate controlled	Federal grant	46.1	46.1
	National party	8.3	8.3
Unlimited campaigns			
	State and local party	22.0[a]	23.0
	Labour[b]	5.0	25.0
Candidate may coordinate	Corporate/Association[b]	1.5	1.0
	Compliance	4.0	2.5
Independent of candidate	Independent expenditures[c]	6.8	0.6
Total		93.7	106.5

Source: Citizens' Research Foundation.

[a]Includes money raised by the national party committee and channelled to state and local party committees.

[b]Includes internal communication costs (both those in excess of $2 000, which are reported, as required by law, and those less than $2 000, which are not required), registration and voter turnout expenditures, overhead and other related costs.

[c]Does not include amounts spent to oppose the candidates: $2.7 million against Dukakis, $77 325 against Bush and $63 103 against Quayle.

and local party spending (soft money), labour unions spent $30 million in parallel campaigning; this amount consisted of voter registration and turnout expenses as well as partisan communication costs to their memberships. Most of this benefited the Dukakis campaign. Other costs outside of the candidate limits and labour spending included minimal corporate spending, candidate compliance costs and independent expenditures. Some of these various costs can be legally controlled by the candidates, some can be coordinated by the campaigns, some are limited, but others cannot be controlled, coordinated or limited.

Legislative Proposals
The experience of the 1988 presidential campaigns led to numerous proposals during the 1989–90 session of Congress to restrict soft money. The House and Senate, both under Democratic control, passed soft money restrictions as part of comprehensive legislation. But differences between the two bodies prevented either campaign reform bill from becoming law before the 101st Congress adjourned in October 1990. (See following section, "The Debate over Legislative Proposals".)

Both bills aimed to prevent a recurrence of the tactics used by the presidential campaigns in 1988. The House legislation would have barred presidential candidates from raising soft money. The Senate proposal would have placed under the limits of federal law all contributions solicited by a national party committee on behalf of a state party organization, thereby curtailing the $100 000 gifts raised in 1988. Both bills also would have sharply restricted the amount of money that a state party could spend on so-called generic campaigns in connection with a presidential race, including voter registration and get-out-the-vote drives.

But the Senate bill went further by placing strict spending limits on generic campaign activities by state and national party committees even when presidential and congressional candidates are not specifically mentioned. In the less stringent House approach, generic campaign efforts that made no mention of federal candidates were left outside the purview of federal law, even if a presidential or congressional candidate might realize some benefit from them.

Both bills would have required disclosure of soft money receipts and expenditures. The FEC passed regulations that went into effect 1 January 1991; these required disclosure and set allocation formulas for generic spending on behalf of the party ticket that may affect the election of federal candidates (*Federal Register* 1990).[11]

Meanwhile, Senate Republicans wanted restrictions on non-party money. They proposed to prohibit tax-exempt organizations from activities on behalf of a particular candidate. This was aimed at organized labour as well as a number of other issue-oriented groups – such as environmental organizations – that have tended to favour Democratic presidential and congressional candidates with various forms of assistance.

In seeking to regulate another device used to skirt campaign spending limits – independent expenditures – the Democrats and Republicans found more common ground. The reason is that legislators in both parties are clearly nervous about becoming victims of the stridently negative advertising that often has characterized independent campaigns. Although the *Buckley* decision found independent expenditures to be a protected form of free speech, both parties in Congress have looked for constitutional ways to discourage them.

The House-passed campaign bill would have required any television advertisement underwritten by independent expenditures to contain a continuously displayed statement identifying the sponsor of the ad. The Senate bill proposed that any broadcaster selling air time to an independent campaign favouring one candidate would then have to sell air time to the other candidate to allow him or her to respond immediately.

The Future of the Presidential Checkoff

While private money has found several channels into presidential campaigns, the flow of available public funding is in danger of slowing to a trickle. It now appears that the Presidential Election Campaign Fund will face severe cash flow problems as early as the 1992 campaign and will be in a deficit situation by the 1996 race unless action is taken.

The $1 federal income tax checkoff has not been increased since its enactment in the *Revenue Act of 1971*, despite the fact that the U.S. dollar is worth about a third of what it was then. Compounding the erosion of the dollar is the eroding support for the checkoff from taxpayers. According to the Federal Election Commission, there has been a 30 percent decrease in taxpayer support for the checkoff since 1980, when checkoff participation was at an all-time high. This translates into tax checkoff rates declining from the high point of 28.7 percent in 1980 tax returns to 20.1 percent in 1988 returns; the 1989 rate on 1988 returns produced $32.3 million – the yearly amounts being aggregated over a four-year period for payouts in presidential election years (Federal Election Commission 1990b). This parallels the drop in checkoff participation in several states (notably New Jersey, Michigan, Minnesota and Wisconsin) that provide public funding to statewide and/or state legislative candidates.

Herein lies a paradox of the U.S. political system: while surveys indicate many voters are convinced that elected officials are being bought off by special interest money, these same voters have shown considerable reluctance to provide the public funding necessary to replace it. Some insights into this conundrum are provided by a series of focus groups sponsored by the FEC in late 1990. The private research firm conducting focus groups reported: "It was often difficult to keep the group focused on the subject at hand (the checkoff) because of their anger at politicians and a perception of wasteful spending by government. Their anger associated with these concerns contaminated their consideration of presidential funding"(Babcock 1991).[12]

The FEC announced in late November 1990 that the presidential public funding program could suffer a cash flow problem during the 1992 presidential race (*Campaign Practices Reports* 1990, 2). To deal with this, FEC and U.S. Treasury officials are currently discussing two plans that would translate into candidates receiving less than the traditional dollar-for-dollar public match on private contributions during the pre-nomination period. Because restricting the availability of public funding in the early going could benefit better-known candidates, the FEC and Treasury are expecting any decision they make to face political and legal challenges.

Both alternatives being considered would require the use of check-off money collected in 1992. That, in turn, would further worsen the deficit projected for the 1996 presidential year. While the FEC is stepping up efforts to educate taxpayers about the checkoff, several commission members said recently that Congress will have to decide whether to make a one-time grant to keep the fund out of debt or totally scrap the checkoff in favour of providing public funding through continuing legislative appropriations – a perilous possibility given U.S. budget deficits (*Campaign Practices Reports* 1990, 3).

Congressional Campaigns

The structure of the law under which members of Congress themselves must stand for election is a hybrid fashioned by legislative and judicial fiat and by FEC regulations and opinions. The absence of public funding for congressional candidates means that there has been no carrot with which to bring about voluntary acceptance of spending limits in House and Senate contests. Reformers subsequently sought to remedy this by lobbying Congress to create a system of expenditure

Table 1.4
Congressional campaign expenditures, 1972–90
(in millions of dollars)

Election cycle	Total	Senate	House
1971–72	77.3	30.7	46.5
1973–74	88.2	34.7	53.5
1975–76	115.5	44.0	71.5
1977–78	194.8	85.2	109.7
1979–80	239.0	102.9	136.0
1981–82	342.4	138.4	204.0
1983–84	374.1	170.5	203.6
1985–86	450.9	211.6	239.3
1987–88	457.7	201.2	256.5
1989–90	445.2	180.1	265.1

Source: Citizens' Research Foundation compilation based on FEC and other data.

limits and public funding similar to the presidential model. But 15 years after the Supreme Court linkage, Congress has yet to enact such legislation.

A very sharp escalation has occurred in spending on contests for Senate and House seats. Table 1.4 shows an increase in total spending from $77.3 million in the 1972 election cycle to $445.2 million in the 1990 cycle. There are 435 House seats elected every two years, and in the aggregate these are costlier than the 33 or 34 Senate seats elected every two years.

Even taking inflation into account, total expenditures in congressional campaigns showed a 160 percent increase between 1976 and 1988 when considered in constant dollars, according to FEC figures. The erosion of the dollar has been such that the $1 000 maximum individual contribution dropped about 60 percent in value between 1975 and 1988 when considered in constant dollars. At the same time, congressional candidates have increasingly pursued the PACs, whose maximum contribution per candidate each election is a higher $5 000.

The combination of escalating campaign costs and diminished participation by individual contributors has given rise to complaints that political challengers are being priced out of the market, while incumbent members of Congress are remaining in office by relying excessively on special interest donations. These two concerns are interwoven through several of the issues that have arisen during the campaign finance reform debate of the late 1980s.

The Rise of PACs

According to FEC figures, there were 608 PACs in existence at the end of 1974, when amendments to FECA loosened restrictions on their formation. By 1990, the number stood at 4 192, almost a sevenfold increase in 16 years. The sharpest increase came among corporate PACs, whose number jumped from fewer than 100 in 1974 to almost 1 800 in 1990 (Federal Election Commission 1990a, 1). There was a surge of new issue and ideological PACs in the early 1980s, but the total numbers have levelled off or even decreased in some categories, as shown in table 1.5.

What particularly disturbs many advocates of reform is the increasing dependence of House and Senate candidates on PACs. PAC donations accounted for 24 percent of the contributions to Senate candidates and 40 percent of the contributions to House candidates during the 1987–88 election cycle; a small downturn to 22 percent in Senate campaigns and 38 percent in House campaigns occurred in the 1989-90 cycle. The growth of PAC contributions to Senate and House candidates over the years is shown in table 1.6.

In contrast, PACs play a relatively minor role in presidential contests. In 1988, these groups accounted for only 1.4 percent of all funding during the pre-nomination period, and four candidates during that period declined to accept PAC money (Alexander and Bauer 1991, 25).

Table 1.5
Growth of Political Action Committees, 1974–90

Year	Corporate PACs	Labour PACs	Others*	Total
1974	89	201	318	608
1976	433	224	489	1 146
1978	785	217	651	1 653
1980	1 206	297	1 048	2 551
1982	1 469	380	1 522	3 371
1984	1 682	394	1 933	4 009
1986	1 744	384	2 029	4 157
1988	1 816	354	2 098	4 268
1990	1 795	346	2 031	4 172

Source: Federal Election Commission.

*This category includes trade associations, membership and non-connected (so-called ideological) PACs.

Table 1.6
PAC contributions to congressional candidates, 1976–90
(in millions of dollars)

Year	Amount
1976	22.6
1978	34.1
1980	55.2
1982	83.6
1984	105.3
1986	132.7
1988	151.2
1990	150.6

Sources: Common Cause (1976); Federal Election Commission (1978–90).

Because many PACs are tied to powerful corporations, trade associations and unions with legislative interests in Congress, critics charge that wholesale vote buying is occurring. Such charges clearly overstate the case; studies of congressional behaviour have indicated that personal philosophy, party loyalties and an aversion to offending voting constituents are more influential factors than campaign contributions in determining the positions taken by members of Congress.

PACs, however, have created further perceptual problems at a time when Congress already is held in low regard by the American public. If PACs have not spawned vote buying, they have created a system in which money and access to legislators have become intertwined. Not only have reformers criticized PACs but so has the Republican congressional leadership in recent years, culminating in President Bush's call for their elimination in his 1991 State of the Union address. This is ironic in view of the Republican record in the 1970s and early 1980s championing business PACs and encouraging their establishment. It was not until business PACs started to give more to Democratic incumbents that Republicans turned against PACs, at least in their rhetoric – they still accept PAC gifts.

PACs have their defenders, who argue that they merely represent the series of competing interests that are an inherent part of the U.S. pluralistic political system; they are hardly monolithic as portrayed. At a time when many bemoan declining citizen involvement in the electoral process, proponents argue that PACs have increased participation by their rank and file.

Finally, they contend that efforts to do away with PACs in congressional races would be as ineffective as the attempt to impose expenditure ceilings in presidential races: PAC money would not disappear but would simply be channelled into less visible, less traceable channels such as soft money and independent expenditures.

Advantages of Incumbency

If reformers believe PACs are inherently corrupting, leading Republicans in Congress have targeted them for very different reasons. The Republicans complain that PAC patterns of contributions in recent years have shown a distinct bias towards incumbent legislators, a significant majority of whom are Democrats.

PACs have become a lightning rod in the debate over whether the advantages of incumbency have become excessive. Most House turnover in recent years has come through retirement, death, members running for higher office, and the redistricting following the decennial census rather than through incumbents being defeated by challengers.

In 1984, when Republican Ronald Reagan won re-election to the presidency in a landslide over Democrat Walter Mondale, the re-election rate of incumbents in the overwhelmingly Democratic House was 96 percent. In 1990, predicted by many to be a year in which a doubting public would turn on incumbents, the re-election rate again was 96 percent. In some years, it has exceeded 98 percent.

Traditionally, the greater prestige and visibility of Senate seats have made them more attractive to political challengers. Even when the odds of defeating an incumbent have been small, well-funded, credible opponents often appeared – hoping for an upset or to use a strong electoral showing as a springboard to a future race for office. However, in the past two elections, there have been increasing signs that the lack of competitiveness affecting House races is seeping into Senate contests as well.

While some political scientists have concluded from the high re-election rates that there exists a "Permanent Congress," in fact, two-thirds of the House has served fewer than 12 years (Edwards 1990), and senators have experienced a 44 percent turnover rate over a nine-year period (Swift 1989).

In 1988, the average winning Senate campaign cost more than $4 million, while many challengers failed to raise even a third of that amount (Makinson 1989, 21). In 1990, of the 31 Senate incumbents seeking re-election, four had no opposition whatsoever and another 11 faced challengers who never presented a credible financial or political threat. Again, in a year in which incumbents were thought to be in disfavour, only one sitting senator was defeated, by a challenger who was outspent 8–1.

The failure of legislative challengers to attain financial competitiveness comes in the face of demonstrations by political scientist Gary Jacobson that money is a much more important campaign resource for non-incumbents than for incumbents (Jacobson 1980, 48–49). And the failure comes at a time when PACs are playing an increasingly important role in funding incumbents' campaigns. According to the FEC, 57 percent of PAC donations went to incumbents during the 1977–78 election cycle; a decade later, that figure had jumped to 74 percent.

Of course, labour PACs supported congressional Democrats strongly throughout this period, including substantial financial assistance to many Democratic challengers. What has angered the Republicans is that business and trade association PACs have shifted their loyalties more and more towards the Democrats. In 1988, 55 percent of business PAC money was funnelled to Democrats, mostly to incumbents. Just six years earlier, Republican congressional candidates got 60 percent of business PAC dollars (Makinson 1989, 15).

The Republicans, a minority in both houses of Congress, contend that their inability to field competitive challenges to Democratic incumbents in many instances is due to a lack of financial support from, among others, the business PACs. In turn, the PACs say that the Republicans often have failed to recruit credible challengers to begin with.

Among the advantages of incumbency are not only the attracting of PAC contributions – in part because of incumbents' use of their legislative committee memberships as bases for fund-raising – but also the franked mail privilege, generous staffing including in home-state or district offices, travel, honoraria, and incumbent-dominated safe districts achieved through decennial reapportionment.

The Costs of Television

The chasing of PAC money, along with the frequent complaints that legislators are paying too much attention to fund-raising and not enough to legislating, are both by-products of the escalating costs of Senate and House campaigns. The professionalization of politics has given rise to computerized campaign headquarters featuring sophisticated and expensive strategies for targeting potential voters and contributors. However, television is repeatedly pointed to as the culprit behind the increasing costs of running for Congress.

Of course, paid television plays a major role in presidential campaigns. But the price tag has been less of an issue, for several reasons. First is the presence of alternative resources in the form of public financing. With soft money increasingly bearing the expense of such nuts-and-bolts activities as voter registration and get-out-the-vote drives, it has left general candidates free to use much of their public subsidy for television advertising. To a considerable extent, the general election public funding to presidential candidates has turned into an income transfer from the U.S. Treasury to private broadcasters.[13] Meanwhile, during the pre-nomination period, state-by-state expense limits and the need to marshal scarce financial resources have limited the use of television. In 1988, television accounted for only 6 percent of all presidential pre-nomination spending (Alexander and Bauer 1991, 35).

At the congressional level, the role of television and its attendant costs have been overstated to a degree. In many House contests, particularly in densely populated urban and suburban areas, the boundaries of a House district are rarely contiguous with the viewership of a broadcast station. There are some 40 congressional districts within the viewing range of New York City stations: some are in New Jersey, some in Connecticut and some in New York. Consequently, it makes little sense to purchase expensive television time to reach many people unable to vote in that district. In these instances, carefully targeted direct mail has been the medium of choice in communicating with voters. In Senate races, which are run statewide, the expense of television is far greater, sometimes as much as 50 percent of the campaign spending.

The federal law governing broadcast stations does not require TV outlets to sell air time to candidates. Section 315 of the *Federal Communications Act of 1934* (the so-called equal time rule) mandates that if one candidate uses a broadcast station, that licensee must provide equal opportunities for all candidates for the same office (whether federal, state or local); this applies to both purchased and free time.

Another part of the law, section 312(a)(7), however, warns that a broadcast station's licence may be withdrawn for "willful or repeated failure to allow reasonable access to or to permit purchase of reasonable amounts of time for use of a broadcasting station by a legally qualified candidate for federal office on behalf of his candidacy." But this does not necessarily translate into the sale of broadcast time; the requirement may be fulfilled by the station's sponsorship of debates or other forums.

In 1972, an amendment to the *Federal Communications Act* (section 315(b)) mandated that broadcast stations cannot charge political candidates more than the lowest unit rate made available to any other advertiser in the same class of time. The rule, which governs the period 45 days prior to a primary election and 60 days prior to a general election, was designed to insure that political candidates received the same discounts as a station's most favoured advertisers.

Some broadcasters, however, have succeeded in frustrating the intent of the rule by selling advertising time on a pre-emptible basis. Because political candidates are advertisers who want time that is not pre-emptible, the "lowest unit rate" for this kind of advertising often has ended up being the highest rate charged by the station. Consequently, critics have complained that the law has done little to hold down political costs.

The Role of Parties

As with many other concerns, the role of the political parties is one that transcends strictly financial issues.

The reforms of the early 1970s sharply curtailed the financial involvement of political parties in both presidential and congressional campaigns, thereby leading to a further weakening of these structures. As noted in the first section, several provisions of the *FECA Amendments of 1979* were designed to respond to these concerns regarding presidential campaigns. In addition, there have been suggestions that the limited ability of the two major parties to finance congressional campaigns has led to diminishing partisan loyalties on the part of legislators, making it increasingly difficult to mobilize votes in Congress.

However, the weakening of the political parties predates the appearance of campaign finance reform on the congressional agenda. To some degree, U.S. political parties have fallen victim to a more educated, more transient, more independent-thinking electorate. Television also has played an important role. Congress has been populated increasingly by non-traditional politicians who, rather than rising through the ranks of political parties, have ignored party structures and used some form of media to get their messages directly to the voters.

In short, parties have lost a great deal of their effectiveness, with many of their functions absorbed by other institutions or left unfulfilled. What the reforms in the political process, including political finance laws, have done is to give rise to a number of institutions, such as PACs, providing candidate support and dialogue with the community. These changes are so basic that it is doubtful that any legislation could succeed in reversing them.

The proposals to reinvigorate parties have, in part, been a response to the rapid growth of PACs. Advocates of this approach argue that channelling money to congressional candidates through political parties, which collect it from a variety of sources, is more desirable than the one-to-one dependence on special interest PACs. The reforms of the 1970s placed strict limits on the amounts of money that national, state and local party committees could give directly to a particular candidate (see table 1.1).

The framework of the law, however, did permit coordinated expenditures under which national and state party committees could pay for certain expenditures undertaken by the candidate. The allowed amount of coordinated expenditures is based on a formula of two cents per voting age population, plus cost-of-living adjustments. In 1990, these expenditures could amount to large sums – as much as $2 million in a California Senate race – and as little as $100 560 in the smallest states. The House limit was $50 280 (see table 1.7). These amounts, which may or may not be spent on specific contests according to the availability of money and candidate need, are disclosed as disbursements by the giving committee(s) but not by the candidates on whose behalf the payments are made; accordingly, the actual costs of some Senate or House campaigns are understated, even in tabulations made by the FEC.

The question of what role to give the parties is not without significant partisan motives. The Republicans, whose national party

Table 1.7
Party spending limits — Senate elections, 1990

State	Voting age population	1990 party spending limits ($)
Alabama	3 010 000	151 343
Alaska*	362 000	50 280
Arizona	2 575 000	129 471
Arkansas	1 756 000	88 292
California	21 350 000	1 073 478
Colorado	2 453 000	123 337
Connecticut	2 479 000	124 644
Delaware*	504 000	50 280
Florida	9 799 000	492 694
Georgia	4 639 000	233 249
Hawaii	825 000	50 280
Idaho	710 000	50 280
Illinois	8 678 000	436 330
Indiana	4 133 000	207 807
Iowa	2 132 000	107 197
Kansas	1 854 000	93 219
Kentucky	2 760 000	138 773
Louisiana	3 109 000	156 321
Maine	917 000	50 280
Maryland	3 533 000	177 639
Massachusetts	4 576 000	230 081
Michigan	6 829 000	343 362
Minnesota	3 224 000	162 103
Mississippi	1 852 000	93 119
Missouri	3 854 000	193 779
Montana	588 000	50 280
Nebraska	1 187 000	59 682
Nevada	833 000	50 280
New Hampshire	828 000	50 280
New Jersey	5 903 000	296 803
New Mexico	1 074 000	54 001
New York	13 600 000	683 808
North Carolina	4 929 000	247 830
North Dakota*	481 000	50 280
Ohio	8 090 000	406 765
Oklahoma	2 371 000	119 214
Oregon	2 123 000	106 744
Pennsylvania	9 199 000	462 253
Rhode Island	767 000	50 280
South Carolina	2 558 000	128 616
South Dakota*	519 000	50 280
Tennessee	3 685 000	185 282
Texas	12 038 000	605 271
Utah	1 076 000	54 101
Vermont*	425 000	50 280

Table 1.7 (cont'd)
Party spending limits — Senate elections, 1990

State	Voting age population	1990 party spending limits ($)
Virginia	4 615 000	232 042
Washington	3 545 000	178 243
West Virginia	1 394 000	70 090
Wisconsin	3 612 000	181 611
Wyoming*	339 000	50 280

Source: Federal Election Commission.

*States with only one representative.

committees have regularly raised more funds than their Democratic counterparts by wide margins in recent years, would like to substantially loosen – if not altogether remove – the current contribution limits and coordinated expenditure limits on party spending in congressional races. Unsurprisingly, the Democrats, who have had trouble matching the Republicans in terms of party money channelled to congressional contests through either means, are leery of such proposals.

The FEC under Fire

The Federal Election Commission is a controversial agency (Jackson 1990; Common Cause 1989). It has been roundly criticized for being too harsh, too lenient, too autocratic, too ineffective, too inconsistent and too insensitive to First Amendment rights as well as to the plight of non-incumbent candidates and grassroots groups.

The Commission was charged with administering the FECA, disbursing public funds to presidential candidates, enforcing the expenditure and contribution limits, and providing comprehensive disclosure of political receipts and expenditures. Observers believe the FEC is or should be at the centre of campaign finance reform. But the FEC looks over its shoulder continually for fear Congress is watching – and would disapprove. As a result, the Commission is less able to carry out its central responsibility to make the *Federal Election Campaign Act* – with its wide scope and extreme complexities – work smoothly and fairly. The Commission has not found a commanding vision that would give the FECA credibility and widespread acceptance.

The *Federal Election Campaign Act* vests the Federal Election Commission with its authority and designates its responsibilities regarding federal election practices. Although the FEC has jurisdiction over civil enforcement of federal political finance laws, it does not have formal authority to act as a court of law. Like other regulatory agencies, it cannot compel a party into a conciliation agreement, to admit a violation or to pay a fine. The Commission can levy a fine upon a party voluntarily participating in conciliation, or it can pursue litigation in the courts. Nonetheless, complaints regarding federal elections must first be approved by a majority of the six-member FEC; only later can redress and non-voluntary compliance be sought through litigation, or through referral to the attorney general. The fact that the FEC membership is divided equally between the two major parties sometimes has made a majority difficult to obtain.

The agency has had to spend considerable time and resources defending itself, often at the expense of administration and enforcement of the law. Budgets are not keeping up with inflation. The constant drumfire of criticism has sapped much of the Commission's vigour, strength and support.

A major criticism of the FEC is that it exercises its enforcement powers too selectively, resulting in unjustified costs and burdens on campaigns that must now employ lawyers and accountants to ensure compliance.

Defenders of the Commission contend that many of the criticisms are unfair because the agency is required to follow the law enacted by Congress and is too often blamed for merely implementing the law. In this view, the fault may lie in the law, but the FEC gets the static. The continuing objections to most facets of the Commission's work are bound to inhibit the healthy functioning of the agency – diminishing its moral authority in administering and enforcing the law.

The most approved and respected functions of the FEC are its disclosure activities – including the easy availability of information through its automated facilities in a ground-floor office – and the compilations of political fund data through its computer services. It can be faulted for not more clearly articulating its many accomplishments in this area and sometimes for its slowness in compiling data in meaningful fashion. Of course, budgetary considerations often slow the compilation process.

In fairness, FEC problems spring less from the agency's shortcomings than from Congress' reluctance to create a truly independent commission. It is the kind of commission the Congress wants, as is apparent in the congressional influence on appointments to the FEC. That, in turn, is reflected in the occasional failure to deal with major campaign finance issues, including two recent cases in which the Commission acted only after being forced to do so by the federal courts.

In discussing the complexities of the *Federal Election Campaign Act*, the late Senator Lee Metcalf once wondered whether office holders should not worry about serving time rather than constituents. His quip, seriously considered, suggests the contradictory nature of the reforms, the conflict between the goals their proponents sought to achieve, and the statutory and procedural constraints their implementation has imposed on the democratic electoral process.

Election commissions are mainly an American innovation. Whether federal or state, they have multiple roles as judge, jury, administrator, prosecutor, enforcer and magistrate. The potential for conflict among these roles is as clear as the tensions they invite and threatens good regulation unless the commissions tread cautiously. Serious enforcement of the law must not chill free speech or citizen participation. An expansive enforcement policy produces an unfortunate political climate. On the other hand, a weak enforcement policy does not raise levels of confidence in the electoral process.

The power to interpret the law is essentially the power to make new law, and the commissions sit astride the political process, empowered to influence the outcome of elections. In these circumstances, legislatures have not been reluctant to restrain the agencies. Yet legislatures have a conflict of interest because their members enact the laws under which they themselves run for re-election. Clearly there is no ideal that can realistically be met.

THE DEBATE OVER LEGISLATIVE PROPOSALS

The 1989–90 legislative session was the closest Congress has come to massively overhauling federal campaign finance laws since the 1974 amendments. This time it was a hint of scandal that prodded both the Senate and the House to pass legislation. But two other factors prevented campaign finance reform from becoming law. One was partisanship: both Democrats and Republicans continued to perceive hidden motives behind each other's legislative proposals. In addition, the long-standing dichotomy between the House and Senate on this issue again emerged. Although both were under Democratic control, the upper and lower houses of Congress were unable to resolve conflicting interests arising from their different approaches to reform.

After a hiatus of more than half a decade, campaign finance reform first resurfaced on the Senate floor in December 1985. Democrat David Boren of Oklahoma and Republican Barry Goldwater of Arizona wanted to reduce the amount a PAC could donate to a candidate. Ironically, most Republicans, who were to embrace such a proposal later, worked to sidetrack this measure. At the time, the Republicans were in control of the Senate and were receiving the majority of donations made by business and trade association PACs.

Democrats regained a majority in the Senate in the November 1986 elections and decided to make campaign finance reform a major issue. Led by Boren, their bill provided direct public financing for Senate candidates who accepted spending limits; also included were aggregate limits on the total amount of money a candidate could accept from all PACs.

A rancorous, eight-month-long debate ensued, in which the Democrats sought without success to shut off a Republican filibuster against the bill. In an unsuccessful attempt to attract Republican support, Boren modified the legislation to provide public funding only to candidates whose opponents exceeded the prescribed spending limits.

Since 1987, Senate and House Democratic leaders have insisted on expenditure limits in congressional races similar to those now in place for presidential campaigns, while Republicans have strongly objected. The issue has become the biggest single obstacle to achieving bipartisan reform.

Many Republicans see spending limits as giving further advantage to incumbent legislators with widespread name recognition at a time when a majority of incumbents are Democrats. Some recent statistics do back up the argument that spending limits could disadvantage challengers. For example, a study by the non-partisan Committee for the Study of the American Electorate found that of 32 winning Senate challengers between 1978 and 1988, only seven stayed within the spending limits proposed by Senate Democrats in 1990 (Peck 1990, 3).

A basic philosophical disagreement also lies behind this dispute. The Democrats insist that rising costs and the escalating money chase cannot be solved unless the total amount of money in campaigns is capped through expenditure limits. The Republicans counter that the chief problem is not the amounts of money, but its sources. They have focused on limiting certain kinds of money considered tainted (i.e., PACs) and replacing it with other sources they regard as more desirable (i.e., donations from individuals and political party money).

The Republicans also oppose public financing, which they tend to regard as an inappropriate use of tax dollars. This is a second major partisan difference between them and the Democrats, although there is by no means acceptance of public financing by all Democrats.

Several factors converged to bring campaign finance reform to the forefront of the legislative agenda when the 101st Congress convened in January 1989. It had become apparent that a bailout of the nation's savings and loan industry was going to cost several hundred billion dollars. Attention focused on the California-based Lincoln Savings & Loan (S&L). It was revealed that Lincoln's owner, Charles Keating, and his associates had given $1.3 million to political and semi-political committees associated with five senators who had met with federal regulators on Keating's behalf.[14]

Then, House members began moving after the 1988 election to give themselves a substantial pay raise, in order to deal with the issue almost two years before they would again face the voters. A fire-storm of protest erupted, and the move was temporarily shelved. To make the pay raise more palatable, House leaders promised action on ethics and campaign reform measures.

House Speaker Jim Wright of Texas, then the subject of an ethics investigation that would ultimately lead to his resignation, appointed a bipartisan task force on campaign reform in January 1989. House Democrats coalesced around two bills proposing campaign spending limits and aggregate ceilings on PAC donations. The chief difference between the two bills was over public financing, reflecting divisions within the Democratic majority on this issue. One bill sought to achieve voluntary compliance with spending limits in return for discounts on postal rates and television ads; the other included public matching funds.

In the Senate, Boren reintroduced his 1987–88 proposal for public financing of Senate candidates only when an opponent exceeds spending limits. The Republicans, led by Senator Mitch McConnell of Kentucky, countered with a cut in PAC contribution limits, an increase in the amount that could be donated by an individual, and fewer restrictions on the money that political parties could give to candidates.

In June 1989, President Bush offered his own proposal. With the Democrats in control of Congress, it was aimed largely at reducing the advantages of incumbency by doing away with most PACs and forcing candidates to "zero out" campaign treasuries after each election. The latter proposal was designed to end the practice whereby incumbents accumulated large "war chests" in an effort to scare away potential challengers. Not surprisingly, the plan was strongly attacked by the Democrats.

By the end of 1989, the co-chairmen of the House task force, Democrat Al Swift of Washington and Republican Guy Vander Jagt of Michigan, reached agreement on some secondary issues. These included guaranteeing priority for political candidates in the purchase of broadcast time, re-establishing tax credits for small donations and doing away with leadership PACs.[15] But, on the major issues – expenditure limits, public funding, PACs and the role of parties – sharp partisan divisions remained.

Just as ethics problems had placed pressure on House Democrats to act on campaign reform in 1989 (ethics controversies forced both Wright and Majority Whip Tony Coelho from office), the Senate came under similar pressure in 1990 as a result of a decision by the Senate Ethics Committee to investigate the five senators involved in the Keating S&L affair. In an effort to avoid a repeat of the 1987–88 battle, the two Senate leaders – Democrat George Mitchell of Maine and Republican Robert Dole of Kansas – named a panel of academic and legal experts to come up with possible solutions.

The panel's recommendations, released in early March, were initially hailed by both political parties as the basis for a possible compromise (Campaign Finance Reform Panel 1990).[16] The panel proposed what became known as "flexible spending limits." Exempt from these limits would be relatively small contributions to Senate candidates from in-state residents, along with spending by political parties for research, voter-registration drives and get-out-the-vote efforts.

The panel sought to compromise between the Democrats' insistence on spending limits and the Republicans' contentions that the chief problem is the source of campaign money. While maintaining a form of expenditure ceilings, the proposal favoured political party contributions and individual donations from voting constituents over PACs and out-of-state individuals – both regarded as major sources of special interest money. In addition, the panel did not recommend direct public financing, an idea strongly opposed by the Republicans. Rather, it suggested reduced broadcast rates and postal discounts combined with tax credits for in-state contributions as incentives for candidates to abide by spending limits.

The political opening created by the panel's report was soon lost amid posturing by Senate Democrats and Republicans, both eager to be seen by voters as wearing the mantle of reform. Although there were also internal differences within each party, the Democrats and the Republicans formulated separate bills as possible substitutes to one that had been reported out favourably by a Democratic-controlled Senate committee.

The Democratic-sponsored bill that passed the Senate in August 1990 proposed that candidates who comply with spending limits be given vouchers with which to buy television time along with discounted mail rates. The Senate legislation also would have provided direct public funding to participating candidates whose opponents exceeded the spending limit in a particular state. The House Democratic bill included free television time and mail discounts. But, reflecting scepticism on the part of some House Democrats regarding the ability of the FEC to administer a program of direct public funding for congressional candidates, the House bill did not provide for such a program.

Another issue to split Democrats and Republicans was how to regulate PACs. In general, the Senate and House Democrats differ on reducing PAC contribution limits or prohibiting PAC contributions entirely, but both have favoured aggregate ceilings on the total any candidate can accept from all PACs. Some Republicans have proposed reducing the current $5 000 per election limit that a PAC is allowed to give to a candidate, while others want to ban PAC contributions entirely. Proposals to reduce contribution limits seem aimed at the Democratic-leaning labour PACs and certain other membership PACs, which have tended to contribute the maximum allowed under law. Some have complained that the Democratic proposals for aggregate limits would enable a candidate to accept large amounts of early "seed money" from well-endowed PACs, thus preventing the smaller PACs from contributing at all if the candidate reached the limit early.

Two provisions faced almost certain judicial challenges if the Senate package had become law: a ban on PACs and a system of contingency public financing. In fact, the Senate bill contained a stand-by scheme for limiting PAC contributions in the event that the ban on PACs was found to be unconstitutional. (Besides corporate, trade association and union PACs, the prohibition included covered "non-connected" or ideological or issue PACs, a move potentially in conflict with constitutional rights.) During the Senate debate, contingency public funding was challenged as a coercive measure because it serves to punish a free-spending candidate by giving public money to his or her opponent.

The House bill, passed several days after the Senate legislation, emerged only after fierce infighting among House Democrats. Those from states likely to lose districts as a result of the 1990 decennial census feared that spending limits would harm their chances for political survival. To satisfy them, the spending limits were loosened for House candidates who survived primary elections with less than two-thirds of the vote. Those complying with the limits were to be rewarded with broadcast and postal discounts.

In contrast to the Senate ban on PACs, the House-passed bill allowed candidates to accept an aggregate amount of PAC contributions equal to half of the spending limit. This clearly reflected House Democratic dependence on PACs: almost 52 percent of the money received by the House Democratic majority during the 1988 campaign came from PACs. The House legislation also gave favoured treatment to those PACs that limited donations from their members to no more than $240 per year. Critics charged that this was simply a move to benefit labour PACs, which rely largely on small contributions.

Negotiations between the House and Senate on the issue were never convened, leaving the future of the matter to the 1991–92 session of Congress. But given the differences between the two houses – along with threats that President Bush would veto any bill calling for spending limits and public finance – few are certain of action in the near future. Nevertheless, both houses of Congress demonstrated in 1990 their ability to pass bills.

THE STATE OF THE STATES

The reforms at the federal level during the 1970s spurred numerous changes at the state and local levels. But recently, the states have often taken the lead while the issue remains stalemated in Congress. The push for reform at the state level comes at a time when many of the problems plaguing the congressional finance system, including heavy reliance on PACs and a shortage of financially competitive challengers, are increasingly present in the campaigns for statewide office and for seats in state legislatures.

As of the end of 1990, all 50 states had some form of campaign disclosure. A majority of states had restrictions on individual donations to a candidate, while half had limitations on PAC contributions.[17] In addition, almost half the states featured direct or indirect public financing for candidates and/or political parties through tax checkoffs or voluntary tax add-ons. Many of the programs provided only modest amounts of public financing.

Several major municipalities, including New York and Los Angeles, the nation's largest cities, provide for public financing (Alexander and Walker 1990).[18]

Following is a look at three political units – New Jersey, Minnesota and New York City – that have put extensive systems into place.

New Jersey

New Jersey adopted public financing of gubernatorial elections in early 1974, six months before Congress expanded the current system of presidential public funding. New Jersey's move also was a reaction to scandal. At the time, New Jersey suffered from a reputation as one of the country's more corrupt states, and public funding was adopted following a period in which several high-ranking public officials were convicted of campaign-related abuses.

New Jersey's program, first implemented in the 1977 general

election, later was extended to cover primaries as well; the gubernatorial races of 1981, 1985 and 1989 featured public funding during both the pre-nomination and general election periods. The New Jersey system is the most generous state program in the country. After raising a "threshold" of $150 000 in private donations, a candidate is eligible to receive $2 in public funding for every $1 raised, up to a prescribed ceiling. In return, he or she must abide by limits on individual contributions as well as overall expenditures and agree to participate in two debates each in the primary and general election.

Beginning in 1989, the expenditure limits and public subsidies were indexed to inflation, mirroring the presidential public funding system. The New Jersey legislature also tied the contribution limits to the consumer price index.

Advocates say that the generosity of the New Jersey system is directly related to its success; gubernatorial candidates of both parties have found it worth their while to accept limitations on spending in return for the substantial public subsidies offered. Of 40 major candidates who have run for the governorship since public funding was enacted, 38 have sought and received the subsidies (Alexander 1989, 9). And, unlike other states, the New Jersey legislature has been willing to appropriate money to supplement receipts from an income tax checkoff.

In the 1989 gubernatorial primary election, public funding accounted for 58 percent of the money spent within the expenditure ceiling (Alexander 1989, table 2, 14). During the general election, the Democratic and Republican candidates each received a public subsidy equal to two-thirds of their spending limits.

Nonetheless, the New Jersey system has not been without its problems; to some extent, it is a case study in the difficulty of seeking to impose expenditure ceilings. In 1977, the spending limit was set at a relatively low level. This ended up placing state Senator Raymond Bateman, the Republican challenger, at a significant disadvantage in his campaign against his better-known opponent, Democratic incumbent Brendan Byrne. "As the public support for the candidates shifted toward Governor Byrne, Senator Bateman, solely because of the expenditure limit, was unable to react and mount an alternative campaign to counteract the growth of support for Governor Byrne," the New Jersey Election Law Enforcement Commission (ELEC) later reported (1982, 17–18).

Based on that experience, ELEC has quadrennially advocated repealing the expenditure ceilings and instead, providing candidates with a base of public funding sufficient to mount a viable campaign. In 1980, the New Jersey legislature voted to do away with the spending ceiling.

Byrne, who had benefited from it, vetoed the measure. In 1989, the legislature raised the ceilings substantially.

As with the presidential candidates, New Jersey gubernatorial nominees have increasingly sought to legally evade spending limits through the use of soft money. In 1989, the state political parties financed a variety of "generic" campaign ads and activities that redounded to the benefit of the gubernatorial candidates (Fitzpatrick 1990, 14–18). In addition, independent expenditure campaigns, used to skirt presidential limits, played a role in the last two governorship races.

In New Jersey, the governor is the only official of the executive branch of government to be popularly elected. To date, the legislature has not chosen to extend public funding to their own election contests. In fact, unlike the gubernatorial race, there are now no limits on how much individuals, businesses, unions and PACs may contribute to legislative candidates. Consequently, much of the special interest money kept out of the governorship election has been diverted into the races for the legislature.

Minnesota
Like the New Jersey system, Minnesota's public funding program also dates back to 1974. However, it owes its creation not to scandal, but to a political tradition of idealistic populism that has made this state one of the most liberal in the United States.

The Minnesota system, although not as well funded as New Jersey's, is more extensive in several respects. It assists political parties as well as candidates. While limited to the general election, it covers all statewide candidates (excluding judicial office). Minnesota also is one of only three states that provide public funding to state legislative candidates. And the state broke new political ground in 1990 when it extended state public funding to elections for Congress. This seems certain to face a constitutional challenge on the grounds that state laws are pre-empted by federal laws in the case of federal elections.

To qualify for public funding in the general election, statewide and state legislative candidates must agree in writing to comply with expenditure ceilings as well as limits on aggregate contributions from individuals, unions, PACs and political parties (corporations are barred from making political donations). Although the Republican candidates for governor declined public funding in 1978 and 1982, the great majority of eligible candidates have opted to accept the money and abide by the limits since the system was first implemented in 1976. In 1986, when both major party gubernatorial candidates accepted public funding, about a quarter of their campaign budgets were underwritten by subsidies (Alexander 1989, 32–33).

Along with Rhode Island, Minnesota currently has the nation's highest tax checkoff for public funding: $5. Initially, candidates of the state's Democratic-Farmer-Labor Party were outdistancing their Republican counterparts in receipt of public funds. But in recent years, Republicans have gained a larger share of the available subsidies (Alexander 1989, 32).

There is mixed evidence as to whether Minnesota's extensive program has achieved a basic goal of public funding systems: to increase the degree of competition among candidates by "levelling the playing field." On the plus side, no one has run unchallenged for statewide office since the law was enacted. All but one of the winning candidates accepted public funding and therefore were constrained by spending limits (McCoy 1987).

However, the benefits of Minnesota's public funding for legislative candidates can be questioned. There is some evidence that candidates in non-competitive races often opt for public financing to pay for their campaigns when the expenditure limits are high enough and the money the program provides is sufficient. But in competitive districts or those in which a strong challenger seeks to unseat an incumbent, candidates may not accept public financing so they can spend as much money as they deem necessary. Generally, Republicans do not participate in public funding as readily as do Democrats.

Expenditure limits also have posed problems for the Minnesota program. In 1980, a year in which both houses of the Minnesota legislature were up for election, the rate of participation in the public funding program dropped to 66 percent from 92 percent four years earlier (Alexander 1989, table 5, 29). At the time, inflation was running in double digits, and the expenditure ceiling had not been raised to take that into account – thereby making the restrictions unattractive to many candidates. After the 1980 election, both spending limits and public funding allocations were tied to the consumer price index, and in the 1990 election the rate of candidate participation was back up to 92 percent.

New York City

Of the four municipalities with public financing, the most extensive program is in New York City. As was the case with the neighbouring state of New Jersey, the New York City program was born of scandal. In response, the City Council in February 1988 enacted public financing legislation, which was signed by Mayor Edward Koch and ratified overwhelmingly by city voters the following November. In 1989, Koch sought re-election under the first test of the new program, losing to David N. Dinkins, then Manhattan Borough president.

Those seeking public funding in New York City must agree to abide by expenditure limits and to demonstrate the viability of their candidacy by raising a relatively modest threshold amount in private donations. Public funds then match private contributions of up to $500 from New York City residents. The program covers all of the city's elected offices: mayor, City Council president, comptroller, the presidents of New York's five boroughs and the members of the City Council.

Candidates participating in the New York City program also must agree to limit individual contributions to $3 000. This is far more restrictive than current New York state law, which sets the individual limit at $50 000.

An assessment of the city's first experience with the new law in 1989 found that it had sharply diminished the role of large contributors – a perennial concern in a city where the powerful real estate industry has often exercised its financial clout in election years.

In terms of candidate participation, the program had its biggest impact in the mayor's race. Five of the six major candidates opted to participate in the program. The Democratic Party nominee, Dinkins, received about 12 percent of his total receipts from public funding; Republican nominee Rudolph Giuliani received about a fifth of his campaign budget from public funds (New York City Campaign Finance Board 1990, 5). In all, 48 candidates who appeared on the ballot in either the primary or general election participated in the program, and 36 received public funds (ibid., 29).

The program was less successful in bringing electoral competition to City Council races, which – with a few exceptions – traditionally have been low-visibility, one-sided contests. While 33 candidates for the 35 council seats opted into the program, only 25 actually received any public funding (New York City Campaign Finance Board 1990, 16). This may change in the 1991 special elections: the City Council is being expanded from 35 to 51 seats and given enhanced power.

CONCLUDING OBSERVATIONS

As noted at the outset, it is risky to draw comparisons between the United States and Canada in view of the significant differences in their political systems. However, in terms of campaign finance, there are several basic realities that underlie both systems as we enter the 1990s:

Professionalized campaigns are here to stay.   The host of professional campaign services relied upon by competitive candidates and parties is costly. No amount of legislative action is going to turn back the clock and de-professionalize campaigns. The issue, rather, is how to finance modern elections in a manner that minimizes the opportunity for corruption, as well as the appearance of corruption.

Money is speech. That tenet lies at the heart of the *Buckley* decision's finding that mandatory expenditure limits were prohibited under the provisions of the U.S. Constitution. But it is a principle applicable to any modern democratic society in which free speech is a basic right. To restrict a candidate's ability to avail himself or herself of the means of promotion can be considered a restriction on speech. Any effort to forestall real or perceived corruption by curtailing the supply of political money must be balanced carefully against basic individual rights.

Unforeseen consequences are inevitable. In democratic pluralistic societies, such as those of the United States and Canada, efforts to regulate the flow of money will never work quite as intended. Some affected parties will seek redress in the judicial process; in the United States, the current structure of campaign finance was shaped almost as much by litigation as by the laws enacted by Congress. The best of intentions often have unintended side effects. In enacting the 1979 FECA amendments, Congress had the purpose in mind of strengthening grassroots political parties. What resulted was the rip tide of soft money that now courses through presidential elections.

The foregoing are among the realities and principles to be kept in mind in evaluating the experience of campaign finance reform and proposing further changes. In the United States, several obvious lessons arise from the experience of the past 20 years:

Expenditure limits develop leaks. Limitations of any kind – whether contribution or expenditure limits – develop leaks. But expenditure limits are the most problematic, as was demonstrated by the Bush–Dukakis race of 1988 and the New Jersey experience (and also, to some extent, by the experience with political interest groups in Canadian elections). In the U.S. political system, candidates at both the federal and state levels have found a multitude of ways to get around the limits by such hard-to-trace forms of political spending as soft money and independent expenditures. The former has reinjected the large contributor into presidential campaigns. The latter has intensified the use of negative advertising, resulting in heightened cynicism in an already disillusioned voting public.

At the congressional level, there is evidence that expenditure limits could place relatively unknown challengers at an even greater disadvantage at a time when races for the House and Senate are growing less and less competitive. The experience at the state legislative level indicates that when a candidate must abide by spending limits to receive public funding, some candidates have chosen to decline public financing. The result is that the candidate must seek that much more private money, which is derived increasingly from groups with interests before the legislature.

Public funding has benefits.   To say that questions can be raised about expenditure limits is not to render the same judgement on public funding. Even with undesirable forms of campaign money coming in through leaky expenditure limits, public funding clearly has displaced a significant amount of private donations in U.S. presidential campaigns. For example, even given the degree to which Dukakis and Bush were able to circumvent the official spending limits in 1988, public subsidies still accounted for significant amounts of their respective campaign budgets. Were that money not available, presidential candidates would likely be forced to do what congressional aspirants already are doing: pursue more PAC money.

From a practical standpoint, the presidential candidates operate under a scheme that has been dubbed floors-without-ceilings. Unrestrained by effective spending ceilings, they nevertheless are given a base of public funding from which to get their messages across through television and other means. In fact, Dukakis' home state of Massachusetts has a floors-without-ceilings system in which candidates receive public funding without committing to spending limits. This idea has met with resistance in Congress and many state legislatures, where some are reluctant to provide taxpayer dollars without attempting to restrain private fund spending. On the other hand, the floors-without-ceilings approach allows the candidates to spend more than the public financing provides without artificial limitations.

Incumbents vs. challengers.   Analysing campaign spending data, political scientist Gary C. Jacobson showed that campaign spending does not have the same consequences for incumbents and challengers alike. Jacobson found that spending by challengers has more impact on election outcomes than does spending by incumbents (Jacobson 1978, 469).

Simply being known and remembered by voters is a very important factor in electoral success. The average incumbent, provided with the resources of office, already enjoys an advantage in voter recognition prior to the campaign. The dissemination of additional information about the incumbent during the campaign, therefore, may often be superfluous even though it helps reinforce voters' opinions. On the other hand, the challenger, not so well known to most voters, has everything to gain from an extensive and expensive effort to acquire voter awareness.

Translated into financial terms, this means that because senators and representatives are generally better known, they usually need less campaign money but are able to raise more. The challengers, while they may need more money, have difficulty in getting it. But when they do, either through providing it to their own campaigns out of their own wealth, or by attracting it, they become better known and are more likely to win. If the incumbent then raises money to meet the threat, spending money helps him or her less per dollar spent than additional dollars spent by the challenger. In summary, those votes that change as a result of campaign spending generally benefit challengers.

Jacobson concluded that any campaign finance policy, such as public subsidies, that would increase spending for both incumbent and challenger would work to the benefit of the latter, thus making elections more competitive. On the other hand, any policy that attempts to equalize the financial positions of candidates by limiting campaign contributions and spending would benefit incumbents, thus lessening electoral competition (Jacobson 1978, 474).

Contribution limits: How high or how low? In setting contribution limits, a balance must be struck between the need to reduce public perceptions of excessive spending and the need for candidates to raise adequate funds to communicate with voters.

No one has seriously advocated a return to the era of the six-figure donor: the presence of $100 000 soft-money contributors in the 1988 campaigns prompted editorial criticism and a negative public reaction. At the same time, setting contribution limits too low can have the effect of turning public officials into non-stop political fund-raisers seeking to collect sufficient money in small lots.

An appropriate limit depends greatly on the political demography of the jurisdiction for which it is intended. But the purpose should be guided by recognition that money is an essential ingredient in political campaigning. Once the decision is made, contribution limits should be indexed to inflation to prevent the type of problem that has arisen in contests for Congress: the erosion of the value of the $1 000 individual contribution limit has, among other effects, provided greater incentives for candidates to seek PAC support with the higher limit of $5 000.

In conclusion, two points are worth considering. First, the impact of money on politics raises concerns on two levels. One level is whether the financing system provides undue influence for those able to contribute, or in the case of PACs, for those able to organize fund-raising of big money in small sums. The other level is the conferring of electoral advantage to those able to raise and spend the most. The regulatory system tries to meet these problems by means of disclosure and limitations, and in the presidential case, public financing, but as illustrated, not always successfully. The search for remedies goes on.

Second, what the federal and many of the state laws – and commissions – have lacked is a philosophy about regulation that is both constitutional in the U.S. framework and pragmatically designed to keep the election process open and flexible rather than rigid, exclusionary and fragmented. Election regulation is essential, but it does not serve the public interest or the political process if it chills citizen participation. It is not desirable for the law to lead election agencies to micromanage political campaigns. More than two decades after major change was initiated, it is not clear that election reform has led to the openness, flexibility and level of participation a democratic and pluralistic society requires.

ABBREVIATIONS

ch.   chapter

Pub. L.   Public Law

ss.   sections

Stat.   Statutes

U.S.C.   United States Code

NOTES

This study was completed in April 1991.

1. This ruling came as part of the *Buckley v. Valeo* case, 424 U.S. 1 (1976), discussed in detail in the first section of this study.

2. This statement appeared in a letter sent by Johnson to Congress on 26 May 1966, in which he proposed the *Election Reform Act of 1966*. Its full text is reprinted in *CQ Almanac 1966* (1967, 1248–49).

3. Taken from a statement by Susan B. King, director, National Committee for an Effective Congress, before House Interstate and Foreign Committee, Subcommittee on Communications and Power, 9 June 1971; quoted in *CQ Almanac 1971* (1972, 888).

4. One of the leaders of the fight to roll back the law in 1967, Sen. Robert F. Kennedy, D–New York, expressed concern that national party chairs would use the money to cajole large states to support the nomination of a particular presidential candidate. A year later, Kennedy mounted an insurgent campaign for the Democratic presidential nomination that was ended by his assassination.

5. The plaintiffs covered a broad ideological spectrum, led by conservative Republican Senator James Buckley of New York and including Eugene McCarthy, a former Democratic senator from Minnesota, and Stewart R. Mott, a large contributor to liberal candidates. The defendants included Secretary of State Francis R. Valeo, the U.S. attorney general, the Clerk of the House of Representatives, the Federal Election Commission and three reform groups: Common Cause, the Center for Public Financing of Elections and the League of Women Voters.

6. Congress reserved the right to veto regulations promulgated by the FEC as well as a number of other independent agencies. This so-called legislative veto was later ruled unconstitutional by the Supreme Court in *Immigration and Naturalization Service v. Chadha* 462 U.S. 919 (1983). The court asserted that Congress was trying to exercise powers reserved to the president under the U.S. Constitution.

7. To put this figure in perspective, some $2.7 billion was spent on all electoral activity in the United States in 1988. Consequently, direct spending by the presidential candidates accounted for almost 20 percent of all political spending.

8. Independent expenditures have come into play in congressional as well as presidential campaigns. In 1980, four liberal senators – including 1972 Democratic presidential nominee George McGovern – were defeated amidst a campaign of ads underwritten by the National Conservative Political Action Committee (NCPAC), the most controversial of the independent expenditure groups of the 1980s. However, most independent spending has been concentrated in presidential contests.

9. The Mondale campaign agreed to pay the U.S. Treasury $350 000, plus an $18 500 civil penalty, for violations of contribution and spending limits growing out of the delegate committee scheme. In addition, the agreement required the Mondale committee to pay $29 640 for exceeding spending limits during the New Hampshire primary. The details of the settlement are contained in FEC MUR (Matter Under Review) #1704.

10. Not every contributor credited with $100 000 gave it all in soft money. Some donated up to the legal limit of $20 000 in hard money to the national party committees. Others gave in varying combinations of hard and soft money totalling $100 000 or more and thus were credited with that amount. Still others gave directly to state party committees rather than routeing the donations through the national parties.

11. The complete regulations are printed in the *Federal Register* (1990), under the Federal Election Commission, "Methods of Allocation Between Federal and Non-Federal Accounts: Payments, Reporting; Final Rule; Transmittal of Regulations of Congress."

12. The focus groups were conducted by Market Decisions Corp., Portland, Oregon, under contract to the FEC. Their findings are contained in "Presidential Election Campaign Fund Focus Group Research," published in December 1990.

13. Bush and Dukakis each received $46.1 million in public funding during the 1988 general election. Dukakis spent just under half that amount ($22.3 million) on paid television, while Bush spent almost two-thirds of the amount of his subsidy ($30.2 million) on television time.

14. The five senators involved in the Keating affair – Democrats Alan Cranston of California, Dennis DeConcini of Arizona, John Glenn of Ohio, Donald Riegle of Michigan and Republican John McCain of Arizona – became known as the "Keating Five." The episode served to highlight the role of soft money at the congressional as well as the presidential level.

15. Leadership PACs are formed by influential members of Congress to funnel money to fellow legislators, thereby allowing the sponsor of the PAC to collect political IOUs and strengthen his or her clout on Capitol Hill.

    The leadership PAC controversy has some parallels to the current debate in Canada over whether spending in contests for party leadership should be regulated.

16. The author of this study served as a member of the six-person panel.

17. For a comprehensive survey of campaign finance laws in all 50 states, see *Campaign Finance Law 90* (1990).

18. There are half a dozen cities and counties that have adopted public finance programs. Besides New York and Los Angeles, they include Seattle, Washington; King County, Washington (the county surrounding Seattle); Tucson, Arizona; and Sacramento County, California. However, the Sacramento and Los Angeles programs are in limbo because of Proposition 73, a state ballot initiative passed in June 1988 that bars public funding of candidates in California. For more information, see Alexander and Walker (1990).

REFERENCES

Alexander, Herbert E. 1989. "Public Financing of State Elections." Paper presented at the State of the States Symposium, Eagleton Institute of Politics, Rutgers University, New Brunswick, NJ.

Alexander, Herbert E., and Monica Bauer. 1991. *Financing the 1988 Election.* Boulder: Westview Press.

Alexander, Herbert E., and Michael C. Walker. 1990. *Public Financing of Local Elections: A Data Book of Public Funding in Four Cities and Two Counties.* Los Angeles: Citizens' Research Foundation.

Babcock, Charles. 1991. "Campaign Tax Checkoff Is Studied." *Washington Post,* 4 January.

Buckley v. Valeo 424 U.S. 1 (1976).

Campaign Finance Law 90. 1990. Washington, DC: National Clearinghouse on Election Administration of the Federal Election Commission.

Campaign Finance Reform Panel. 1990. "Campaign Finance Reform: A Report to the Majority Leader and Minority Leader, United States Senate." Washington, DC.

Campaign Practices Reports. 1990. "Tax Checkoff, Presidential Primary Financing in Jeopardy as FEC, Treasury Prepare Stopgap Plan." Washington, DC: Congressional Quarterly.

Canadian Study of Parliament Group. 1990. "Reform of Electoral Campaigns." Keynote address, "Reforming Canada's Electoral Campaigns," by Patrick Boyer, MP. Toronto.

Common Cause. 1989. "The Failure-to-Enforce Commission." Washington, DC: Common Cause.

Corrado, Anthony. 1990. "The Pre-Candidacy PAC Loophole." *Boston Globe,* 6 May.

CQ Almanac, 1966. 1967. Washington, DC: Congressional Quarterly.

CQ Almanac, 1971. 1972. Washington, DC: Congressional Quarterly.

Edwards, Mickey. 1990. "What 'Permanent Congress'?" *New York Times,* 5 January.

Federal Election Commission. 1990a. "FEC Releases 1990 Mid-Year PAC Count." Washington, DC.

———. 1990b. "Presidential Fund Income Tax Checkoff Status." Washington, DC.

Federal Register. 1990. 55 (26 July): 26058–73.

Fitzpatrick, Bob. 1990. "Soft Money on a Hard Roll." *New Jersey Reporter,* February, 14–18.

Germond, Jack, and Jules Witcover. 1985. *Wake Us When It's Over: Presidential Politics of 1984.* New York: Macmillan.

Harvard University. John F. Kennedy School of Government. Institute of Politics. 1979. "An Analysis of the Impact of the Federal Election Campaign Act, 1972–78." Study prepared for the U.S. Congress, House Administration Committee. Washington, DC: Government Printing Office.

Houston, Paul. 1988. "Bush, Dukakis Got Record Big Gifts." *Los Angeles Times*, 10 December.

Immigration and Naturalization Service v. Chadha 462 U.S. 919 (1983).

Jackson, Brooks. 1990. *Broken Promise: Why the Federal Election Commission Failed.* New York: Priority Press.

Jacobson, Gary C. 1978. "The Effects of Campaign Spending in Congressional Elections." *American Political Science Review* 72:469–91.

———. 1980. *Money in Congressional Elections.* New Haven: Yale University Press.

Makinson, Larry. 1989. "The Price of Admission: An Illustrated Atlas of Spending in the 1988 Congressional Elections." Washington, DC: Center for Responsive Politics.

McCoy, Mary Ann. 1987. "Public Financing and Expenditure Limits." Paper presented at a meeting of the Commission on Government Integrity, Buffalo, NY, 23 October.

New Jersey Election Law Enforcement Commission. 1982. "New Jersey Public Financing: 1981 Gubernatorial Elections." Trenton, NJ.

New York City Campaign Finance Board. 1990. "Dollars and Disclosure: Campaign Finance Reform in New York City." New York.

Peck, Louis M. 1990. "Campaign Financing." Issue Brief No. 101–08. Washington, DC: Congressional Quarterly.

President's Commission on Campaign Costs. 1962. *Report, Financing Presidential Campaigns.* Washington, DC: Government Printing Office.

Swift, Al. 1989. "The 'Permanent Congress' Is a Myth." *Washington Post Weekly Edition*, 26 June.

United States. *Federal Corrupt Practices Act of 1925*, Feb. 28, 1925, ch. 368, title III.

———. *Federal Election Campaign Act of 1971*, Pub. L. 92–225, Feb. 7, 1972, 86 Stat. 3 (1973), codified and amended in 2 U.S.C. 432 and 18, 47 U.S.C.

———. ———. *Amendments of 1974*, Pub. L. 93–443, Oct. 15, 1974, 88 Stat. 1263.

———. ———. *Amendments of 1976*, Pub. L. 94–283, May 11, 1976, 90 Stat. 475.

———. ———. *Amendments of 1979*, Pub. L. 96–187, Jan. 8, 1980.

———. *Revenue Act of 1971*, Pub. L. 92–178, Dec. 10, 1971, ss. 701–703, 801, 802, 85 Stat. 497, 560–74 (1972).

———. *Revenue Act of 1978*, Pub. L. 95–600, Nov. 6, 1978, 92 Stat. 2763.

2

THE EVOLUTION OF CAMPAIGN FINANCE REGULATION IN THE UNITED STATES AND CANADA

Robert E. Mutch

THE PROBLEM OF money in elections is as old as elections themselves, and legislative attempts to regulate that money have changed with its sources and uses. The modern era in American politics began in the early 19th century, when elections ceased to be contests among upper-class factions and came to be fought by professional, middle-class politicians organized into parties. With the parties came a new source of money to finance the election expenses, which wealthy politicians had once paid out of their personal fortunes: the parties exacted financial support from those they had placed in government jobs by assessing office holders a fixed percentage of their salaries, usually 2 percent.

Civil service reformers opposed the practice of political assessments, and their attempts to free government employees from political control were also the first American attempts to regulate campaign funds. Congress made several such attempts, beginning in the 1830s, but reformers did not succeed until a disappointed office seeker assassinated President James A. Garfield in 1881. The *Pendleton Act* of 1883 created a class of federal government workers who had to win office by competitive examination, and it prohibited the solicitation of political contributions from these workers. Subsequent legislation, which continued well into the 20th century, further diminished the importance of the civil service as a source of party funds. But these laws, however significant their impact on campaign finance, were primarily intended to reform and improve the federal civil service.

State legislatures passed the first laws aimed directly at the use of money in elections: from 1890 to 1904, 21 states adopted "corrupt practices acts," which were more or less closely patterned after Great Britain's *Corrupt and Illegal Practices Prevention Act* of 1883. Some of these laws followed the example of one part of the British Act by limiting campaign spending, while others set their own example by banning corporation contributions. Most, however, imitated the other main provision of British law by relying primarily upon disclosure, or "publicity" as it was then called. British law required candidates to appoint agents, who then had to account publicly for all money received and spent in the campaign; the American version of this "agency doctrine" was to assign these responsibilities to campaign committee treasurers. None of these laws was effective (Belmont 1905, 171–79; Bryce 1903, 148–49).

Canada did not develop a modern party system until the 1896 general election, and national party financing thus remained a minor factor in Canadian elections until the end of the 19th century. Canadian politicians also never resorted to the American practice of systematically assessing civil service salaries to raise campaign funds. Canadian campaign finance after Confederation fell into two patterns: either candidates for office paid their own election expenses, even into the 20th century, or they were personally paid by party leaders. As late as 1930, Conservative leader Richard Bedford Bennett paid most of his party's election expenses out of his own pocket (Seidle 1980, 143–45; Ward 1972, 336; Paltiel 1970, 20–21, 29).

When Canada did develop modern parties, its political fund-raising became a far more centralized operation than has ever been the case in the United States. Perhaps this development was in part a continuation of the pre-modern pattern whereby party leaders assumed personal responsibility for election expenses. Probably, however, the main reason is that a parliamentary system concentrates governmental authority in the Cabinet, thus encouraging similar concentration within the parties themselves.

Canada's two major parties resemble their otherwise dissimilar American counterparts in their extensive financial reliance on business and a few wealthy individuals. From the late 19th century on, the primary source of political money for Liberals, Conservatives, Republicans and Democrats (apart from civil service assessments and politicians' personal fortunes) has been corporations and wealthy business people. In both countries, too, it was a scandal concerning business money that led to the first federal regulations of campaign financing.

THE POLITICS OF REGULATING CAMPAIGN FUNDS

The United States

Congress passed the first federal campaign finance law in 1907, in response to revelations from a 1905 New York State investigation into the insurance business. The investigators discovered that insurance companies had secretly contributed large sums to Republican presidential campaigns in 1896, 1900 and 1904. Congressional reformers proposed two remedies: to prohibit corporations from making campaign contributions, and to require national party committees to disclose their receipts and expenditures. Several states had already tried both approaches. By 1911, Congress had enacted both measures and had added a ceiling on campaign spending by congressional candidates.

For more than 30 years, Congress did little more than revise and recodify the laws enacted in this initial burst of legislative innovation. Then, in the 1940s, a Republican–Southern Democratic congressional majority responded to increased labour political activity by extending the corporation ban to cover labour unions. After the same conservative majority also extended civil service protections against political assessments in a move to stop the New Deal, Democrats retaliated by imposing contribution limits as well as expenditure limits on national campaigns. The civil service protections remain in force, but the limits soon proved to be ineffective.

The 1950s and 1960s saw rising concern about the rapidly increasing cost of campaigning in the television era and about the consequences of the resulting scramble to accumulate ever-larger political funds. In 1966–67, largely in response to these financial pressures, Democrats in Congress passed – and then repealed, amid furious partisan and intra-party debate – a program of public financing for presidential campaigns. Public and private groups also studied the problem of campaign finance: President Kennedy appointed the Commission on Campaign Costs in 1962, and two private groups, the Committee for Economic Development (a big business group) and the Twentieth Century Fund (a foundation) addressed the problem in 1968 and 1969. In 1970 Democratic majorities in Congress enacted a bill to limit media spending in campaigns, only to see President Nixon veto it.

Congress put the cap on this "middle period" of American campaign finance regulation by enacting the *Federal Election Campaign Act of 1971* (FECA). The FECA followed the advice of the 1960s studies by repealing contribution and expenditure limits, although it imposed new limits on spending for the broadcast media. The Act also took the first steps toward reviving the 1966 Act for public financing of presidential campaigns and, in its only genuinely reformist section, greatly strengthened disclosure requirements.

The late 1960s and early 1970s saw a steep drop in public confidence in American political leaders. A study of public opinion polls concluded that this "virtual explosion of antigovernment sentiment" had much to do with the Vietnam War, but what is important here is that this political environment was ideal for the creation of Common Cause in 1970 (Lipset and Schneider 1983, 16; McFarland 1984).

Common Cause can be seen as a descendant of the National Publicity Bill Organization (NPBO), in that both are in the Progressive, "good government" tradition. But the earlier group was formed for the sole aim of enacting a national disclosure law, and it ceased to exist once this goal had been attained. Common Cause remains active because it sees itself as a "citizens' lobby," for which campaign finance is but one item in a broad agenda. In the fertile soil of public discontent, the group grew quickly, building a national membership and attracting to its Washington office people with legal, lobbying and congressional staff experience.

As the 1972 campaign drew near, Common Cause turned its attention to campaign finance. One of its first projects was to monitor the newly strengthened disclosure law and to publish the financial data in the candidates' reports. Since the new law did not take effect until 7 April 1972, Common Cause asked all candidates voluntarily to release information for funds raised before that date. Most complied, but some, notably President Richard M. Nixon, running for re-election, did not. The group filed suit, and when it became clear that the case would be heard before election day, thus ensuring maximum publicity, the president's campaign committee voluntarily released the data. Among the contributions listed were one for $1 million and another for $2 million, the largest ever recorded.

The Watergate scandal further depressed popular confidence in the country's political leaders and raised Common Cause's standing with the press and public. On the evening of 17 June 1972, Watergate Hotel security officers discovered five Nixon campaign committee employees inside the burgled offices of the Democratic National Committee. Investigations into this break-in soon turned up violations of election law, mostly illegal contributions from corporations and foreign nationals, cash contributions, and reporting failures (Alexander 1976, chaps. 3 and 13). A White House attempt to cover up the affair failed in the face of congressional and press investigations and eventually resulted in President Nixon's resignation and the inauguration of the country's first unelected president, Gerald R. Ford.[1]

Watergate was for Common Cause what the 1905 New York insurance investigation had been, on a smaller scale, for the National Publicity Bill Organization. Although the 1971 FECA was barely a year old, the scandal prompted the Senate to amend it, and Common Cause became the best known of the several interest groups that lobbied Congress on campaign finance reform. In 1974, after months of debate, Congress re-enacted contribution and spending limits, established a public financing program for presidential elections, and created an independent agency to administer and enforce the law.

Shortly after passage of the 1974 FECA Amendments, conservative and libertarian opponents of the new law, headed by Senator James Buckley (Rep., New York), challenged its constitutionality in federal court. They targeted every part of the law, thus making the Supreme Court's decision in the case, *Buckley v. Valeo* (1976), a landmark opinion in campaign finance law. The challengers were most successful on expenditure limits. Arguing that spending money in a campaign was equivalent to political speech, they charged that contribution and spending limits violated First Amendment guarantees of free speech. The Supreme Court agreed and struck down all spending limits except those accepted voluntarily by presidential candidates as a condition of receiving public financing for their campaigns.

In these actions we can find themes that appear throughout the development of American campaign finance law. The major themes are the role of scandal in prompting legislation, the importance of public interest groups in promoting reform, debate over the political influence of wealth (specifically the proper roles of corporations and labour unions) and the difficulties of drafting election laws for a federal system.

Corporations and Labour Unions

The politically sophisticated had long known, or at least suspected, that corporations were contributing large sums to the Republican party, but this fact did not become public knowledge until September 1905. In that month, a New York State legislative committee investigating the insurance business discovered that the country's three largest life insurance companies had secretly financed the 1896, 1900 and 1904 Republican presidential campaigns. Although such contributions were not illegal at the time and the absence of a national disclosure law meant that no one would have been required to reveal them, the corporations nonetheless disguised their contributions as individual gifts. This attempt at concealment suggests that the insurance executives knew their actions, if made public, would be widely regarded as illegitimate.

The political influence of wealth was not an entirely new phenomenon in the United States, but the rise of the large corporation in the 1890s gave it new prominence. Lord Bryce noted that the "growth of vast fortunes has helped to create a political problem," adding that "it is through corporations that wealth has made itself obnoxious" (Bryce 1903, 856). Ironically, civil service reform promoted this trend, for by slowly cutting off the most important source of political funds, it forced the parties to turn to private business. The Senate first showed concern about the political role of business in 1895, when a coalition of progressive Democrats and Republicans tried and failed to appoint a special committee to investigate corporate influence in congressional elections (U.S. *Congressional Record* [hereinafter *CR*] 4 May 1895, 4769, and 18 Dec. 1895, 230). In 1897, reacting to corporate support for the 1896 Republican presidential campaign, four states that had voted for the Democratic candidate – Nebraska, Missouri, Tennessee and Florida – prohibited campaign contributions by corporations. The 1905 New York disclosures revealed even broader opposition to corporate political contributions, as was evident from the editorial pages of newspapers across the nation. Both Republican and Democratic papers condemned corporation political contributions. The *New York Tribune*, the Republican party's flagship paper, was especially eloquent: "A corporation is not a citizen ... and attempts by it to exercise rights of citizenship are fundamentally a perversion of its power. Its stockholders, no matter how wise or how rich, should be forced to exercise their political influence as individuals on an equality with other men. This is the basic principle of democracy, and forgetfulness of it is responsible for many corporation abuses and for much of the popular prejudice against incorporated wealth" (*New York Tribune*, 20 Sept. 1905).

The consensus against corporation political contributions extended even to the courts, which interpreted corporation law as forbidding the practice.[2] This consensus guaranteed that editorial pressure for remedial legislation would be brought to bear on both Congress and the White House.

The National Publicity Bill Organization (NPBO), a public interest group formed immediately following the revelations, enlisted several prominent men – state and federal office holders, college presidents, business executives and even some labour leaders – to form a focal point for this pressure.[3] NPBO, as its name implies, advocated a federal publicity law, but it also saw publicity as a way to deal with corporation political money.

The founder of the group was Perry Belmont, a wealthy New York Democrat whose brother, banker August Belmont, was a leading contributor to the Democratic party. Just months before the New York State legislative hearings, Perry Belmont wrote an article claiming that a federal disclosure law would "secure the freedom of elections from improper influences," chief among which were corporations. He wrote that "contributions by corporations should be restricted," but he preferred to rely upon publicity as an aid to private stockholders' suits and did not press for prohibitive legislation (Belmont 1905, 185, 182).

It was one of NPBO's few Republican members, William E. Chandler, a former U.S. senator from New Hampshire, who was chiefly responsible for congressional passage of a ban on corporation contributions. He drafted and first introduced the bill early in 1901, shortly after the Boston & Maine Railroad, which dominated New Hampshire politics, successfully opposed Chandler's re-election. The bill did not come to a vote in 1901, but newspapers revived it immediately after the 1905 New York insurance hearings, and Chandler himself eagerly sought someone to reintroduce it in the Senate (Richardson 1940, 361, 489–91, 632, 636).

Chandler failed to find a Republican willing to sponsor his bill. This is an important point, because most accounts give credit for the eventual law to the Republican then occupying the White House, Theodore Roosevelt. The issue was a delicate one for the President, as the revelation that corporations had financed his 1904 campaign came less than a year after his own carefully phrased rebuttals, during that campaign, of Democratic charges that he had accepted such money. Three months after the revelation, in his message to the Fifty-Ninth Congress, the President advocated both a publicity law and a ban on corporation contributions. His advocacy of campaign finance reform went no further, however: no one in his administration drafted bills embodying the suggested regulations, and the President lent none of his considerable political weight to any of the reform measures introduced by others (Roosevelt 1952, 1009, 1101–102; *CR*, 5 Dec. 1905, 96).

After failing to persuade a member of his own party to introduce his bill, former Senator Chandler chose an old ally to sponsor it, South Carolina Democratic Senator Benjamin R. Tillman. Republicans controlled both houses of Congress, and the reluctance of Senate Republicans to introduce a reform bill drafted by a member of their own party did not augur well for that same bill's chances of passage when sponsored by a Democrat. But Tillman kept the issue alive in floor speeches and in calls for investigations into the financing of presidential elections, and it was probably his persistence, as well as the upcoming 1906 midterm elections, that convinced the Privileges and Elections Committee to report out a weakened version of the bill. Two weeks later, the Senate passed the bill without debate (*CR*, 9 June 1906, 8162; U.S. Senate Report [hereinafter S. Rept] 3056 (59th Cong.)). After waiting seven months, the Republican-controlled House also passed the bill, with minimal debate and by an unrecorded voice vote (*CR*, 21 Jan. 1907, 1452–54).

The revelation of the secret insurance company financing of Theodore Roosevelt's 1904 presidential campaign led to enactment of the 1907 Act, and it was publicly disclosed labour contributions to his Democratic cousin Franklin's 1936 and 1940 campaigns that prompted Republicans and conservative Democrats to extend the prohibition to unions. Labour unions had never spent much money on elections, so it was a great shock to Republicans when the United Mine Workers and other unions gave nearly $800 000 to President Roosevelt's 1936 re-election campaign (S. Rept 151 (75th Cong.), 127–31). In 1943, with both public opinion and the Roosevelt administration aroused over a long wartime coal strike, conservative elements of both parties saw their best chance to move against unions.

Democrats still had a majority in Congress, but Republicans had so increased their number in both houses that they could outnumber Northern Democrats three to one by joining with Southern Democrats, as they did on labour issues. House members of this conservative coalition had already tried to pass a separate bill banning union contributions, only to see the House Labor Committee reject it on the grounds that it discriminated against unions by imposing on them restrictions not applied to other unincorporated associations (*CR*, 3 June 1943, 5341). They fared better by adding the identical provision as a floor amendment to a Senate-passed bill restricting strikes in war-related industries. President Roosevelt vetoed the bill, but the Republican–Southern Democratic coalition managed to muster the two-thirds majority of both houses needed to override the veto (*CR*, 3 June 1943, 5328–47; 4 June 1943, 5390; 25 June 1943, 6487–89, 6548–49). The bill, a wartime measure only, was terminated six months after the president declared an end to hostilities.

The same coalition had an even easier time making the ban permanent in the Republican-controlled Eightieth Congress (1947–48), despite vigorous opposition from Northern Democrats and the two main labour organizations, the Congress of Industrial Organizations (CIO) and the American Federation of Labor (AFL). The conservative majority not only re-enacted the ban as part of the Taft-Hartley labour-management relations act but extended it to cover expenditures as well as contributions, and primaries and nominating conventions as well as general elections (Congressional Quarterly 1947, 279–308). Attempts by congressional conservatives to curb labour political activity only increased it. Unions went to court several times in the 1940s and 1950s to defend the legality of their political expenditures, and they met with much success.[4]

Labour's most significant act in the 1940s was to invent the political action committee. In direct reaction against the 1943 wartime ban, CIO created the Political Action Committee (CIO-PAC) to participate in the 1944 elections. So as not to fall under the strictures of the 1943 law, the funds CIO-PAC contributed to federal candidates came not from the treasuries of member unions but from voluntary contributions by rank and file members of those unions: thus, the PAC was technically not a union. Passage of the *Taft-Hartley Act* in 1947 had a similar result: the more moderate AFL created its own political arm, Labor's League for Political Education, and appealed for contributions from its 8 million members. These were the first PACs.

If unions could not use dues money for political purposes even when the decision to do so was made by majority vote of union members or their elected representatives, then members would have to be systematically solicited to contribute more money on top of their dues. Unions designed PACs to accomplish this end – to collect and distribute large sums of money collected in small amounts from large numbers of people. By the 1960s, PACs had become the primary vehicle for labour political activity. It was also in the 1960s that the labour political committees first came under attack.

In 1968 the federal government indicted a St. Louis local of the Pipefitters' Union for using its PAC to violate the 1947 prohibition against union political contributions. The Department of Justice alarmed labour by arguing that even if the local could show that member contributions to the PAC were voluntary, such contributions were still illegal because the PAC's overhead was paid directly out of the union treasury and its officers were also officers of the union, who solicited members at work (*Pipefitters* 1972). Since most union PACs were similar to that of the Pipefitters' St. Louis local, the government's victories in the district and circuit courts threatened the election activity of all unions. Labour's fears mounted when two national business organizations announced plans to seek further restrictions on labour PACs; when the government initiated a suit against the Seafarers' Union PAC; and when conservative Republicans tried to amend the 1971 FECA, on which Congress was then working, to restrict labour political funds. In the interval between the Supreme Court's agreement to hear the case on appeal and actual argument before that court, AFL-CIO decided to seek a more favourable amendment to that election law.

In 1971 Rep. Orval Hansen, a moderate Republican from Idaho, introduced the labour-backed amendment, which explicitly legalized the establishment of PACs (*CR*, 30 Nov. 1971, 43379). Hansen's amendment covered corporations as well as unions, but since most corporations contributed through individual executives rather than PACs, its main impact was on labour. Most House Republicans and Southern Democrats opposed the amendment, but it passed. It became law when the Senate also accepted it. Six months later, the Supreme Court ruled that the Pipefitters' PAC did not violate federal law, firmly establishing the legality of union political funds.

Corporations did not form PACs until after 1974. In the post-Watergate FECA Amendments, Congress dramatically altered patterns of corporate political giving by imposing strict and enforceable ceilings on individual contributions. A corporation's primary political resource is its treasury, and for decades business giving had been conducted through individual contributions by corporate executives. Companies found it easier than unions to evade the prohibitions enacted against them and so saw little reason to establish PACs.[5] The 1974 limits changed matters and began what has aptly been termed the explosive growth of corporate PACs.

Disclosure

In his 1905 article, National Publicity Bill Organization (NPBO) founder Perry Belmont argued against new laws to punish the improper use of money in elections. Rather, he sought "prevention by indirection" through the "turning on of the light" by disclosure, the method also preferred by the states that had enacted corrupt practices acts (Belmont 1905, 182, 185).

Political and constitutional problems prevented the reformers from turning on a light of very high intensity, however. The major political problem was that most NPBO leaders were Democrats and that congressional Republicans blocked passage of NPBO's bill for four years. Another problem was one of constitutional structure, that of states' rights in a federal system, which raised doubts about congressional authority to legislate in the area. What made this issue so serious was that it became intertwined with partisan politics, because Southern Democrats, still resentful of post–Civil War legislation, were particularly sensitive to it. The result was that NPBO wrote a weaker bill than the one it had first intended to propose.

Perry Belmont had argued that "Congress may assume the entire control of the election of representatives" and also "has complete and paramount jurisdiction over the choice of presidential electors" (Belmont 1905, 180).[6] He changed this view at the behest of former Senator William Chandler. Chandler reminded his fellow reformers that only 11 years earlier (when Democrats had gained control of the White House and both houses of Congress for the first time since the Civil War) the Democratic party had repealed the postwar laws giving the federal government authority to punish electoral corruption in the states of the old Confederacy. Southern Democrats had argued then that the federal government had no constitutional authority to regulate state elections, and NPBO decided not to offend whatever sensibilities remained on that score. The bill they drafted required the reporting of contributions and expenditures only by political committees that were active "in two or more states"; that is, it applied only to the national committees and the congressional campaign committees of the two major parties, not to the campaign committees of congressional candidates. Rep. Samuel McCall (Rep., Massachusetts), an NPBO member, introduced the bill in the House of Representatives early in 1906, at the start of the Fifty-Ninth Congress.

The Republican majority on the House Elections Committee rejected the bill. Pointing out that contributors could evade disclosure simply by routeing their money through state and congressional district campaign committees, the chairman went so far as to call the bill "futile nonsense" (CR, 26 May 1906, 7474). Committee Democrats then threw aside their states' rights concerns by drafting a bill requiring disclosure even by state and congressional district campaign committees, but the majority rejected that as well. The Republicans then introduced their own bill, which never made it to the floor and died with the end of the Fifty-Ninth Congress (CR, 26 May 1906, 7468, 7475; U.S. House Report [hereinafter H. Rept] 5082 (59th Cong.), 15).

Rep. McCall and NPBO reintroduced the same bill in 1908, in the Sixtieth Congress, with similar results. This time, Republican congressional leaders were also feuding with President Roosevelt and vowed to obstruct almost all legislation except appropriations bills (New York Tribune, 23 May 1908, 1). The reformers tried once more in the Sixty-First Congress and were finally successful, or partly so. The original bill had required only post-election disclosure, but the second time around Rep. McCall and former Senator Chandler added a pre-election disclosure requirement, and they kept this feature for their third try. Although the Elections Committee waited nearly a year before holding yet another hearing on the already much-discussed bill, it reported it favourably, and the House passed it after only minimal debate. The Senate also passed it, after deleting the pre-election reporting requirement, and President Taft signed it into law (H. Rept 928, S. Rept 681 (61st Cong.); CR, 18 Apr. 1910, 4926–36, and 2 June 1910, 8753–54).

The Democrats had a chance to shape their own reform legislation when they won a majority in the House in the 1910 mid-term elections. Early in 1911 the Elections Committee, now under Democratic control, reported out a bill restoring the pre-election reporting requirement that Senate Republicans had deleted the previous year. The ensuing floor debate concerned Democratic sensitivity to states' rights, a sensitivity that now reappeared in full force after the brief momentary lapse of 1906. Southern Democrats, who occupied nearly half the party's seats in the lower chamber, opposed disclosure requirements on state and congressional district campaign committees and in primary elections on the grounds that these were wholly under state jurisdiction.[7] By pressing these issues, Republicans very nearly split their opponents along sectional lines. The Democrats decided that party unity was of paramount importance, however, and the House eventually passed their pre-election reporting bill unanimously (CR, 14 Apr. 1911, 254–69).

Senate Republicans, still in control of the upper chamber, renewed the effort to split the Democrats. The Privileges and Elections Committee kept the pre-election disclosure provision but added the very same primary and general election disclosure amendment that the House had defeated. Southern Democrats were not as influential in the Senate, though, and their northern colleagues joined Republicans in approving the amendment in floor debate. Democrats also added another feature, a spending limit for congressional candidates, which also passed (S. Rept 78 (62d Cong.); CR, 17 July 1911, 3005–20).

Senate Republicans had, in effect, called the House Democrats' bluff. Reformers in the lower chamber could now either back down to keep peace within their own party or confront intraparty divisions head-on and also challenge the sincerity of the Republicans' own newly zealous reformism. They chose the latter course and accepted the Senate amendments in conference committee. After a spirited and unusual three-way floor debate among Republicans and Northern and Southern Democrats, House members passed the bill (H. Rept 147 (62d Cong.); CR, 17 Aug. 1911, 4087–4102).

Congress made two changes in the disclosure law in 1925. Following the Supreme Court's 1921 decision in U.S. v. Newberry, Congress repealed the requirement that candidates report their primary election finances (see the following section on contribution and expenditure limits). The Teapot Dome scandal prompted the only other amendment of disclosure requirements before 1971. President Harding's secretary of the interior secretly leased government oil reserves at Teapot Dome, Wyoming, to private developers in return for bribes. One of these developers had also contributed to the Republican National Committee, contributions that went unreported because of a loophole in the law: the 1910–11 law required disclosure only in election years, and the developers had contributed in a non-election year. In the *Federal Corrupt Practices Act of 1925*, Congress amended the law to require national party committees to make quarterly reports in non-election years (Mutch 1988, 24).

For 46 years after enactment of the *Federal Corrupt Practices Act of 1925*, Congress did nothing to strengthen disclosure of campaign financing. Enforcement remained poor, which is not surprising in light of the fact that those charged with the duty of reporting violations to the attorney general were the clerk of the House and the secretary of the Senate, both employees of the very people the regulations were supposed to restrain. Although some of the ad hoc congressional committees appointed after each election to compile and publish financial data did good work, most information that reached the public did so through the efforts of private individuals and groups. Political scientists Louise Overacker and James K. Pollock did excellent work in the 1920s and 1930s, and in the 1950s the Citizens' Research Foundation was spun off from the research team assembled to compile what became the best of the congressional campaign finance reports, that of the Senate Privileges and Elections Subcommittee on the 1956 election. Until the rise of Common Cause in the 1970s, the Citizens' Research Foundation was almost the only source of campaign finance data. This situation changed in 1971.

In the *Federal Election Campaign Act of 1971*, Congress took a very large step toward an effective disclosure law. First, Republicans and reform-minded Democrats tried and failed to establish an independent agency to administer disclosure. Republicans wanted such an agency because the congressional officers responsible for that task under the terms of the *Federal Corrupt Practices Act of 1925* were appointed by and accountable to the majority party in their respective chambers, which for the past 18 years had been the Democrats. Ironically, it was the Democratic congressional leader most hostile to reform who proposed the compromise measure eventually enacted as part of FECA.

Rep. Wayne Hays (Dem., Ohio), who chaired the House Administration Committee, suggested that the congressional officers retain their powers over congressional campaign financing but that the comptroller general – head of another independent agency, the General Accounting Office (GAO) – be given responsibility for administering the new law for presidential candidates. Both houses accepted the compromise and required the three supervisory officers to devise uniform procedures.

The GAO acts as an agent of Congress in its normal functions, but it is still independent, which is to say that its staff is not appointed by or responsible to any member of Congress. This insulation from political pressures allowed GAO to propose higher standards for disclosure than either of the congressional officers had in mind. The eventual compromise still reflected a significant strengthening of disclosure requirements.

Watergate revealed the inadequacy of even the strengthened 1971 provisions and revived congressional support for an independent election agency to administer and enforce campaign finance law. Still, even Watergate could not reconcile some members of Congress, House Democrats in particular, to the idea of relinquishing administration of that law, and in 1974 lawmakers devised a Federal Election Commission (FEC) that was independent in name only.

The Senate had approved a plan under which a six-member commission would have been constructed in the same manner as other independent agencies. These agencies are defined as independent because the president appoints their commissioners, subject to Senate confirmation, to fixed terms of office. Fixed terms free agency officers from partisan political pressures, and executive-legislative cooperation in the appointment process ensures that appointees enjoy broad support. It was precisely this independence to which House Democrats objected, and the Senate reluctantly agreed to a scheme under which Congress would appoint four of FEC's six commissioners and would also exercise veto power over its regulations.

FECA opponents argued in *Buckley* that the new commission should be abolished because its structure violated the separation of powers and because, in the performance of its duties, it would endanger freedom of speech. The Supreme Court ruled that FEC's functions were executive and judicial and that under the Constitution the legislature could not exercise them; but the Court gave permission to the agency to continue operating, provided Congress reorganized it along the lines of other independent agencies. The lawmakers complied with this ruling in the 1976 FECA Amendments, giving FEC six commissioners, three from each of the two major parties, to be appointed by the President and confirmed by the Senate. It continues in this form today (Mutch 1988, 83–91).

Contribution and Expenditure Limits

During Senate debate on the 1911 disclosure bill, freshman Senator James A. Reed (Dem., Missouri) offered an amendment setting limits on congressional campaign spending. Under existing conditions, he contended, the only people who could run for office were the rich and candidates willing "to accept contributions from those institutions which may be interested in legislation" (*CR*, 17 July 1911, 3006, 3011). Congress passed this limit, but the U.S. Supreme Court weakened it 10 years later in *U.S. v. Newberry* (1921).

In 1921 the Court overturned a lower court's conviction of Senator Truman Newberry (Rep., Michigan) for exceeding the 1911 spending limit in his primary campaign. The Court, however, handed down its decision in three separate opinions, which left the validity of primary regulation unclear. Four justices concluded that Congress had constitutional authority over general, but not primary, elections; another four decided that Congress could not effectively regulate the former without also regulating the latter. The ninth justice broke the tie by voting with the first four. He did so, however, on the grounds that, while Congress did have the authority to regulate primaries, the 1911 statute did not cover Senator Newberry's primary campaign, because it had been enacted prior to ratification of the constitutional amendment that provided for direct popular election of U.S. senators, and thus prior to the existence of senatorial primaries (*U.S. v. Newberry* 1921, 239, 258, 282; Mutch 1988, 16–18).

There were two interpretations of this confusing ruling. One was that Congress lacked *constitutional* authority to regulate primaries at all; the other was that it lacked only *statutory* authority to regulate senatorial primaries, a shortcoming that could be remedied simply by re-enacting the 1911 law. The new Republican administration of Warren G. Harding opted for the former, and so advised Congress. In the *Federal Corrupt Practices Act of 1925*, a Republican-controlled Congress overturned the Republican–Northern Democratic victory of 1911 and repealed the primary regulation provisions of that year's law (Mutch 1988, 18–21).

Repeal meant that federal campaign spending limits would not apply to primaries, and the *Newberry* decision also weakened their force in general elections. Senator Newberry had argued that the limit applied only to candidates, not to campaign committees, and that he could not be held accountable for his committee's spending, since he had no knowledge of its members' activities. The Court, while not ruling on limits, appeared to agree that limits applied only to the candidates' own money or to expenditures made with their knowledge and consent. This interpretation permitted candidates to evade the limits at will. As Louise Overacker observed, it simply required "the astute candidate to be discreetly ignorant of what his friends are doing" (Overacker 1932, 271). The next set of limits to evade came in 1940.

The 1940 contribution and expenditure ceilings began as a Democratic plan to scuttle a Republican–Southern Democratic tightening of civil service regulations. The *Pendleton Act of 1883* had created a "classified," or competitive, section of the federal civil service and had removed it from political pressures, both by opening positions only to those who passed competitive examinations and by prohibiting the government employees who filled these positions from engaging in political activity. But most federal government employees held positions that were "unclassified," or politically appointed, and thus were still vulnerable to political pressures to contribute time and/or money to campaigns for elective office. President Franklin Roosevelt greatly expanded the federal bureaucracy to carry out his New Deal and thus also increased the number of government workers who held "unclassified" positions. In 1939 anti-Roosevelt Democrats, who opposed both the New Deal and Roosevelt's decision to run for an unprecedented third term in the White House, joined with Republicans to pass the *Hatch Act*, which extended civil service regulations to cover most of the federal workforce that had not been covered before (*New York Times*, 3 Aug. 1939, 1).

The *Hatch Act* explicitly prohibited the solicitation of political contributions from many federal employees, but no such law protected state government workers, who were still an important source of congressional campaign funds. In 1940 the same coalition of Republicans and conservative Democrats reunited in the Senate to extend the 1939 *Hatch Act* to cover state employees who were paid at least partly from federal government funds.

A vocal minority of Senate Democrats opposed the bill. Indiana Senator Sherman Minton argued that the second *Hatch Act* aimed to "purify the little fellows": Democrats who financed their campaigns by collecting small amounts from public employees rather than large amounts from corporations and wealthy families (*CR*, 13 Mar. 1940, 2791–92). These opponents attempted to undermine Republican support for the Hatch bill by adding amendments the Republicans could be expected to oppose. They were successful in attaching a $5 000 contribution limit, a move designed to curb the generosity of the Republicans' wealthy supporters. Republicans predictably opposed the limit while Democrats, even those in the conservative coalition, supported it. Republicans then confounded the hopes of the limit's backers by voting unanimously to pass the bill to which it was attached (*CR*, 13 Mar. 1940, 2790–91, and 14 Mar. 1940, 2853).

The House substantially weakened the contribution ceiling by passing a Republican amendment to exempt state and local committees.

But the House also added a Democratic amendment setting a $3 million expenditure limit for national political committees, another attempt to restrict Republicans, who usually outspent Democrats. The Senate accepted both House amendments, and the bill was enacted in time for the 1940 campaign (*CR*, 10 Mar. 1940, 987, and 10 July 1940, 9463–64; Putney 1940, 292).

The House's weakening of the contribution limit proved sufficient to permit wealthy contributors to continue giving at their accustomed high levels as long as they routed their gifts through state and local, rather than national, party committees. Republicans also showed Democrats how to evade the spending limit – by claiming that it applied not only to the two parties' national committees but also to non-party, or "independent," committees promoting presidential candidates. A large number of such committees appeared during the course of the 1940 campaign, and by election day both parties had greatly exceeded the $3 million limit (*New York Times*, 4 Aug. 1940, 2; S. Rept 47 (77th Cong.), 6; Overacker 1932, 30–36). Having learned how to evade the law they had just passed, both parties ignored it for the next 30 years. Although Democratic reformers in Congress, notably Senator Thomas C. Hennings (Dem., Missouri), attempted to strengthen the limits throughout the 1950s, they failed to overcome Republican–Southern Democratic opposition and often failed even to secure the support of their own party leaders.

By the 1960s, the rising costs of running television campaigns had begun to attract the attention of groups outside Congress. President Kennedy's Commission on Campaign Costs, the Committee for Economic Development, and the Twentieth Century Fund all expressed concern about candidate dependence on large contributors. The Committee for Economic Development, a big-business group, observed in 1968 that "undue reliance on relatively few heavy donors" was one cause of the "deplorable reputation of political financing in this country" (Committee for Economic Development 1968, 51). While expressing the same fear of the undue influence of wealth that had long motivated liberal reformers, these three groups nonetheless recommended repeal of contribution and expenditure limits on the grounds that they were unrealistic and unenforceable (ibid., 53; U.S. President's Commission 1962, 17–20; Twentieth Century Fund 1970, 7–19).

Not everyone was convinced that limits were unworkable. In 1971 Common Cause brought suit against the Republican and Democratic parties. By seeking an injunction against the methods both parties used to evade contribution and expenditure ceilings, the reform group sought to ensure adherence to those limits in the 1972 election. The legal action, however, had the opposite effect: the unpleasant prospect of having to defend their upcoming campaign practices in court appears to have driven many otherwise reformist Democrats into the conservative camp (Mutch 1988, 67–68).

For the FECA of 1971, Democrats, who had comfortable majorities in both houses of Congress, joined Republicans in repealing contribution and expenditure limits. Far from moderating their opposition to limits, Republicans had by 1971 developed explicitly ideological arguments in favour of unrestricted giving and spending in election campaigns. Money, they claimed, was equivalent to speech in the context of a campaign, so restrictions on the amounts one could give or spend amounted to restrictions on speech and thus violated the First Amendment's guarantee of free speech. The Democrats' objections were of a more practical nature. Their 1968 presidential campaign had plunged the party deeply into debt, and they feared that contribution limits might prevent them from raising enough money to mount a viable campaign in 1972.[8] The only limit remaining was a new one imposed on broadcast spending.[9]

The Watergate scandal, with its revelations of $1 and $2 million contributions and illegal expenditures, convinced Congress that ceilings had to be re-enacted. The Senate Rules Committee stated that "political financing during 1972 has caused changes in attitude toward limitations on both contributions and expenditures." Even Republicans who only a few years before had doubted the constitutionality of limits supported them in the wake of Watergate. House Republicans supported re-enactment and pointedly referred to "abuses that became apparent in the 1972 campaign" (S. Rept 93-310 (93d Cong.), 5; H. Rept 93-1239 (93d Cong.), 115). In 1971 bleak financial necessity forced Democrats into an alliance with Republican opponents of past Democratic reforms; but in 1974 urgent political necessity created by an angry public forced Republicans into an alliance with Democrats to re-enact and strengthen those very reforms.

The Supreme Court also went along with the new legislation, up to a point. The justices agreed that contribution ceilings were a constitutional means of preventing "the actuality and appearance of corruption," noting that "the deeply disturbing examples surfacing after the 1972 election demonstrate that the problem is not an illusory one" (*Buckley*, 26, 29–30). The Court took a very different position on expenditure limits. Adopting the same argument Republicans had employed in congressional debate on the 1971 FECA, the Court struck down spending limits as violations of First Amendment guarantees of free speech (see the section on constitutional issues later in this study).

Public Financing of Presidential Elections

Public financing of presidential campaigns has always been a Democratic idea, and with a few exceptions Republicans have always opposed it. A Democratic member of the House of Representatives introduced the first bill to effect such financing just after the 1904 presidential campaign. No one took the idea seriously then, but it did not go away, and over the next 10 years several people suggested it as a remedy for the corruption engendered by large private contributions. Democrats raised the idea again in the 1950s and 1960s, but it was not until 1966 that Democratic Senator Russell Long of Louisiana introduced a public financing bill.

The Senate Finance Committee was considering several campaign finance bills in the summer of 1966. Senator Long, who chaired that committee, had no trouble getting his measure reported out, but he must have had doubts about Senate reception of his unprecedented move, for he attached it as a rider on a House-passed tax bill. Tax measures reaching the upper chamber often become "Christmas tree" bills, on which senators hang all sorts of pet projects, because they are almost certain to pass. Removing any one of the amendments is difficult, because so many senators have an interest in at least one of them that it is nearly impossible to get a majority against any of them. At the end of the session, with nearly one-third of the senators having already left town, the Senate passed Long's bill over Republican opposition.

Surprisingly, Rep. Wilbur Mills (Dem., Arkansas), who chaired the House tax-writing committee, Ways and Means, also supported it. The House, with only a bare majority of members present, passed it. Perhaps this can be explained by the unsurprising fact that by this time Long's rider had won the enthusiastic backing of President Lyndon Johnson, who was at that time still planning to run for re-election in 1968. Another factor may have been Rep. Mills's own presidential aspirations: in 1968 he briefly campaigned for the Democratic nomination. Thus, the bill became law; but not for long.

When the Senate reconvened early in 1967, Democratic opponents of Long's act joined Republicans in a joint attack. Most Northern Democrats actually supported some form of public funding and objected to Long's measure because it would have given money to the party rather than to the candidates. The Democratic party has always been more decentralized than the Republican and much more heterogeneous as well, embracing a wide variety of social and economic groups, characteristics that have encouraged factionalism and distrust of whoever happens at the time to be in control of the White House and/or the national party apparatus. Much Democratic opposition to Long's plan was actually opposition to President Lyndon Johnson, and the factional infighting that finally resulted in the repeal of public financing in 1967 was part of the larger intraparty battle that eventually led Johnson to decide against running for re-election in 1968 (Mutch 1988, 35–40).

As part of the 1967 compromise reached between Long and his opponents, the voluntary income tax checkoff – the method by which he would have financed presidential campaigns – was not repealed; rather, it was postponed until Congress could decide how to distribute the checked-off dollars. Democrats did not revive it until 1971, when they were deeply in debt and seeking a way to finance their 1972 presidential race. Once again, they added it as a rider on a tax bill.

This time the Republicans responded with a lengthy filibuster and tied up the Senate for days, debating and defeating Republican amendments to the Democrats' rider. Another difference was that the White House was occupied by a Republican, Richard Nixon, who vowed to veto the tax bill if Congress passed it with the public financing rider intact. The combatants accepted a compromise that resembled the one struck in 1967: the income tax checkoff would be retained but would be postponed until 1973, after the upcoming presidential election. President Nixon compromised also: he repeated his opposition to public financing, but he signed the bill. By 1973, of course, revelations of President Nixon's campaign fund-raising methods had renewed support for this controversial proposal.

Three features of the 1973–74 attempt were different from previous attempts to enact public financing. First, a Republican congressional leader, Senator Hugh Scott of Pennsylvania, was one of two co-sponsors of the bill that eventually passed; second, the sponsors of that bill tried for the first time to include congressional elections; third, for the first time since Congress debated the first laws, interest groups were deeply involved in drafting and passing the legislation. Twice in 1973 the Senate Rules Committee held hearings on campaign finance legislation, and twice the committee failed, or refused, to report out any public funding measure. Senators Scott and Edward Kennedy (Dem., Massachusetts) had already drafted a bill, but so had other senators. It was at this point – when it was clear that Democratic party leaders were not going to take the lead on the issue and that following normal Senate procedure of going through a committee was not going to produce a public financing bill – that interest groups became crucial.

The two interest groups most active in the Senate were Common Cause and the Center for the Public Financing of Elections, created for the sole purpose of enacting a public funding law. The AFL-CIO also lobbied for such a law, chiefly in the House. These lobbies did the hard work of building a coalition around a single bill, spending many long days trudging from one senator's office to another piecing together the compromises that would broaden support for the bill.

When the three groups had hammered a bill together, Senators Scott and Kennedy introduced it as a rider on a debt ceiling bill. Although Republicans and Southern Democrats still opposed public financing, especially of congressional campaigns, enough of them joined Northern Democrats to pass the bill and send it down to the House.

So deeply did the House oppose public funds for congressional elections that the lower chamber voted to send the bill back to the Senate. Behind-the-scenes negotiations between House and Senate leaders resulted in a compromise under which the House agreed to accept publicly financed presidential campaigns if the Senate agreed to exclude congressional campaigns. Republicans and Southern Democrats then halted Senate debate on the bill by launching a four-day filibuster that ended only when the bill's supporters agreed to send it back to committee.

Early in 1974 the Senate Rules Committee reported out a public financing bill much like the one the Senate had passed and the House had rejected. The committee's change of heart probably can be explained by increasing support for reform in general and for public funding in particular. Nonetheless, the bill faced another filibuster as soon as debate resumed. The same factors that had changed attitudes on the Rules Committee also made the filibuster harder to maintain, and after 11 days the Senate passed the bill once more, again over Republican and Southern Democratic opposition. House opposition to publicly funded congressional elections had not abated, however. After voting it down in floor debate, the two chambers went to conference committee, where House opposition to the inclusion of congressional elections proved to be so much stronger than Senate support for it that both houses agreed to drop the measure and unite behind presidential public funding (Mutch 1988, 118–31).

Canada

Canada adopted its first campaign finance law, a disclosure requirement, in 1874, only seven years after Confederation and more than 30 years before America's first federal regulation in this field. Parliament passed this first law in response to revelations of business contributions to the governing party's re-election campaign (which came to be known as the Pacific Scandal) and used British law as a model.

" The parliamentary sessions of 1906 and 1907 were among the most scandal-ridden on record," according to one authority, and they set the stage for the next round of reform legislation (Canada, Committee 1966, 18). Sir Wilfrid Laurier's Liberal government responded in 1908 by strengthening disclosure and prohibiting corporation political contributions. What makes the latter interesting here is that it was enacted partially in response to the American scandals concerning the 1904 Republican presidential campaign.

In 1920 Sir Robert Borden's Conservative government further strengthened disclosure and also extended the 1908 corporation prohibition to cover unincorporated associations. After a decade of protest from parliamentary progressives that this extension was aimed at farmers' and labour organizations, it was quietly repealed. For 50 years after the 1920 laws, Parliament passed no significant election funding reforms, and it was prompted to act only by further scandal, domestic and American, and by provincial example.

Quebec took the first step. Late in 1956 *Le Devoir*, a Montreal newspaper, published a detailed analysis of that year's provincial election. *Le Devoir* may not have surprised its readers by estimating that the ruling Union Nationale party had spent at least $1.25 million to win re-election (and more than three-fourths of the seats in the provincial assembly), but its report that the party outspent the Liberals, its only serious rival, by eight to one, "blew the lid off" (Angell 1966, 283). The Montreal newspaper and the Salvas provincial Commission of Inquiry (Quebec, Commission of Inquiry 1963), which was appointed to investigate corruption in the Quebec government, pierced the veil of secrecy cloaking the Union Nationale's financing and provided much information for public discussion.

The Liberal party won a slim majority of seats in the 1960 Quebec election and began work on legislation to fulfil its campaign promise of electoral reform. The party commissioned a study of relevant legislation elsewhere, devoted most of its 1961 convention to the subject, and in 1962 introduced a comprehensive reform bill. The proposed legislation reintroduced the doctrine of agency that Great Britain had pioneered in 1854, imposed spending limits on parties and candidates, required disclosure of contributions and expenditures, and provided for partial government subsidies to candidates. The 1962 election, in which the Liberals increased their majority, slowed but did not stop the bill's progress. When the new legislature met in 1963, it made a few minor amendments and passed the bill. Quebec's new law attracted much attention, which, combined with a minor scandal at the national level, led to a re-examination of federal legislation (Angell 1966).

In 1964 Lester Pearson's federal Liberal government appointed a five-member special committee to study "the problem of rising election expenses and make recommendations" (Canada, House of Commons *Debates* [hereinafter House *Debates*], 27 Oct. 1964, 9457). One of the five members, Professor Norman Ward, later observed that "it was not wholly coincidence" that the Rivard scandal immediately preceded appointment of the committee (Ward 1972, 347). Lucien Rivard was a drug smuggler whom the United States sought to extradite. Rivard's underworld associates went through a minor official in Pearson's government to contact the Montreal lawyer who was representing the United States, offering him a $20 000 bribe and $50 000 for the Liberal party if he would not oppose bail (*New York Times*, 25 Nov. 1964, 8, and 30 June 1965, 13). This sordid affair was only the most serious of several small scandals afflicting the Pearson government, and a scandal involving party funds at the same time as Quebec was making headlines with its new law must have been sufficiently embarrassing to impel some action. The government's failure to take action on the special committee's impressive final report, however, raises the suspicion that commissioning the study had been mainly symbolic.

That committee, which became known as the Barbeau Committee after its chairman, Alphonse Barbeau, issued recommendations for new legislation that were largely based on Quebec's 1963 act, which Barbeau had helped to draft. The Committee suggested that Parliament impose spending limits on campaign advertising, require parties as well as candidates to disclose contributions and expenditures, subsidize candidates for a part of their campaign expenses, and establish a registry of political finance to administer and enforce the law (Canada, Committee 1966, 41–45, 50–52, 54–56, 58–62). These recommendations went even further than the innovative Quebec law, which may have encouraged government inaction despite "extraordinarily detailed [media] coverage from coast to coast" (Ward 1972, 340). Even the new Liberal Prime Minister, Pierre Trudeau, who had said in 1968 that he gave top priority to the Committee's report, did little until 1970 (Seidle 1980, 185).

In 1970 Parliament created another special committee to study election expenses, known after its chairman, Hyliard Chappell (PC, Peel South), as the Chappell Committee. By this time, Nova Scotia had already adopted new legislation similar to Quebec's, and Saskatchewan and Manitoba were re-examining their statutes (Seidle 1980, 189; Ward 1972, 341). Like the Barbeau Report, the Chappell Committee endorsed spending limits on candidates and parties and endorsed partial public subsidies for candidates' campaign expenses, but it opposed disclosing the names of contributors as well as the establishment of an enforcement agency (Seidle 1980, 187–88; Ward 1972, 342). One year later, the Trudeau government embodied some of the two committees' recommendations in an election expenses bill that met a mixed reception in the House of Commons. That bill did not even get to second reading before the government dissolved Parliament for the 1972 general election (Seidle 1980, 189–92).

The Progressive Conservatives made significant gains in the October election, and Pierre Trudeau returned as prime minister of a minority Liberal government. In the summer of 1973, the government introduced another election expenses bill, Bill 203. It was stronger than its predecessor, a feature probably resulting from the government's dependence upon the New Democratic Party for a parliamentary majority and from the Watergate scandal then unfolding in the United States.

The NDP parliamentary leader, David Lewis (York South), explained the "vast improvements" in the bill by stating that "my party, my colleagues and myself stand for certain things in the realm of election expenses" (House *Debates*, 12 July 1973, 5554). Another NDP member, Leslie Benjamin (Regina–Lake Centre), said "with some reluctance" that Bill 203 was also the result of "something that is presently going on in another country" (House *Debates*, 10 July 1973, 5482). Members of the two traditional parties also referred to Watergate throughout committee deliberation on the bill. On the first day that the Privileges and Elections Committee considered Bill 203, Terry O'Connor (PC, Halton) explained why he thought the country needed it: "To eliminate the public suspicion which has existed for so long in our system of financing candidates and parties ... events of the past year and a half in the United States with respect to Watergate and related matters have caused ... additional suspicion in the Canadian system ... that situation has played some part in our thinking here in Canada" (Canada, House of Commons, Standing Committee on Privileges and Elections [hereinafter P&E], *Minutes*, 10 Oct. 1973, 12:15–16). Once again an American scandal had interacted with Canadian events to produce reform legislation.[10]

Like the post-Watergate legislation then under consideration in Congress, Bill 203 was a most complex piece of legislation. It emerged from the Privileges and Elections Committee intact in all of its major provisions, but there were some challenges and disagreements.

Disclosure

Although few details of what became known as the Pacific Scandal have emerged, it is known that businessmen bidding for the government contract for the Canadian Pacific Railway gave a large sum of money to Prime Minister Sir John A. Macdonald, whose Conservative party then went on to win re-election in 1872. The government resigned when the payment became public knowledge a year later, and Alexander Mackenzie's Liberal party beat the Conservatives badly in 1874 (Wearing 1988, 123; Canada, Committee 1966, 13–14). The new Liberal government enacted the *Dominion Elections Act* of 1874, which included a provision for publicizing campaign spending.

The new law closely followed the British *Corrupt Practices Prevention Act, 1854* and required candidates to appoint agents who would be responsible for paying all campaign expenses. These agents were further required to submit a statement of those expenses to a returning officer, who was in turn directed to insert an abstract of it in a local newspaper within 14 days (Seidle 1980, 146–47). The 1891 McGreevy Scandal, another incident concerning business financing of the governing Conservative party's re-election campaign, prompted that government to enact a law defining bribery of candidates as a corrupt practice (Canada, Committee 1966, 17).[11]

The 1905 New York insurance investigation also affected Canadian politics. Although Parliament was not in session when the hearings began or during the testimony about political contributions, Canadian newspapers covered the New York events as closely as did their American counterparts. When the Tenth Parliament convened for its second session early in March 1906, Sir Wilfrid Laurier's Liberal government had already appointed a commission to investigate Canadian insurance companies (the Speech from the Throne mentioned "the investigation ... in the neighbouring Republic") and also promised a bill to amend the *Dominion Elections Act* (House *Debates*, 8 Mar. 1906, 6). The government did not present a bill that session or the next. The government did not act until March 1907, in the fourth session, when it submitted amendments that slightly strengthened disclosure and banned corporation contributions. The government bill, which became law in 1908, strengthened the agency doctrine by providing that to make campaign contributions "otherwise than to the agent will be illegal" (House *Debates*, 9 Mar. 1908, 4568).[12]

Initially, the Laurier government also proposed that the election "agent should be required to make public ... the amount and source of all election contributions he has received" (House *Debates*, 9 Mar. 1908, 4568). This would have brought Canadian law in line with the 1883 British Act, but the provision did not make it into the 1908 law, and Parliament did not enact it until 1920 (Canada, *Dominion Elections Act*, s. 79(1)(*e*)).

The 1920 legislation also created the position of chief electoral officer (CEO). This official was charged with supervising elections "with a view to ensuring ... compliance with the provisions of the Act." The law did not give the CEO authority to enforce those provisions, however, although he could report to the House of Commons on any matter arising in the course of an election (ibid., s. 19(*b*)).

The Barbeau Committee stated in its 1966 report that "after 1920, whatever innovating spirit Parliament had once possessed concerning election expenses seemed to disappear altogether" (Canada, Committee 1966, 22). What is surprising is that this spirit failed to reappear despite the eruption in 1931 of one of Canada's worst scandals, the revelation that the Beauharnois Power Corporation had contributed a large sum of money to finance the governing Liberal party's unsuccessful re-election campaign.[13] Nonetheless, Parliament passed no legislation for the next 50 years and failed even to bring Canadian law fully up to the British standard of 1883 by, for example, setting campaign spending limits (Seidle 1980, 171–73).

The Barbeau Committee hoped to prod Parliament out of its lethargy and recommended establishment of a registry of election and political finance that would serve as a depository of candidate and party financial reports, would audit those reports, and would enforce the elections act. In 1971, Parliament's Chappell Committee (Canada, House of Commons 1971) disagreed on this point and suggested retaining the chief electoral officer with added duties. The Barbeau Committee had decided that the chief electoral officer, who was responsible for election administration – "the management and control of the official election machinery and procedure" – should not take on the very different task of enforcing the financial provisions of the proposed law (Ward 1972, 342).

Bill 203 did not include any provision for such a registry, choosing instead to follow the Chappell recommendation. In committee, Joe Clark (PC, Rocky Mountain) tried to amend the bill "in effect to empower the Office of the Auditor General to act as an agent of enforcement of the bill," and he mentioned Watergate, as well as experience with the 1874 and 1908 acts, in expressing his concern that the law would be useless unless enforced. The vice-chairman ruled this amendment out of order (P&E *Minutes*, 6 Dec. 1973, 24:43, and 11 Dec. 1973, 25:4). The CEO, Jean-Marc Hamel, on being informed of the powers he would exercise under the proposed act, stated that he would appoint a director of election expenses to administer its provisions (P&E *Minutes*, 18 Oct. 1973, 12:14).

Corporations and Unions

The most striking feature of the 1908 law was a "provision prohibiting any company from contributing any amount whatever to an election campaign fund" (House *Debates*, 9 Mar. 1908, 4568). If this reflected American influence – Congress having passed the 1907 Act one year earlier – it appears to have been exerted through the Conservative party. Opposition leader Robert L. Borden had suggested a corporation ban early in 1906, shortly after addressing an American national conference on electoral reform in New York City. In 1908 Borden also supported a private bill, introduced by G.O. Alcorn (Cons., Prince Edward Island), which he tried unsuccessfully to substitute for the government's corporation contributions provision. Alcorn said he had patterned his measure after the New York State law (House *Debates*, 15 Mar. 1906, 244; 2 Jan. 1908, 1677–79; 5 May 1908, 7860–62; 3 July 1908, 11927–29; *New York Times*, 7 Mar. 1906, 7; 8 Mar. 1906, 5). Editorials in two Toronto newspapers suggested an explanation of the two parties' positions on corporation contributions. Both the liberal *Globe* and the conservative *Daily Mail* gave front-page coverage to the 1905 New York insurance hearings but drew different conclusions from them. The *Daily Mail* denounced the insurance company contributions as a "gross ... abuse of trust" and warned that "there would be no limit to the possibilities of political corruption" should Parliament permit such activities (21 Sept. 1905, 6). The *Globe* was critical, too, but also suggested that the companies' money may well have been spent in the policy holders' best interests (19 Sept. 1905, 6). These differences continued to appear in the two papers' coverage of later events. In 1908 the *Globe* ignored Alcorn's bill, emphasizing instead the publicity provisions of the government measure (23 Jan. 1908, 3, and 10 Mar. 1908, 3). The *Daily Mail* gave front-page coverage to Alcorn's bill (23 Jan. 1908) and followed with a telling editorial revealing the reason for partisan differences on the ban: "It is firmly believed that the Government derives most of its corruption money from corporations. It gives the franchise or the legislation, and takes the cash by a circuitous route for use in elections. [Alcorn's bill] will protect the honest elector, whose vote is nullified by the vote of the bought elector, and it will defend the public from corporation concessions" (*Daily Mail*, 24 Jan. 1908, 6).

The most troublesome provision in the 1908 ban was an exemption for organizations "incorporated for political purposes alone." Alcorn charged that the government had crafted the exception to protect Liberal organizations – the bill's sponsor, Justice Minister A.B. Aylesworth, later mentioned the Ontario Liberal Association as the kind of group included under the excepting clause. These organizations, said Alcorn, were then free to "collect and distribute in the most corrupt manner possible an election fund of any size" (House *Debates*, 5 May 1908, 7930).[14] Conservatives either changed their minds about the dangerous character of this clause or took the Liberals' suggestion that their own supporters incorporate, for they did not avail themselves of the opportunity to delete it after they came to power in 1911.

In 1920 Sir Robert Borden's Conservative government introduced its own amendments to the *Dominion Elections Act* and broadened the corporation ban to include unincorporated as well as incorporated companies and associations. This move immediately caused some members of Parliament to suspect that the government intended to undercut the growing power of the new farmers' organizations that had sprung up in the West (House *Debates*, 26 Mar. 1920, 783, 1170–71; 10 Feb. 1925, 347, 350; 19 June 1925, 4553). These farm organizations did eventually incorporate so as to qualify for the exemption, but it turned out that most labour unions were unable to do the same. As the Fourteenth Parliament's two Labour party members explained in 1925, most Canadian unions were affiliates of American ones and were thus bound by American union constitutions, which did not permit incorporation. In the same year the Labour members failed, after much debate, both to repeal the entire section and to insert a specific exemption for unions. It was Liberals who defeated these attempts; both Conservatives and Progressives supported at least one of the Labour moves. A similar attempt failed again in 1929, but another succeeded in 1930 almost without debate.[15]

Expenditure Limits

By 1973, expenditure limits for candidates had been a feature of British law for 88 years, and both the Barbeau and Chappell committees had recommended limits on spending. Bill 203 also followed Chappell here, by setting limits on spending by parties as well as by candidates.

Privy Council President Allan J. MacEachen (L, Cape Breton Highlands–Canso), who introduced the bill, said in committee that he regarded spending limits as the bill's most important feature, and probably most members agreed.[16] There was dissension, however. Frank Howard (NDP, Skeena), who probably spoke on this bill more than any other member, both in committee and on the floor of the Commons, joined forces with Flora MacDonald (PC, Kingston–The Islands) in attempts to lower the limits on both parties and candidates, but they were badly beaten (P&E *Minutes*, 22 Nov. 1973, 20:27–28; 27 Nov. 1973, 21:3, 15; 4 Dec. 1973, 23:12–14).

Both the Barbeau and Chappell committees had opposed contribution limits, and Bill 203 did not include them. But Howard did try to insert a provision that all contributions "shall be in Canadian funds and directly from Canadian sources." His stated reasons were to allay suspicion that the NDP was financed by American unions and to prevent American corporations from financing the Liberals and Conservatives. This move also failed (P&E *Minutes*, 27 Nov. 1973, 21:7, 48–53). Frank Howard and a handful of other NDP members made a final, predictably futile, attempt to attach their amendments on the floor of the Commons in the report stage (House *Debates*, 18 Dec. 1973, 8177, and 20 Dec. 1973, 8942).

Public Financing
Public financing was far less controversial in Canada than in the United States, but Bill 203's provisions for partial subsidies did meet serious resistance from two directions. Most serious in practical terms was the NDP's insistence that the threshold for subsidies be lowered from 20 percent of the vote to 15 percent. The issue was whether the 20 percent level so discriminated against minor parties as to "aid unduly the established parties."[17] As they had on the issue of expenditure limits, NDP members made futile attempts to amend the bill in committee, then lost again on the floor. The difference here was that they won behind the scenes. The NDP leader, David Lewis, told Leslie Seidle that he met with Allan MacEachen privately to tell him that if the government did not lower the threshold his party would not support the bill. On the last day of debate at the report stage, the government announced a new threshold of 15 percent (Seidle 1980, 201).

From the opposite end of the ideological spectrum came a complaint curiously similar to the one that American conservatives were raising in Congress. Conservative Terry O'Connor acknowledged that subsidies would be needed because the disclosure provisions would discourage large donors. Nonetheless, he stated that it had been his party's position since the Chappell Committee that "we not depart ... from the principle of requiring candidates and parties to rely on the freely given private donation as the chief source of financing ... It is wrong in principle to require that the taxpayers ... under compulsion be required to support parties and candidates with whose philosophy ... a majority may disagree" (P&E *Minutes*, 6 Dec. 1973, 24:31). O'Connor then moved to amend the bill by reducing the federal subsidy. No NDP members were present that day, and the vote on the amendment was a tie: six Conservatives against six Liberals. The Committee's vice-chairman, Douglas Stewart (L, Okanagan–Kootenay), broke the tie by voting against the amendment.

The NDP members also succeeded in amending the tax credit for campaign contributions. The provision that had been in Bill C-211 was altered to encourage small donors, who were, not coincidentally, an important NDP financial resource (Seidle 1980, 202).

Conclusion

Scandal – the sudden revelation of a hitherto secret and widely disapproved practice – has spurred reform in both countries. All three of the elements just mentioned must be present: the practice must be one the public regards as illegitimate; those engaged in it therefore try to conceal their involvement; their involvement is nonetheless revealed. This revelation creates a press and public outcry that lawmakers must satisfy by legislation. Most American campaign finance regulation is the product of just two scandals, that involving the 1904 Republican presidential campaign, and Watergate. Oddly, most Canadian law in this area also is the result of just two scandals, the Pacific Scandal and Watergate.[18]

To produce significant campaign finance reform, a scandal must involve the financing of a successful campaign. This is why one of the biggest American scandals of the 20th century, Teapot Dome, resulted only in a slight strengthening of disclosure requirements: the funding of President Harding's 1920 election was a minor issue, almost unnoticed in the allegations of the misuse of public office. The Pacific Scandal, the 1905 New York insurance investigation and Watergate all produced significant reform because all involved the financing of successful national campaigns.[19]

The two big American scandals also underscore the importance of public interest groups in the United States. The persistence of the National Publicity Bill Organization (NPBO) and Common Cause had more to do with enacting reform legislation than any actions taken by the president or congressional leaders, and this fact marks a fundamental difference between the United States and Canada. By embodying press and public opinion in a scandal and focusing popular pressure on Congress, interest groups fill the vacuum left by the absence of institutionalized leadership on campaign finance issues. The two major parties are notoriously lacking in formal policy-making capacity, but election reform also lacks the sources of leadership enjoyed by other policy areas: the presidency, congressional committees, and interest groups with a continuing interest in the subject.

Not one of the American campaign finance laws enacted from 1907 to 1979 was the result of presidential initiative, something that probably cannot be said of any other policy area. Canadian governments introduced the 1874 *Dominion Elections Act* and its 1891, 1908 and 1920 amendments, as well as the *Elections Expenses Act* of 1973–74; only the 1930 repeal of the corporation and union prohibitions originated in a private member's bill. All American legislation from 1907 to 1979 originated in Congress. Indeed, Congress enacted the 1943 and 1947 union bans over presidential vetoes, repealed the 1966 public financing act, despite strong presidential support, and passed the 1974 FECA Amendments notwithstanding doubts expressed by presidents Nixon and Ford.

Even congressional committees provided no leadership. The House Administration and Senate Rules committees, which have jurisdiction over this legislation, are primarily "housekeeping" committees, with low prestige and high turnover, and they therefore have not acquired a core membership of experts to whom fellow members look for guidance.[20] Much of the expertise in other policy areas also resides in interest groups, which provide representatives and senators with information as well as drafts of bills. But there is no interest group with a continuing stake in campaign finance, because Congress itself is the only constituency whose interest in the subject need not be kindled by scandal. Thus, while members of Congress themselves have drafted most campaign finance legislation, these members have been "freelancers" with no institutional power base, and they have needed the assistance of outside groups – NPBO, Common Cause, Center for the Public Financing of Elections and AFL-CIO – in building coalitions with their colleagues and keeping the pressure on them.

Finally, it must be added here that Common Cause differs from the other interest groups in that it did more than respond to the Watergate scandal. It actually helped create it. It created a national audience for campaign finance information by its volunteer work in collecting and publishing congressional candidates' disclosure reports. The group also filed suit against President Nixon's 1972 campaign committee, forcing it to release information on those who had contributed before the 1971 FECA went into effect, thus revealing some extremely large contributions. Some of the most troubling contributions made to the President were those revealed as a result of Common Cause's actions.

Interest groups, public or otherwise, have not nearly as important a role in Canadian legislation on this subject. The reason for this difference lies in the two countries' very different constitutional structures. Congress is a far stronger legislative body than the Canadian Parliament, but its power is both formally and informally fragmented: formally, in that it is shared equally by House and Senate and is distributed among a large number of standing committees and subcommittees in both houses; informally, in that the Republican and Democratic parties exercise almost no discipline over their members. The American parties are not so much organizations dedicated to attaining and exercising power as loose collections of political entrepreneurs, each of whom must win re-election as an individual. Thus, American interest groups have vastly more points of access to legislative power than their Canadian counterparts have, as well as greater opportunity to affect, even to initiate, policy. In Canada, on the other hand, where "legislative decision making ... is highly centralized and party discipline is almost complete ... interest group representation has less power to explain legislative outcomes" (Thompson and Stanbury 1979, 25).

Canada's more limited opportunities for interest group influence over public policy may explain the absence north of the border of a public interest group like NPBO or Common Cause. Economic interests – business, labour, agriculture, the professions – sometimes face the same restricted access to policy makers. But it is far easier to organize small numbers of people whose livelihoods are directly affected by government policy than to do the same with large numbers of people who share no more than an interest in "good government." Moreover, the members of economic interest groups are members not because they made a conscious decision to join and pay dues, but simply by virtue of the fact that they share a common way of making a living. The immediacy of this interest makes it necessary to be in frequent contact with government policy makers, even where, as in Canada, the formal structure of government offers fewer opportunities for affecting policy. Add this lower probability of affecting policy to the difficulty of recruiting members for a public interest group, and Canada's failure to produce an organization similar to the NPBO is understandable.

Centralization of power in the Canadian cabinet and comparative lack of opportunity for interest group influence may also explain why there has been less campaign finance legislation north of the border than there has been to the south. We may assume that most legislators, American and Canadian, normally prefer not to regulate their campaign practices and do so only under extraordinary pressure. Scandals can produce such pressure, but only if they are exploited by reformers, as NPBO and Common Cause did in 1905–10 and during Watergate. The absence of such groups in Canada means that those best fitted to exploit scandal are the parties themselves. Since the parties naturally resist election expenses reform, they are likely to respond to scandal with merely symbolic acts, such as the appointment of special committees in response to the Beauharnois and Rivard affairs.

The ability of Canadian governments to brush off domestic scandal raises the question of why they responded substantively to American scandals in 1908 and 1973–74. The answer may be that they responded for the same reason American governments did – because American interest groups made sure to keep media attention focused on the scandalous events and on their own reform agenda. A loud, splashy American scandal cannot help but attract the Canadian media, and its coincidence with some smaller-scale domestic unpleasantness, as in fact happened in 1908 and 1973, may have been sufficient to tip the balance in favour of remedial legislation.

Only Canadian parties whose electoral future is at stake are likely to exploit public discontent in order to push for real reform, as did the Quebec Liberals in the 1950s and the NDP at the federal level in the 1970s. Both are unusual cases. As with Common Cause in Watergate, the Quebec Liberals did not simply respond to crisis but helped create it through articles written by the Liberal journalist (and later Liberal member of the provincial assembly) Pierre Laporte. The NDP, as a minority party and one on the left, was serious about reforming election financing, whereas the conservative minority party, Social Credit, voted against the 1974 legislation. The NDP's ability to influence legislation, however, derived less from its own commitment to reform than from the Liberals' poor performance in the 1972 general election.

One final note about interest group activity in the two countries: the more numerous opportunities for interest group influence on policy in the United States have led not only to the creation of public interest groups but also to lobbying on campaign finance issues by economic interest groups. In 1905 both business, through the National Civic Federation, and labour, through AFL President Samuel Gompers, lobbied for a disclosure law. In the 1960s the Committee for Economic Development, another business association, did a study of campaign finance and issued recommendations for reform. In the 1970s AFL-CIO lobbied for publicly financed presidential campaigns and other reforms. Given Canadian interest groups' more restricted access to lawmakers, corporations and unions north of the border are unlikely to squander contacts they need to pursue goals that are of immediate interest to their own constituencies by deploying them on issues of more general concern.

The differing roles of socio-economic interests in the two countries also appear in their very different legislation regarding business corporations, farmers' organizations and labour unions. The United States banned corporate contributions in 1907 and union contributions in 1943, and both laws remain in force. Canada prohibited corporation and union contributions in 1908 and 1920 but repealed both in 1930, before the United States had even considered legislating on unions.

Parliament was clearly less committed to these prohibitions than Congress was, and while the reasons for this difference are unclear, some explanations will be ventured.

Congress banned contributions from both sources in response to crises. In 1907 a Republican-dominated Congress reluctantly (and solely in response to the tireless efforts of outside reformers, backed by press and public opinion) prohibited a source of campaign funds that leaders of both parties had publicly branded as illegitimate. No such crisis occurred in Canada. Indeed, given Canadian press coverage of the New York revelations, along with Sir Robert Borden's contacts with American electoral reformers, it is possible that the 1908 law was more a reaction to the American scandal than to domestic events. Certainly, there were Canadian scandals involving corporation money – the Pacific and McGreevy affairs cannot have been forgotten – but it does seem that, unlike the American events, they involved government contractors. Like Teapot Dome, these events merely added new chapters to the age-old story of greedy businessmen and corrupt officials seeking to enrich themselves at public expense, a story that predates both democracy and industrial capitalism. The 1905 New York revelations were a different matter. It is unlikely that the corporations that financed Theodore Roosevelt's run for the White House were entirely disinterested, but it is also true that they did not give with the expectation of immediate financial gain. The growth of the large corporation was a revolutionary social and economic development, and when these financial giants began to participate in electoral politics, people began to fear that they endangered democracy. No such concern preceded enactment of the Canadian prohibition, and it may well be that its absence in 1908 made it easier to repeal the prohibition in 1930.[21]

Congress also enacted the ban on union contributions in response to crisis, although only the Republican–Southern Democratic majority saw it as such. Labour unions grew in both membership and political activity in the 1930s, and their decision to throw their resources behind President Roosevelt marked a significant divergence in the two parties' financial bases. The Republicans' successful anti-union alliance with Southern Democrats in the 1940s threatened Northern Democrats much as the 1907 Act had threatened Republicans.

If Conservatives and Liberals in Parliament were responding to a similar crisis in 1920, the threat appears to have come not from the few small unions in existence at the time, but from the growing, and politically active, Progressive and farmers' organizations in the West. Western MPs not only subscribed to such Progressive goals as the initiative, referendum and recall, but they greatly alarmed their fellow members by having financed their campaigns with large numbers of $1 contributions, solicited door-to-door.[22] By 1930, those farmers' organizations had incorporated, and it was clear that the 1920 law was not going to stop their political activity. On the other hand, the law did restrict labour unions, most of which, being affiliates of American unions, were legally unable to incorporate. Labour's interest in repealing the legislation was obvious. The major parties' interest in accommodating the unions is less clear, but it should be pointed out that neither in 1920 nor in 1930 did the unions pose nearly as great a threat to the Liberals and Conservatives as American unions did to Republicans and even to conservative Democrats in the 1940s. There was in Canada, moreover, the very important influence of the British example: the very existence of the British Labour party was an argument against the Canadian prohibition, and J.S. Woodsworth (Labour, Winnipeg) reminded his colleagues that British Conservative leader Stanley Baldwin had opposed a similar prohibition in the United Kingdom (House *Debates*, 19 June 1925, 4557–58, and 26 June 1925, 4972–73).

The American debate featured philosophical/legal arguments about the differences between corporations and unions that did not appear in Canada. Corporations are profit-making organizations, investment in which government protects by grants of limited liability; although the corporations' internal governments are theoretically democratic, they rely on a property-based suffrage (not one vote per person, but one vote per share) that has long since been abolished in politics; they also permit proxy voting, by which shareholders allow elected officers and/or directors to cast their votes for them. Unions are unincorporated, non-profit associations of individuals; internal union government is more democratic in theory than in practice, but even the theory is more democratic than that of corporations, votes being distributed one to each member. Democrats raised these differences time and again during committee hearings and congressional debate on the 1943 and 1947 laws forbidding union contributions. Democrats insisted that unions, as voluntary associations, should not be denied political rights, and Republicans insisted on treating unions and corporations as similar organizations requiring similar treatment. (In recent years, the American debate over the proper political role of corporations has been raised in the courts. See the following section on constitutional issues.)

Federalism was not an obstacle to national legislation in Canada, but it was once a serious obstacle in the United States. Long before the Civil War, Southern politicians fervently believed that states retain much of their sovereignty under the Constitution, and this belief outlasted the Civil War by more than a century. The NPBO's fear of offending

Southern sensitivity about states' rights in 1906 led it to draft a disclosure bill that would not apply to campaign committees operating entirely within one state, i.e., the vast majority of such committees. In 1911 Republican hopes of arousing Southern ire ironically resulted in a strengthening of disclosure. Ten years later, Republicans undid that victory by repealing primary coverage for all federal campaign finance laws, an action that remained in effect until 1971.

Doubt as to Congress' authority to regulate elections in a federal system was much less evident in the 1970s, but there are still some interesting differences between legislation in the two federations. Although the states enacted the first American campaign finance laws, this did not lead to pressure on Congress to do the same. The states followed Congress' lead in this policy area, both in the early years of the century and in the 1970s. In Canada, on the other hand, provincial legislation appears to have had more influence on Parliament.[23] This was certainly true in the 1960s and 1970s, when Nova Scotia, Saskatchewan, Manitoba and Ontario were studying Quebec's innovative 1963 law. It may be the informal structures of power that explain this difference.

It has long been recognized in the United States that political careers start at the state or local level and progress up to the national, where there is another status difference between the House of Representatives and the Senate. This status hierarchy makes it unlikely that Congress, which is composed of politicians who regard themselves as having "graduated" from state legislatures, will be much influenced by the action of those whom they see almost as apprentices. There appears to be no such status ladder for Canadian politicians. V. Peter Harder discovered not only that two-thirds of Canadian MPs had held no prior elective office, just the opposite of the American case, but also that Canadian politicians were as likely to make their careers in provincial legislatures as in Parliament (Harder 1979, 338). The smaller status differences between legislators at the two levels in Canada, and their rough similarity of experience, may cause Parliament to heed the provinces more than Congress does the states.

CONSTITUTIONAL ISSUES

The major issue raised by the *Federal Election Campaign Act* (FECA) is expressed in the phrase "money is speech," which is a condensation of the conservative proposition that spending money for political communication is equivalent to the communication itself. A corollary argument is that restricting such spending is equivalent to restricting political speech and thus violates constitutional guarantees of free expression. Conservatives successfully used this argument in 1971 to persuade

Congress to repeal contribution and spending limits. Although in the wake of Watergate this same argument failed to sway a Congress determined to re-enact those limits, it did convince a majority of the Supreme Court, in *Buckley*, to strike down spending limits as unconstitutional.

Buckley eliminated candidate expenditure ceilings as a legislative issue, but controversy continues to swirl around independent spending on behalf of or in opposition to candidates. The Supreme Court struck down limits on such expenditures in presidential elections in 1985 but continues to face difficult cases involving independent spending by corporations. Independent, or "third-party," expenditures also have been the chief constitutional issue in Canada, where the issue arose later than in the United States and is far from having run its course.

The United States

Independent spending first appeared in the 1940 American presidential campaign, after Congress imposed a $3 million annual spending ceiling on national political committees (see the section on disclosure in the United States in the first part of this study). As soon as this law took effect, Republican lawyers interpreted "national political committees" as meaning only the national committees of the two major parties, and not non-party organizations operating independently. This interpretation quickly spawned a profusion of groups, most supporting Republican candidates and each claiming to have no connection with official party organizations. Instead of the $3 million envisaged by Congress, Democrats spent $6 million to re-elect President Roosevelt, and the Republicans spent $15 million trying to oust him.

Independent spending first appeared as a transparent evasion of campaign spending limits, and it was immediately clear that limits would not be effective until something was done about evasion. For 30 years Congress went back and forth between two solutions. The first was to require a candidate to authorize one or more committees to raise and spend money for his or her campaign, to permit spending only by authorized committees, and to treat all such committees as a single unit bound by one spending limit. The second, simpler, method was to impose spending ceilings on any independent committee.

The first method was proposed as early as 1944, but Congress did not make it law until 1971. In the FECA of that year, Congress limited spending on print and broadcast media and reinforced that limit by prohibiting publishers and radio and television stations from charging for any political advertising not authorized by the candidate it promoted. Republicans had raised First Amendment objections to this authorization method in the 1950s, and they raised them again, to no avail, in 1971. In 1973 a federal district court struck down the law as an unconstitutional abridgement of speech (*American Civil Liberties Union*).

When amending the FECA in 1974, Congress adopted the second approach, setting a $1 000 limit on the amount any individual or committee could spend on behalf of a candidate and not counting that amount against the candidate's own limit. Congress also tightened the definition of independent expenditures by exempting from the ceiling expressions of opinion on political issues that did not expressly advocate the election or defeat of specific candidates. The Senate Rules Committee offered the new law as "the best compromise of competing interests in free speech and effective campaign regulation" (S. Rept 93-689 (93d Cong.), 19). Shortly after passage of the 1974 FECA Amendments, a libertarian-conservative coalition challenged their constitutionality.

Reformers had sought financial equality among candidates since the first candidate spending limits enacted in 1911. Judging private campaign funding against the standard of "one person, one vote," liberals regarded political contributions "as an especially important kind of vote" and viewed "people who give in larger sums or to more candidates than their fellow citizens [as] in effect voting more than once" (Heard 1960, 48–49). Only in the 1970s, on the other hand, did conservatives begin to raise reasoned argument against limits, leading Congress to balance libertarian and egalitarian values. By the time the *Buckley* challenge was filed, conservative legal scholars had developed an explicitly libertarian defence of unlimited giving and spending in election campaigns. They argued that giving and spending for political purposes are more like speaking than voting and that restricting contributions and expenditures actually restricts speech and is therefore unconstitutional. This is the argument denoted by the phrase "money is speech."

The U.S. Supreme Court accepted this argument and ruled that the 1974 law suppressed expression by "restricting the voices of people and interest groups who have money to spend" (*Buckley* 1976, 17). The justices rejected egalitarian arguments in favour of limits by reformulating them, via the money-speech equation, as attempts to suppress speech: "[T]he concept that government may restrict the speech of some elements of our society in order to enhance the relative voice of others is wholly foreign to the First Amendment" (ibid., 48–49).

The Court found limits on independent expenditures to be doubly wrong: they not only suppressed speech, but they suppressed speech that was ineffective. Congress had restricted such spending to reinforce candidate and party limits, to prevent the kind of evasion that had appeared in the 1940 presidential election. The Court, however, did not believe that independent committees could be of any assistance to candidates. The justices ruled that the very independence of a spender, the "absence of prearrangement and coordination ... undermines the value of the expenditure to the candidate" (ibid., 47). Congress had not, according to the Court, closed a loophole, for there was no loophole to close.

The argument resumed in 1980, when some Ronald Reagan supporters announced the formation of two independent expenditure committees to promote his presidential candidacy. The Federal Election Commission filed suit, contending that each of the new groups had to abide by the 1974 law's $1 000 limit. The *Buckley* contenders had somehow overlooked this provision, applying only to publicly funded presidential candidates, and it was still on the books in 1980. Perhaps the FEC hoped that the courts would uphold the provision because the Supreme Court had retained spending limits on publicly funded presidential campaigns. This did not happen. Although the Court deadlocked on this case, it struck the limits down in a similar 1985 decision.[24]

The reformers lost on independent spending, but one of their primary concerns, accountability, was reviewed in the 1980 election case. Accountability was central to the question of independent expenditures: parties and candidates are accountable to voters, but to whom are independent spenders accountable? The 1980 pro-Reagan committees portrayed themselves as the means through which "thousands of small voices" could make themselves heard in presidential elections. Common Cause challenged that claim, finding the groups to be flimsy counterfeits of political organizations because their speech was not that of their members, who did no more than make a money contribution, but was that of their unelected fund-raisers and managers. This was not an issue for the Court, though, perhaps because it clung to the conviction that independent spending, accountable or not, is unlikely to benefit the candidates it promotes (Mutch 1988, 76–80).

While these cases were being argued, a separate set of cases involving corporations was moving through the courts. These, too, used *Buckley* as a precedent, but in combination with another case, *First National Bank of Boston v. Bellotti* (1978). In the Boston case, the State of Massachusetts prosecuted the First National Bank and several other corporations for violating a ban on business political spending by opposing an income tax submitted to voters in a referendum. Massachusetts argued that corporations cannot have opinions and do not have the same First Amendment speech rights as individuals. The Supreme Court countered that the issue was not whether corporations had speech rights but whether the state law abridged speech: "We hold that it does ... We thus find no support ... for the proposition that speech that otherwise would be within the protection of the First Amendment loses that protection simply because its source is a corporation" (ibid., 776, 784).

Taken together, *Buckley* and *Bellotti* have far-reaching implications. By ruling that money is constitutionally protected speech even when it is in a corporate treasury, the Court also ruled that the distinction between individuals and corporations is without constitutional significance. Using these two decisions as precedents, the Court could strike down the federal 1907 Act and all remaining state bans on corporation political spending. Far from taking advantage of this opportunity, however, the justices have in recent cases resurrected pre-*Bellotti* arguments in favour of regulation, thus producing a welter of contradictory opinions. Two recent cases in point involve independent spending by corporations.

During the 1978 congressional election, Massachusetts Citizens for Life (MCFL), a non-profit advocacy corporation created to oppose abortion, issued a voter guide to pro-life candidates. The FEC brought suit under the 1907 Act but lost in the Supreme Court (*MCFL* 1986). It was not that the Court found the Act to be an unconstitutional suppression of corporate speech; indeed, it even cited with apparent approval pre-*Bellotti* rulings upholding congressional intent to curb the political influence of " 'large aggregations of capital' "(ibid., 257). Rather, the Court decided that because the 1907 law targeted business corporations, it did not apply to advocacy corporations such as MCFL. Because MCFL had no stockholders, did not accept business money and was formed for purposes of political advocacy, it could not serve as a conduit for corporation money and was financed by individuals who supported its anti-abortion policy. It was not that the Massachusetts group "merely poses less of a threat of the danger that prompted regulation. Rather, it does not pose such a threat at all" (ibid., 263).

The next corporate independent spending case to reach the Court was that of the Michigan State Chamber of Commerce, a non-profit corporation that had violated state law by spending treasury funds on behalf of a candidate for the state legislature (*Austin* 1990). The Court, relying heavily on *MCFL*, found for the state on the grounds that the Chamber of Commerce, unlike the Massachusetts pro-life group, was more than an advocacy organization and that more than three-fourths of its members were business corporations. The significance of this decision does not lie in its upholding of prohibitions on corporation political spending, for that conclusion was expected given the Michigan Chamber's claim that it be accorded the same exemption granted to MCFL. Rather, it lies in the vigorous dissents of the Court's three Reagan appointees, all of whom insisted that corporations are voluntary associations of individuals and as such have First Amendment speech rights. These three were the youngest members of the Court, and if they are representative of the pool of appointees from which future justices will be chosen, *Buckley* and *Bellotti* may yet lead to repeal of the 1907 Act (Mutch 1990).

Canada

In Canada the issue of third-party spending first appeared when Parliament imposed limits on party and candidate spending in 1973–74. The Barbeau Committee had foreseen the impossibility of enforcing restrictions on party and candidate expenses if spending by "corporations, trade unions, professional and other groups" was not also restricted: "If these groups are allowed to participate actively in an election campaign any limitations or controls on the political parties or candidates become meaningless. In the United States, for example, *ad hoc* committees such as 'Friends of John Smith' or 'Supporters of John Doe' commonly spring up to support a candidate or party. Such committees make limitations on expenditures an exercise in futility, and render meaningless the reporting of election expenses by parties and candidates" (Canada, Committee 1966, 50). With the American experience in mind, the Committee recommended that for the duration of the campaign (from the date of issuing the writ dissolving Parliament until polling day), third parties be prohibited from making expenditures on behalf of or in opposition to candidates and parties. The Chappell Committee agreed in 1971; and in 1972 and 1973, in bills C-211 and C-203, the Trudeau government banned campaign spending by third parties without the "actual knowledge and consent" of candidates or parties. No member of the Privileges and Elections Committee considering Bill C-203 objected to the prohibition, and it became law in 1974 as section 70.1(1) of the *Canada Elections Act*, enacted by section 12 of the *Election Expenses Act*.[25]

Section 70.1(1), which resembles Congress' 1971 "candidate authorization" approach to the problem, is balanced by a definition of election expenses that resembles Congress' 1974 "express advocacy" definition of independent spending: third parties can make expenditures to promote policies, but not to promote candidates or parties. This definition permits "recognized opinion groups ... to operate during a campaign" without running afoul of the prohibition on independent spending (House *Debates*, 10 July 1973, 5477). Parliament then added a mitigating provision that neither the Barbeau nor Chappell committees had suggested: section 70.1(4) allowed third parties charged with making expenditures to support or oppose a candidate or party to claim that they incurred the expenses "for the purpose of gaining support for views ... on an issue of public policy" and that they did so "in good faith," i.e., not in collusion with any party or candidate. The U.S. Supreme Court struck down the American limits before anyone discovered how difficult it would have been to enforce them, but Parliament soon learned just how broadly its "good faith" defence could be interpreted.

In a 1976 Ottawa by-election, a union local hired an airplane to fly over the electoral district trailing a banner urging those below to "vote but not Liberal." Despite the fact that the banner referred only to a registered party, not to a policy, the union local's president defended the action by claiming that he had incurred the expense only to oppose the government's anti-inflation program. The Office of the Chief Electoral Officer decided to prosecute, but late in 1977 a trial court judge, in *R. v. Roach* (1977), acquitted the union official.

This decision dismayed several members of Parliament, which was just then considering Bill C-5 to amend the *Canada Elections Act*, and of the all-party "ad hoc committee," which was considering amendments to that bill.[26] Chief Electoral Officer Jean-Marc Hamel, whose office had already decided to appeal the case, said that "there is no doubt that the decision of the court has pointed out perhaps a weakness in the act" and suggested ways of amending section 70.1 (P&E *Minutes*, 16 Nov. 1977, 1:19). The ad hoc committee, which "had a number of discussions" of the case, proposed an amendment to section 70.1. The House of Commons, however, did not even consider that amendment: since the amendment was to the parent act rather than to Bill C-5, floor consideration during the report stage required unanimous consent, which was withheld by a single vote (House *Debates*, 15 Dec. 1977, 1926–27, and 16 Dec. 1977, 1959).

In June 1978 an appeal court refused to allow the Crown's appeal in *R. v. Roach* because it could "not be proven" that the local's expenditure had been "for the purpose of ... opposing directly a registered party" and because the president "was clearly expressing the views of his association on an issue of public policy" (1978, 741, 742). Two weeks later the Trudeau government withdrew Bill C-63, which included another amendment to section 70.1, after the same Conservative MP, stating that "it goes to the fundamental right of freedom of speech in this country," again refused to give the bill unanimous consent (House *Debates*, 29 June 1978, 6872).

Chief Electoral Officer Jean-Marc Hamel suggested amending section 70.1 in his 1979 *Statutory Report* (Canada, Elections Canada 1979), and in his 1983 report he listed amendments recommended by the ad hoc committee.[27] At the committee's request, CEO Hamel forwarded these proposed amendments to President of the Privy Council, Allan J. MacEachen, to be embodied in legislation. In October 1983, Parliament unanimously passed the resulting legislation, Bill C-169, which repealed section 70.1(4). In light of later events, it is worth noting that Chuck Cook, the Conservative MP who spoke on behalf of Bill C-169, although emphasizing that "all parties were involved in open discussion" of it and that he was "delighted to see this bill go through," suspected "that any number of groups in the country may wish to challenge" the amendments to section 70.1, as it struck him "as somewhat of an interference with the rights of an individual to lobby on behalf of a political party or candidate." Although the New Democratic Party had pressed for amending the section since immediately after the first *Roach* decision, the party's spokesperson acknowledged that the third-party spending provision "may be … hard to enforce under the Charter of Rights," but added that "it is incumbent upon the House not to follow the American example" on independent spending (House *Debates*, 25 Oct. 1983, 28296–99).

Two months after the 1983 amendments received royal assent, the National Citizens' Coalition (NCC) challenged the constitutionality of section 70.1(1)'s ban on third-party expenditures. That prohibition, NCC charged, limited the freedom of expression guaranteed by section 2(*b*) of the 1982 *Canadian Charter of Rights and Freedoms* and was thus unconstitutional. Curiously, the very first precedent the NCC cited in its written argument in Alberta Queen's Bench was the United States Supreme Court decision, *Buckley v. Valeo*.[28]

Even section 70.1's supporters acknowledged that it limited freedom of expression during an election by those who were neither candidates nor registered parties. The crucial question before the court concerned section 1 of the Charter – whether the third-party ban was a "reasonable" abridgement, such "as can be demonstrably justified in a free and democratic society." Patrick J. McCaffery, acting for the attorney general, argued that the ban was reasonable because it protected the "equality and fairness" that were the goals of the spending limits imposed on parties and candidates. "[T]he statutory objective of equalizing electoral opportunity and ensuring the right to an informed vote cannot be achieved if individuals and groups … are permitted to operate outside the rules relating to election expenses."[29]

Mr. Justice Medhurst disagreed. He acknowledged that limits on the freedom of expression should be assessed on the basis of the harm their absence would cause to other values in society. But he ruled that there "should be actual demonstration of harm ... to a society value before a limitation can be said to be justified. In my view ... [the third-party ban] has not been shown to be reasonable or demonstrably justified" (*National Citizens' Coalition Inc.* 1984, 264).

The 1984 election was already underway when the court handed down its decision, and the Liberal government decided not to appeal. Prime Minister Brian Mulroney's Conservative government, which won parliamentary majorities in the 1984 and 1988 general elections, has also not appealed the decision. The Commissioner of Canada Elections decided during the 1984 election that, pending a definitive ruling by the Supreme Court, his office would not enforce section 70.1 anywhere in the country (Seidle 1985, 128–30; Hiebert 1989–90, 79; Ewing 1988, 594–604).

CONCLUSION

The 1982 *Canadian Charter of Rights and Freedoms* introduced an "American" element into Canada's British-style constitutional system. Judicial review of legislation means granting some of Parliament's lawmaking function to the courts, thus leading the two institutions to "check and balance" each other with shared power. It may well be many years before Canadian judges write legislation with the facility of their American counterparts, but the *National Citizens' Coalition* decision demonstrates that Canada has already taken a significant step toward Americanizing the politics of campaign finance reform.

Regulating campaign finance requires, by its very nature, the balancing of competing values. Even disclosure, the least controversial regulation in both countries, is acceptable only on the grounds that the public's right to know who finances the campaigns of those who govern them outweighs the privacy rights of donors. Disclosure requirements probably owe their broad acceptability to the fact that they are the least intrusive means of dealing with the central problem of all campaign finance law, the proper role of wealth in a democracy. Limits are the most intrusive means and hence the most controversial.

Buckley and *National Citizens' Coalition* are alike in that both represent successful libertarian legal challenges to legislation aimed at equalizing political resources. But the two rulings occurred in different political contexts. The decision to impose limits probably was made more easily in Canada, while the challenge to that act was more broadly successful in the United States. The disciplined parties fostered by parliamentary systems can deal with one another as corporate bodies. Once Watergate had quickened the pace of reform north of the border, the parties were able to work out mutually acceptable legislation and to institutionalize further negotiation through the ad hoc committee.

Interparty agreement on spending limits probably was aided in Canada by the fact that the two largest parties have traditionally relied upon the same source – business corporations – to pay for their campaigns. Political survival in America's separation-of-powers system, on the other hand, does not require cohesive, hierarchical party organizations. The absence of party structures conducive to interparty negotiation is compounded by socio-economic differences between Republican and Democratic constituencies. Republican opposition to limits reflects the views of wealthy conservatives, as well as that party's reluctance to give up a financial advantage over the Democrats. Congress' passage of the sweeping 1974 FECA Amendments did not evolve naturally out of bipartisan agreement that new legislation was needed; rather, it was forced by circumstances. Watergate's negative impact on the Republican party's public image gave congressional Republicans a short-term interest in supporting Democratic reforms they had previously opposed. Thus, the two different systems produced, for very different reasons, two similar "liberal" laws.

Conservative objections to the 1974 laws in the two countries were also similar. Conservative MPs in Canada opposed limits and public financing, the same measures that Republicans and Southern Democratic members of Congress protested in the United States. Conservative and libertarian groups outside the legislatures of both countries also opposed these sections of their respective 1974 laws. A parliamentary system offers minority parties little opportunity to obstruct or even significantly delay government bills, though, and offers even less opportunity to interest groups. Such parties instead devote their efforts to modifying bills: the NDP, as a government coalition partner, may have influenced the drafting of Bill C-211, but it was the Conservatives who were most effective in amending it in the Privileges and Elections Committee. The American system, by contrast, offers minority parties and interest groups endless opportunities for delaying legislation, and the U.S. Senate is obstructionist heaven. Neither Republicans nor Southern Democrats used these opportunities to block limits, but they did weaken and delay public financing. Watergate may have caused Republicans on Capitol Hill to deem it unwise to oppose limits, but interest groups outside Congress faced no such constraint. It was they who continued the battle in the courts, and it was their legal victory over limits that made it unnecessary for Republicans to resume their political opposition in Congress.

Conservatives and libertarians won court battles against liberal laws in both countries, but the larger legislative role of U.S. courts gave American challengers the greater victory. In invalidating Parliament's prohibition of independent spending, Mr. Justice Medhurst ruled against only one resolution of the conflict. It is possible that the same court would uphold a measure that did not ban but only limited such spending. Congress passed just such a limit, only to see the Supreme Court invalidate it as well as limits on candidates. By ruling that spending is equivalent to speaking and cannot be limited, the Court did more than strike down one resolution of the conflict between equality and liberty; by finding liberty to be the supreme good, it declared the conflict itself to be illegitimate.

Egalitarians promote limits as a means of retarding the tendency of unequally distributed wealth to become the basis of a similarly unequal distribution of political power. Libertarians and conservatives oppose limits on the grounds that government has no business restricting the freedom of law-abiding citizens. Conflict between equality and liberty appears to be inescapable in a democracy, and any resolution is likely to be impermanent. If this is so, the problem is not how the conflict is to be resolved, but who shall attempt resolution. Elected legislators are the obvious choice, as they are the locus of power in a democracy. But the courts should also play a part, and the issue on both sides of the border is how great a part.

ABBREVIATIONS

c.	chapter
CR	*Congressional Record*
D.L.R. (3d)	Dominion Law Reports, Third Series
D.L.R. (4th)	Dominion Law Reports, Fourth Series
en.	enacted
E.R.	English Reports
F. Supp.	Federal Supplement
H. Rept	House Report (U.S.)
N.Y.	New York Court of Appeal Reports
P.	Pacific Reporter
P&E	Privileges and Elections Committee
Pub. L.	Public Law
R.S.C.	Revised Statutes of Canada
s. (s)	section(s)
S.C.	Statutes of Canada
S. Ct	Supreme Court Reporter (U.S.)
S. Rept	Senate Report (U.S.)
U.S.	United States Supreme Court Reports

NOTES

This study is complete as of 25 March 1991.

1. Ford, a former Republican Representative from Michigan, had been appointed Vice-President after Spiro T. Agnew resigned for reasons not connected to Watergate.

2. In *McConnell* (1904) the Montana Supreme Court ruled against a silver-mining company that had made a political contribution, on the grounds that its charter did not authorize such action; in 1907 the New York Supreme Court reached the same conclusion about New York Life's contribution to the Republican party's 1904 presidential campaign (*People ex rel. Perkins*).

3. A list of NPBO members was printed in the *Congressional Record* (6 May 1906, 7471–72).

4. The most important labour cases were *U.S. v. CIO* (1948) and *U.S. v. UAW* (1957).

5. Compare Canadian Labour MP William Irvine's 1925 observations on the same subject: House *Debates*, 19 Feb. 1925, 347.

6. The cumbersome method of electing an American president requires explanation. The president is elected by the Electoral College, which is composed of presidential electors, who run on partisan tickets in state elections. A state has as many electors as it has members in the U.S. House of Representatives and Senate. Thus, the president is not elected by a national popular majority but by adding the results of 50 state elections. The electors cast their ballots for president and vice-president in their state capitals in the December immediately following the election, and these ballots are counted before a joint session of Congress the following January. The casting and counting of Electoral College votes is only a formality today, as the people know as soon as the November elections are over which presidential candidate received a majority of electoral votes.

7. Primary elections are held to select party nominees for elective office. Because the South was solidly Democratic in the first half of the 20th century, the real contest for congressional seats was among contenders for the Democratic nomination. The general election, in which Republicans put up only token opposition or none at all, merely ratified the primary decision. For Congress to require disclosure in general elections, but not in primary elections, would thus have effectively excluded almost one-third of congressional Democrats from its coverage, something Republicans understandably did not want to do.

8. See the testimony of Ralph K. Winter, Attorney General Richard G. Kleindienst and Lawrence O'Brien, in United States, Congress (1971a, 182–83, 518, 566–67, 583, 638–39; 1971b, 51–54, 203).

9. Democrats had passed such a limit in 1970 but without a majority large enough to override President Nixon's veto. In 1971 President Nixon surprised even his own party by supporting the limit (Mutch 1988, 69).

10. Leslie Seidle's interviews with officials in the Office of the Chief Electoral Officer corroborated the view "that Watergate provided a 'big push' towards legislation" (Seidle 1980, 195, n. 1).

11. The 1874 *Dominion Elections Act* had already followed the British example by defining as corrupt such practices as personation, bribery of voters, treating, and undue influence: ss. 75, 92–95, 98.

12. American influence of a less wholesome kind was reflected in the third provision of the 1908 law, which prohibited foreigners from participating in Canadian elections. Electoral corruption was a serious problem in both countries, but more frequent elections in the United States had created a large number of operatives whose skill in the arts of vote fraud inspired such admiration north of the border that both Canadian parties imported Americans to assist in general election campaigns.

13. The Beauharnois scandal aroused public suspicion of corruption in Quebec's Liberal government, which was defeated in 1936 by provincial Conservatives in alliance with a reformist Liberal faction. The Conservative Premier, Maurice Duplessis, then created his own Quebec nationalist party, the Union Nationale. Corruption in the Union Nationale government finally led to a Liberal victory in 1960, and then to Quebec's famous *Election Act* of 1963. In a very indirect way, the scandal did produce campaign finance reform (see Regehr 1990, 182–84; Angell 1966).

14. Alcorn's criticism is interesting in light of his claim to have followed the New York law, which also exempted "a corporation or association organized or maintained for political purposes only" (1906 Laws of New York 470, chap. 239).

15. On the incorporation of farmers' groups after 1920, see remarks of Brown and MacPhail (House *Debates,* 19 June 1925, 4553 and 4562, respectively). On the inability of unions to incorporate, see remarks of Labour MPs William Irvine and J.S. Woodsworth (ibid., 19 Feb. 1925, 348, and 19 June 1925, 4557, respectively). For Irvine's attempts to repeal the ban and to win an exemption for unions, see his remarks (ibid., 19 Feb. 1925, 347–52, 19 June 1925, 4552–62, 26 June 1925, 4970–75 and 28 May 1930, 2712–14). For Conservative support for repeal, and even for exempting unions, see remarks and vote of the Leader of the Opposition, Arthur Meighen (ibid., 19 June 1925, 4552–53 and 26 June 1925, 4974); for Progressive support of exemption, see remarks and vote of parliamentary leader Robert Forke (ibid., 19 Feb. 1925, 350–51 and 26 June 1925, 4974).

16. An exception was Paul Dick (PC, Lanark–Renfrew–Carleton), who thought disclosure was the most important feature and wondered why

candidates' spending should be restricted (P&E *Minutes,* 30 Oct. 1973, 15:29–30).

17. P&E *Minutes,* 25 Oct. 1973, 14:22. The problem of minor parties and independent candidates was also a difficult problem for American public financing (Mutch 1988, 139–44).

18. The importance here assigned to scandal in promoting campaign finance reform raises in some minds the question of why Congress passed the *Federal Election Campaign Act of 1971* (FECA) in the absence of one. A large part of the answer must be that the 1971 Act resembles the genuine reforms of 1907–11 and 1973–74 less than the *Federal Corrupt Practices Act of 1925.* Both were less innovations than revisions and recodifications of existing law, and both repealed important sections of that law: the 1925 Act repealed disclosure and spending limits for congressional primaries, and the 1971 Act repealed contribution and spending limits. The one notable innovation of the 1971 FECA was a greatly strengthened disclosure provision, which does have the distinction of being a reform enacted without the goad of scandal. Perhaps the best explanation of this Act is that offered by the Comptroller General, who in the course of enforcing the new law observed that its requirements "came as a distinct shock to most candidates for federal office" (United States, Office of Federal Elections 1975, 1). He suspected that Congress simply had not realized how much change it was bringing upon itself.

To say that scandal spurs campaign finance reform is not to say that all legislation in this area must be preceded by scandal; it is to say that when such legislation is not produced by scandal, it is likely to be ineffective. The contribution and expenditure limits of 1940 and the Long public financing act of 1966 are cases in point. Both may be considered genuine reforms in the abstract; but they were also partisan and factional moves that, not having the backing of public opinion, did not earn the respect of the partisans at whom they were aimed. Republicans announced a legal rationale for evading the 1940 limits almost as soon as they were enacted, barely troubling themselves to conceal their disdain for the new laws. The Long act was the work of Senate insiders, and when it came under attack at the next session of Congress it could be defended only by parliamentary manoeuvres, and only for a short time. The very different reception accorded the same measures after Watergate is instructive: bipartisan majorities voted in favour of limits, and Republicans opposed public financing not with cynical evasions but with principled objections.

It should be unnecessary to add that scandal, important as it is, can do no more than further reform by dramatizing the issues around which reformers have organized and by prodding lawmakers into action; it cannot create those issues. Indeed, scandal itself may be impossible without well-defined issues. It is not at all clear, for example, that the activities revealed at the 1905 New York insurance hearings would have been considered scandalous if no one had given any thought to the propriety of corporation political contributions before those hearings took place. The precondition of scandal is the fact that politicians, opinion makers and the general public have all given some thought to the practice in question and have judged it to be offensive. Scandals are enabling events, not causes.

19. The fact that the campaigns in question were successful means that the guilty parties were in office when the scandals broke. Liberal defeat in the 1930 Canadian general election may help explain why the Beauharnois affair produced no reform legislation: the wrongdoers did not benefit from their activities, thus there was no public demand that they give up the fruits of their crimes. Still, 1931 does seem to have been the most opportune moment for the victorious Conservatives to propose limits on election expenses, a policy that would have restricted them far more than the better-financed Liberals and also would have been in accord with British precedent.

20. Senators Thomas C. Hennings, Jr. (Dem., Missouri), and Albert Gore (Dem., Tennessee), who chaired the Senate Privileges and Elections Subcommittee, are exceptions to this generalization. One accustomed to congressional standing committees, membership on which changes only every two years, can at first be quite confused by the ease with which members on Canadian parliamentary committees vanish and are replaced.

21. Only once did any Canadian MP make the kind of argument that characterized the American debate, and that was 12 years after enactment: in 1920 the Acting Solicitor General, Hugh Guthrie, when asked why the Borden government's enlargement of the ban did not extend to individual contributions, replied that "an individual has a heart and soul and mind of his own, and he has a right to vote ... The case is different with a company" (House *Debates*, 26 Mar. 1920, 781).

22. For Progressive views, see remarks of MP Oliver R. Gould (United Farmer, Assiniboia) (House *Debates*, 13 April 1920, 1172, 1178–81). For criticism of the Progressives, see the remarks of Herbert M. Mowat (Unionist, Parkdale) and John W. Edwards (Cons., Frontenac) (House *Debates*, 13 April 1920, 1176–78 and 1186–87).

23. Norman Ward wrote that, "as has been common in Canada's electoral history, the provinces were the pioneers, and Parliament the follower" (Ward 1972, 338). Seidle also commented that "ideas have often drifted upwards from the provincial level in Canada" (Seidle 1980, 174).

24. *FEC v. Americans for Change* (1982) and *FEC v. NCPAC* (1985).

25. The Committee made one minor amendment, to protect party agents, in s. 70.1(1)(*b*) (see P&E *Minutes*, 12 Dec. 1973, 24:47).

26. The "ad hoc committee" came into being informally, as a result of Chief Electoral Officer Jean-Marc Hamel's efforts to involve the political parties in developing uniform interpretations of the 1974 *Election Expenses Act.* It continued to meet after that Act became law, and meets under the chairmanship of the Commissioner of Election Expenses (Carter 1979, 89–91).

27. *National Citizens' Coalition* (1984). Written Argument of Attorney General, First Submission, 52–55, 57–59; Canada, Elections Canada 1983, 74.

28. *National Citizens' Coalition* (1984). Written Argument of Plaintiffs, First Submission, 2, n. 2.

29. Ibid. Written Argument of Attorney General, First Submission, 85.

REFERENCES

Acker, Eric C. 1979. "The Birth of the Election Expenses Bill." In *The Canadian House of Commons Observed,* ed. Jean-Paul Gaboury and James Ross Hurley. Ottawa: Éditions de l'Université d'Ottawa.

Alexander, Herbert E. 1976. *Financing the 1972 Election.* Lexington: Lexington Books.

American Civil Liberties Union v. Jennings 366 F. Supp. 1041 (1971).

Angell, Harold K. 1966. "The Evolution and Application of Quebec Election Expense Legislation, 1960–66." In Canada, Committee on Election Expenses. *Report.* Ottawa: Queen's Printer.

Austin v. Michigan Chamber of Commerce 110 S. Ct. 1391 (1990).

Belmont, Perry. 1905. "Publicity of Election Expenses." *North American Review* 180:166–85.

Bryce, James. 1903. *The American Commonwealth.* Vol. 2. New York: Macmillan.

Buckley v. Valeo 424 U.S. 1 (1976).

Canada. *Canada Elections Act,* R.S.C. 1970, c. 14 (1st Supp.), s. 70.1, en. 1973–74, c. 51, s. 12.

———. *Canadian Charter of Rights and Freedoms,* ss. 1, 2, Part I of the *Constitution Act, 1982,* being Schedule B of the *Canada Act 1982* (U.K.), 1982, c. 11.

———. *Dominion Elections Act,* S.C. 1874, c. 9, ss. 75, 92–95, 98.

———. *Dominion Elections Act,* S.C. 1920, c. 46, s. 79.

Canada. Committee on Election Expenses. 1966. *Report.* Ottawa: Queen's Printer.

Canada. Elections Canada. Various years. *Statutory Report of the Chief Electoral Officer as per subsection 59(1) of the Canada Elections Act.* Ottawa: Minister of Supply and Services Canada.

Canada. House of Commons. Special Committee on Election Expenses. 1971. *Report.* Ottawa: Queen's Printer.

———. Standing Committee on Privileges and Expenses. Various issues. *Minutes of Proceedings and Evidence.* Ottawa: Queen's Printer.

Carter, David. 1979. "Implementation of the Election Expenses Act." In *The Canadian House of Commons Observed,* ed. Jean-Paul Gaboury and James Ross Hurley. Ottawa: Éditions de l'Université d'Ottawa.

Christian, W., and C. Campbell. 1990. *Political Parties and Ideologies in Canada.* Toronto: McGraw-Hill Ryerson.

Committee for Economic Development. 1968. *Financing a Better Election System.* New York: CED.

Congressional Quarterly. 1947. *Almanac.* Washington, DC: CQ.

Ewing, K.D. 1988. "The Legal Regulation of Campaign Financing in Canadian Federal Elections." *Public Law* (Winter): 577–608.

FEC v. Americans for Change 455 U.S. 129 (1982).

FEC v. Massachusetts Citizens for Life Inc. (MFCL) 479 U.S. 238 (1986).

FEC v. NCPAC 470 U.S. 480 (1985).

First National Bank of Boston v. Bellotti 435 U.S. 765 (1978).

Harder, V. Peter. 1979. "Career Patterns and Political Parties at the National and Sub-National Levels in the United States and Canada." In *The Canadian House of Commons Observed,* ed. Jean-Paul Gaboury and James Ross Hurley. Ottawa: Éditions de l'Université d'Ottawa.

Heard, Alexander. 1960. *The Costs of Democracy.* Chapel Hill: University of North Carolina Press.

Hiebert, Janet. 1989–90. "Fair Elections and Freedom of Expression Under the Charter." *Journal of Canadian Studies* 24:72–86.

Lipset, Seymour Martin. 1990. *Continental Divide: The Values and Institutions of the United States and Canada.* New York: Routledge.

Lipset, S.M., and William Schneider. 1983. *The Confidence Gap.* New York: Free Press.

McConnell v. Combination Mining and Milling 79 P. 248 (1904).

McFarland, Andrew. 1984. *Common Cause: Lobbying in the Public Interest.* Chatham: Chatham House.

Mutch, Robert E. 1988. *Campaigns, Congress, and Courts: The Making of Federal Campaign Finance Law.* New York: Praeger.

————. 1990. "Corporation Political Spending and the First Amendment." Paper presented at the American Political Science Association annual meeting, San Francisco, 30 August–2 September.

National Citizens' Coalition Inc./Coalition nationale des citoyens inc. v. Canada (Attorney General) (1984), 32 Alta. L.R. (2d) 249 (Q.B.).

Overacker, Louise. 1932. *Money in Elections.* New York: Macmillan.

Paltiel, Khayyam Zev. 1970. *Political Party Financing in Canada.* Toronto: McGraw-Hill.

People ex rel. Perkins v. Moss 187 N.Y. 410 (1907).

Pipefitters v. U.S. 407 U.S. 385 (1972).

Putney, Bryant. 1940. "Money in Politics." *Editorial Research Reports,* April 15.

Quebec. Commission of Inquiry Concerning the Purchasing Methods Used in the Department of Colonization and the Government Purchasing Service from July 1st, 1955 to June 30th, 1960. 1963. *Report.* Montreal.

R. v. Roach, Provincial Court (Criminal Division) Judicial District of York, Toronto, 24 Oct. 1977; affirmed (1978), 101 D.L.R. (3d) 736 (Ont. Co. Ct.).

Regehr, T.D. 1990. *The Beauharnois Scandal: A Story of Canadian Entrepreneurship and Politics.* Toronto: University of Toronto Press.

Richardson, Leon Burr. 1940. *William E. Chandler, Republican.* New York: Dodd, Mead.

Roosevelt, Theodore. 1952. *The Letters of Theodore Roosevelt,* ed. Elting E. Morison. 8 vols. Cambridge, Mass.: Harvard University Press.

Seidle, F. Leslie. 1980. "Electoral Law and Its Effects on Election Expenditure and Party Finance in Great Britain and Canada." D.Phil. dissertation, Oxford University.

————. 1985. "The Election Expenses Act: The House of Commons and the Parties." In *The Canadian House of Commons: Essays in Honour of Norman Ward,* ed. John C. Courtney. Calgary: University of Calgary Press.

Thompson, Fred, and W.T. Stanbury. 1979. "The Political Economy of Interest Groups in the Legislative Process in Canada." Montreal: Institute for Research on Public Policy.

Twentieth Century Fund. 1970. *Electing Congress.* New York: Twentieth Century Fund.

United Kingdom. *Corrupt and Illegal Practices Prevention Act, 1883* (U.K.), 46 & 47 Vict., c. 51.

————. *Corrupt Practices Prevention Act, 1854* (U.K.), 17 & 18 Vict. c. 102.

U.S. v. CIO 335 U.S. 106 (1948).

U.S. v. Newberry 256 U.S. 232 (1921).

U.S. v. U.A.W. 352 U.S. 567 (1957).

United States. *Federal Corrupt Practices Act of 1925,* Feb. 28, 1925, ch. 368, title III.

———. *Federal Election Campaign Act of 1971,* Pub. L. 92–225, Feb. 7, 1972.

———. *Hatch Act.*

———. *Laws of New York* 1906 470, ch. 239.

———. *Pendleton Act of 1883* (Civil Service Act), Jan. 16, 1883, ch. 27.

United States. Congress. 1895–. *Congressional Record.* Washington, DC. (Specific issues are identified in the text as *CR,* followed by date and page.)

———. House. *Reports.* (Specific reports are identified in the text as H. Rept, followed by report and Congress numbers.)

———. Senate. *Reports.* (Specific reports are identified in the text as S. Rept, followed by report and Congress numbers.)

———. Senate. Committee on Commerce. 1971a. *Hearings on the Federal Election Campaign Act of 1971.* 92d Cong., March–April.

———. Senate. Committee on Rules and Administration. 1971b. *Hearings on the Federal Election Campaign Act of 1971.* 92d Cong., 24–25 May.

United States. Office of Federal Elections. 1975. *Report of the Office of Federal Elections of the General Accounting Office in Administering the FECA of 1971.* Washington, DC.

United States . President's Commission on Campaign Costs. 1962. *Financing Presidential Campaigns.* Washington, DC.

Ward, Norman. 1949. "Electoral Corruption and Controverted Elections." *Canadian Journal of Economic and Political Science* 15:74–86.

———. 1972. "Money and Politics: The Costs of Democracy in Canada." *Canadian Journal of Political Science* 5:335–47.

Wearing, Joseph. 1988. *Strained Relations: Canadian Parties and Voters.* Toronto: McClelland and Stewart.

3

INNOVATION AND EQUITY
The Impact
of Public Funding

Jane Jenson

ANY REFORM OF legislation regulating party finance and election expenses is only as effective as its contribution to creating a societal consensus that healthy democratic politics exist. Recreating that consensus among Canadian citizens is the most compelling task facing us at this time. The country is at a crossroads. Part of the current debate – beyond the constitutional controversies, disputes over economic restructuring and the rights of all segments of the population – involves the well-being of democracy. Indeed, many observers of the Canadian electoral and party systems agree that these central democratic institutions are at risk.[1]

In the past decades, since the 1964 Committee on Election Expenses (the Barbeau Committee) first set out its proposals (Canada, Committee 1966), the legitimacy of elections and the representational capacity of political parties have declined for several reasons. A major one is the sense that parties have not succeeded in incorporating the new demands expressed by their varied constituencies, so that aggrieved citizens turn to other channels for representation. The most extreme expression of concern about this process comes from those Canadians who consider the 1988 election "stolen" by the activities of moneyed "third parties." Other reasons are found in the party system's inability to sustain its legitimacy in the face of powerful social changes in the direction of bureaucratic decision making, executive governance and social-movement politics.

Cross-national comparative observation demonstrates that such loss of party and electoral representational capacity is not inevitable, however. Many European countries in the 1970s experienced challenges and trends similar to those that provoked the "decline of party" discussion in Canada at the time.[2] Extra-parliamentary protests – both pacific and violent – rocked the countries of Western Europe. Social movements of all types claimed that *no* traditional party could *ever* represent their new demands and that new types of action in the streets, the home and the community were necessary. Yet the 1980s have demonstrated that party systems in many of these countries have subsequently opened themselves to the basic demands of such groups, absorbing the extra-parliamentary dissent and achieving new legitimacy. The party systems that had seemed "frozen" in 1921 thawed sufficiently to accommodate the entry of new actors, and the health of these democracies has improved.[3] Indeed, representational legitimacy is expanding, with new enthusiasm for Europarliamentary elections. That Parliament – long the "joke" of representative bodies – owes part of its new-found popularity to its rightful claim that it is "accommodative."

This re-legitimatization of party and electoral politics following the challenges of the 1970s has not occurred in Canada. Instead "party decline" goes on and, as the last election demonstrated, is even intensifying as many ordinary citizens question the justice of the 1988 results, despite the solid majority produced.

By presenting comparative material from several Western European countries, this study first makes an argument about public funding that is somewhat at variance with the "conventional wisdom" of a good part of the literature that has influenced Canadian thinking about these matters. It explores the ways in which state support for parties and electoral democracy have implications for processes of representation. It does so by focusing on a theme central to the Barbeau Committee – that of fairness as reflected in procedures for public funding. While some aspects of the regulations of party and election financing have translated that Committee's equity concerns into legislation over the years, the issue of fairness of access for innovative ideas and parties has received less attention. The premise of this research study is that the short shrift granted to such questions of access has contributed to the current crisis of confidence, because innovation in issues and by actors has been hindered.

Second, the study argues that in the regime for public funding, the overwhelming emphasis on the parties' ability to raise and spend money challenges another notion of fairness. Most systems for allocating such public funds do so according to the number of votes received. Canada is different. By rewarding spending rather than vote-getting (in the case of reimbursement procedures) and fund-raising (in the case of tax credits), the representation of politics provided via such a funding regime is that "money talks" more than votes. This is a perversion of the fundamental principles of liberal-democratic politics.

Third, this study argues that public funding that seeks to strengthen parties as organizations and party systems as representational complexes has proven more responsive to the new demands of the last decades and has better met the basic goal of equal opportunity for actors representing innovative world views and emerging social groups. Rather than contributing to the "petrification" of the existing systems, programs that recognize that parties serve as a crucial bridge between the citizen and the state have helped these countries to be tolerant of and receptive to innovation. Such politics have been more adaptive than those that assume that the basic tie of democracy is one between the individual candidate and the voter. Moreover, rather than becoming excessively bureaucratized and expensive, politics in party-oriented countries are characterized by extensive ongoing political debate and less exclusive attention to elections as the sole moments of democratic politics.[4] Thus the decline of an active and participatory citizenry is not necessarily the price of continuous state funding of political parties. Indeed an argument about the opposite outcome is sustainable.

State Subsidies as Gatekeepers

Within the realm of electoral reform and party financing, regulations for recognition of parties and public funding are only a part of the whole. Yet because they serve as gatekeepers in the process of innovation and renewal of national party systems, they are crucial factors that deserve careful attention. Recognition and subsidization of parties can open the door to new parties as they seek to mobilize around issues or positions that are less well represented by existing formations. In turn, public perception of expanded access contributes to the acknowledgement of party politics as a route to innovation and to higher levels of support for the political process.

Of the five goals sometimes identified as being associated with the regulation of elections, public funding might be used to achieve all of them. These goals, suggested by the Ontario Commission on Election Expenses and developed by Adamany and Agree (1980), are

- to achieve equality of opportunity in a liberal democracy characterized by inequalities in the distribution of wealth;
- to make enough money available that competitive campaigns can exist;

- to allow new entrants, while not encouraging frivolous candidates or propping up decaying political organizations;
- to reduce the opportunity for undue influence; and
- to prevent corruption.

Despite some agreement about goals, however, several questions about design structure immediately arise. Many choices are available, and the mechanisms selected will affect whether the gatekeeping effects of public funding will be equitable and tolerant of political pluralism or whether they will be exclusionary.

The four relevant questions about funding mechanisms are: when, to whom, for what and how will public funds be allocated?

Funding may come at the time of the election, or it may be spread over the whole inter-election period. The recipients may be party organizations or they may be individual candidates and legislators. Moreover, national party organizations may collect the funds or they may go to subnational units, in regions or provinces, or to specialized subgroups, like youth and women's organizations. The third issue concerning what is to be supported is complicated. Campaign expenses may be the focus; public funds may be provided to cover mailing, broadcasting, travel or other campaign costs. On the other hand, the price of "being" a party, of maintaining a complex organization, may provide the rationale for subsidizing staff, broadcasting, research and other costs. Sometimes state subsidies are in kind, with the state paying the costs of activities – broadcasting, publicity and space, for example – that parties might otherwise assume. Finally, funds may be granted as direct subventions, as specific grants and services, or as indirect subsidies (tax credits being the best example here).[5]

In this study it will become clear that these choices have been made in a wide variety of ways in different jurisdictions, resulting in different combinations of specific mechanisms. Most of the analysis focuses on the when, to whom and for what questions because they have the greatest impact on the gatekeeping aspects of public funding and thus on representation in its broadest sense.

Party politics and elections set out rules for social choice by which, among other things, any society pronounces whether it is open or closed to the demands of all its citizens. In that process, the society represents itself to itself. At the root of the representational process is, then, the question of power. Who will have the power to make their voices heard and their demands met in the political arena? Who can, and will, exercise the power that comes from being the legitimate representative of the citizenry? Under what conditions and in what ways will that power be institutionalized in a system of political parties? And, finally, how will political institutions exercise the power to represent the citizenry to itself, by setting the boundaries of recognized political discourse and by identifying legitimate political actors and actions?

These questions are all engaged in any discussion of public funding for parties and elections. Any comparative analysis quickly reveals that such questions about power and representation have been answered very differently across time and across space.

This study bases its claims on consideration of several other ways of conceptualizing the representational process than that predominant at the federal level in Canada. The argument in brief is that equity and innovation – and therefore popular consensus about the well-being of democracy – are supported by public funding that rewards vote-getting more than fund-raising and spending, which covers more than the election period, which goes to parties more than candidates, and which is designed to meet the costs of being a party in a liberal-democratic polity.

A central theme of this study is, then, that the mere presence of public funds is not sufficient. They must be provided in ways which are non-exclusionary and tolerant of political pluralism. Only with that additional criterion will they do more than reinforce the power of the existing actors. Only then will they expand the boundaries of the representational system in inclusionary ways.

What Is the Proper Comparison?
A crucial step in any analysis is the identification of appropriate comparative cases. Very often discussions of electoral reform and party financing compare Canada to the United States, not only because of the long-standing tendency to make this comparison for all matters, but also because the regulatory systems in the two countries have developed in part through cross-fertilization (Alexander 1980, 338). Nevertheless, there are important differences between the two countries that make it legitimate to wonder whether other comparisons might not be more appropriate.

The party system in the United States is a very decentralized one, formed by a loose alliance of candidates running under the same party label. Both congressional and national party organizations are only weakly institutionalized, giving little consistent content to the language of politics. Voters gain only a small amount of information about the candidates' likely behaviour in Congress from the party label.[6] Moreover, candidates and elected officials are very much on their own for raising money and responding to the pressures of organized interests, whether ordinary lobbyists or Political Action Committees. As a result of these characteristics of the party system, the regulations of election financing emphasize the individual candidate. Only presidential elections are subsidized and only if the candidates accept voluntary spending limits.

The Canadian tradition of responsible government implies a greater commitment to the party. Disciplined parties are crucial to the working of Parliament, which in turn gives meaning to the party label that represents a particular – albeit very broad – policy stance. Thus the term "party" makes a great deal more sense in the Canadian context than it does in the United States.

Despite the importance of parties for organizing the work of Parliament, however, there has been an overly long maintenance of the fiction that for electoral purposes, the *primary* democratic link is between individual candidates and voters. A consequence of stressing this "fictitious bond" has been that public funds for reimbursing campaign expenses have gone disproportionately to individual candidates. Less thought has been given to developing and sustaining strong and representative national parties. In Canada, despite the constitutional centrality of parties for organizing Parliament, direct funding programs have tended to treat the political party as if it existed only to contest elections and serve as a vehicle to meet the needs of candidates.

This outlook has positioned Canada at variance with almost all countries with programs that directly fund political parties. These countries usually make annual allocations rather than only election-related ones, doing so in recognition of the importance of political parties to the polity (Alexander 1989, 13).[7] Moreover, public support for parties in the inter-election period (via the tax credit) exists in a form that downplays any notion of the parties sharing responsibility with the state for a healthy representational system. The money from tax credits appears to be simply a relationship between parties and supporters, because tax expenditures of this sort are rarely considered by popular perception a subsidy or even a state initiative.

Therefore, in thinking again about public funding in Canada it is instructive to examine closely the efforts of several European countries to support parties. Such a study can provide clues for thinking about ways to maximize fairness and pluralism in the representational process; it suggests, therefore, some possible routes to regeneration of popular support for the institutions of liberal democracy in Canada.

Political parties in many European countries are valued participants in liberal democratic politics, being generally considered crucial intermediary bodies between citizens and the state. This appreciation arises from a number of sources. In some cases, analyses of history have spotlighted the contribution of weak party systems to breakdowns of liberal democracy, especially in the interwar years. Also important were the legacies of visions of society as stratified, not simply in terms of socio-economic characteristics but also institutionally. These discourses, shared by Tories, Catholics and leftists, translated into an enthusiasm for institutional bridge building.[8] The underlying notion was that if society were something more than, or other than, a collection of individuals facing the state, then institutions ought to be designed so as to represent correctly the density and complexity of such social ties.[9]

Parties were designated as one such institution. As a result, their ability to remain autonomous of other strong social actors as well as of other institutions became as much a goal as did their responsibility for providing a channel of representation for citizens to the state.[10] State subsidies appeared to their advocates as a mechanism to provide that autonomy and thereby to help sustain the representational capacity of the party system. At the same time, however, the logic of such thinking about parties meant that it was important to encourage responsiveness. Existing parties could not be permitted to gain such an advantage that challengers would be discouraged. Indeed, recognition of the institution of the party – rather than simply the particular incumbents in place – created a universe of political discourse in which support for principles of equality of opportunity and the reactive capacity of the whole party system could gain wide acceptance. While fears of "petrification" became an important theme in considerations of proper procedures for public subsidy programs, experience demonstrates that explicit attention to that danger has, in fact, helped to minimize it.

Not all European countries share exactly the same ideas about representation, of course. There have been variations in specific regulations that depend upon the particularities of each history and culture. Therefore, it is worthwhile to explore them separately. Nevertheless, as this discussion has already indicated, certain of these countries do share a commonality. For them, "party finance" dominates "election finance," with the goal being to encourage national parties. Before examining these cases, however, it is useful to reconstruct Canada's own experience with electoral reform and party finance. This past has established the discursive terms for considering both the present and the future.[11] It is within the boundaries of this discourse that dialogue about the future will emerge.

DEFINITIONS OF FAIR ELECTIONS IN CANADA

The laws now regulating election and party finance at the federal level derive from the political conditions and controversies of the mid-1960s. In February 1964 the federal government disclosed that a process of reform would begin. In October of that same year, Secretary of State Maurice Lamontagne announced the terms of reference of the Committee on Election Expenses. These were to "inquire into and report upon the desirable and practical measures to limit and control federal election expenditures." With this assignment the Committee – which eventually became known as the Barbeau Committee – went to work.[12] Only later, at one of its early meetings, did the scope of the Committee expand to include consideration of "raising" money as well as spending it. Thus, from the beginning, the discourse of regulation was bounded by considerations of spending.

Despite rather limited terms of reference, however, the announcement made by the Secretary of State cast a broad net, linking the democratic system itself to the question of election expenditures. He said: "It is the first time in our country that a study of this kind has been undertaken and that a government has declared its intention to take effective steps to limit election expenditures. As a result of those steps we hope that our political life will be improved and will reflect more faithfully our democratic ideals" (quoted in Paltiel 1970, 134–35).

The first part of this study explores the ways in which the original conceptualization of restrictions on electoral spending and party finance embedded particular visions of liberal democracy, elections and party politics into the legislation that was passed during the 1970s and revised in subsequent years. These visions were a product of the historical moment, reflecting a specific understanding of how to address the problems being experienced at that time. Some attention to the conceptualizations of representation that motivated this first effort is crucial because that wave of reform established the terms of the discourse within which considerations of these matters still take place. And, as we will see, they are quite limited. Therefore, some expansion of the discursive range is appropriate – even necessary – for the different future of the 21st century.

What Were the Problems Faced at the Time?

Concern about party finance and election expenses emerged simultaneously in several jurisdictions; Canada was not alone in devoting attention to these matters. Although considerations of the issue and the solutions proposed differed quite widely across the several jurisdictions, there were some similarities.

By the late 1950s it was becoming increasingly obvious to participants and observers alike that party systems were undergoing transformations. Moreover, the new communication technologies, in the context of these shifts in the party system, were causing the costs of maintaining parties and organizing elections to soar. These two changes fed into long-standing apprehensions about the ways in which money could pervert the institutions of liberal democracy. Indeed, concern with corruption was itself sufficient in some jurisdictions to motivate a process of reform, even in the absence of much attention to changes in the structure of liberal-democratic representation.

Canadian discussions in this first wave spotlighted costs and corruption. There was also a concern with "equity" and equality of opportunity. Reformers articulated the goal of sustaining the party and electoral systems so that competition among conflicting positions could be resolved peaceably, and public confidence increased (Paltiel 1970, 164).

From the perspective of the last decade of the century, this goal is to be applauded. It should also be retained for the future. Nevertheless, although representations of equitable institutions and fair practices that informed the first wave of reform were appropriate to that time, they are somewhat less apposite for ours. We need to retrieve the equity goal and reassess it in light of conditions in the new century, for which the second wave of reform is now preparing. In doing so, the issue of public confidence reappears.

Undertaking such a retrieval involves deconstructing the impact of the earlier moment, because it is those representations that not only inform many current presumptions about equity but also have empowered the actors – the parties and the administrative institutions – in whose hands the process of regulation now rests.

The next section of this study proceeds to an exploration of these matters by recounting the concerns that motivated the first wave of reformers and by analysing the varied impact of their decisions on the system of meanings and practices facing us now.

Several Crucial Ideas about Reform

There are at least five different themes about the need for reform that can be drawn out of the writings by and about the Barbeau Committee. Some of them are quite straightforward, requiring little amplification, while others call for some elaboration. Each is dealt with separately below, ordered not according to their importance for the reform process but for ease of explication.

The first motive, and the easiest to understand, followed from the dilemmas posed for the party system by frequent minority governments, which brought not only governmental instability but also numerous elections. Between 1960 and 1974 there were six federal elections, only two of which produced majorities in Parliament. Moreover, there were several structural factors that made minority governments a likely permanent feature of the federal scene. The newborn New Democratic Party (NDP) gave the appearance that it would remain a significant "third party," being more solidly financed and somewhat more "modern" than its predecessor, the Co-operative Commonwealth Federation.[13] Second, in 1962 the Créditistes surfaced "out of nowhere" to capture 26 seats in Quebec.[14] Finally, Diefenbaker's populist leadership of the Progressive Conservative (PC) Party and the frequent elections of the late 1950s and 1960s clearly unveiled an electoral map deeply divided by region, in which national coverage by either of the two major parties, except in exceptional circumstances like the 1968 election, seemed no longer likely.[15] For these three reasons, then, a multi-party system appeared here to stay.

The fear of minority governments had two identifiable consequences. The first was to put the issue of money – of spending, that is – clearly on the political agenda. Parties confronted with the costs of frequent campaigns and the new technology of television found themselves hard pressed to keep their heads above water. A second consequence was rising concern that the political system was fragmenting. When minority government reappeared in 1957, politicians, journalists and other observers began to wonder whether the parliamentary system might collapse or alter in unexpected ways.[16] "Majority government" became a big election issue. In 1965 Prime Minister Pearson called on the voters to support the Liberals, saying, "we need in this country ... a five-year plan for action, rather than a five-month plan." He blamed the small parties for the problem, claiming they considered "the great challenges facing the country were less important than giving third, fourth, and fifth parties a veto over everything the government tried to do." The very parliamentary process was at stake, according to Pearson (quoted in Beck 1968, 377–78). The voters agreed, when 58 percent of them said in 1965 they were very likely or fairly likely to switch parties to obtain a majority and when 55 percent in 1974 stated a clear preference for majority government (Clarke et al. 1979, table 8.8, 259).

This was the context in which the Barbeau Committee and Parliament did its work. It is hardly surprising, then, that they focused primarily on the ways election spending could be regulated, especially by setting limits, and by meeting costs through reimbursements and tax credits. Also important for the discussion was the issue of broadcasting time, including provisions for free-time broadcasts and reimbursements of parties' costs. Nor is it surprising that the Barbeau Committee spent little time – as revealed by the relative silence of the report and the published research studies – on the question of access of new parties to the federal process.[17] The very high thresholds set for registration and reimbursement not only effectively blocked supposedly "frivolous" candidates from taking advantage of the newly instituted public funds but also decreased the likelihood of further fragmentation of the party system.

The fear of minority government thus contributed to the "fear of frivolity," especially at public expense. Such consternation thereby became a deeply embedded element of the discourse of election financing at the federal level. It superseded any notion that liberal democracy might be better served by a respect for "difference" and/or political pluralism. Fear of frequent elections, as well as changing technology, also made raising and spending money the major topic considered by the Committee.

The notion that high thresholds represented a commitment to "seriousness" derived not only from the prevailing concern about minority government. Contributions also came from the experience of Quebec, which provided an important model to the federal Committee (Paltiel 1970, 134). In 1960 the Liberal party of Quebec promised reform of election financing, to achieve two goals:

- a cleansing to overcome the corrupt practices that had characterized the Duplessis years – electoral finance reform was only one of the many mechanisms designed to differentiate the "new broom" Liberals from their predecessor and competitors (Angell 1966, 293, 296); and
- a reduction of election costs: in comparative terms, more was spent on elections in Quebec than in the other provinces.[18]

With this 1960 announcement Quebec initiated a move toward election finance reform in Canada. As such it was a model for the rest of the country. But a more direct impact from Quebec came with the appointment of Alphonse Barbeau to head the federal committee. Barbeau had previously chaired the commission that designed the reform the Quebec Liberals proposed at their 1961 convention.[19]

The legacy of the Quebec model was twofold. Most obviously, it encouraged attention to reform of electoral finance as a means of simultaneously controlling corruption and costs. Thus the sources of funds were to be reported, agents required, and limits set. This approach informed the later federal agenda. But the other legacy of the Quebec experience was as influential, if less examined at the time.

A proposal that came out of the 1961 Quebec Liberal convention incorporated a plan for partial reimbursement of candidates' and parties' costs by the state. Here the thresholds for subsidy were high. Candidates would be eligible for reimbursement only if they received at least 20 percent of the vote. Parties were to have some costs reimbursed if they had a leader, a program and candidates in at least 50 percent of the constituencies and they received 10 percent of the total vote (Angell 1966, 292–93). But by the time Bill 15 (*Quebec Election Act*) was introduced in 1962, the thresholds for party registration and reimbursement had become even more stringent. To become a "recognized political party," and therefore have the right to spend any money at all during an election campaign, a party had to have a leader and an official agent and have nominated candidates in three-fifths of the constituencies.[20] Candidates eligible for reimbursement were those of the two parties that had received the most votes in the last election or received no less than 20 percent in the current one.

Objections to these thresholds stressed the potential negative consequences for minor parties – which under these rules might not be able to spend any money at all – and for independent candidates. In response to criticisms about the anti-democratic nature of such limits and the advantages thus granted to existing large parties, Premier Lesage clearly articulated the notion of "serious party" with which the reformers were working. He said, "a party, to be serious, must have a reasonable, or at least mathematical chance of forming a government" (quoted in Angell 1966, 297).

It is unnecessary to document the debate on this bill in committee, in the legislature and in the press or to delineate the amendments that ultimately lowered the threshold for registration and recognized the needs of independent candidates. What is more relevant is that after all the adjustments, subsidy provisions continued to favour the parties that had done best, or second-best, in the previous election (Paltiel 1970, 120). Moreover, all discussion necessarily took the form of trying to moderate a very stringent set of proposed standards.

Most relevant for our purposes is the notion embedded in the discourse right from the beginning – that there was little need to equalize opportunity for all potential candidates and parties and encourage political pluralism. The goal was precisely the opposite, to limit the number of candidates and parties to those that seemed "reasonable" or "reasonably able to form a government." Representation of politics as wide-ranging debate among pluralistic alternatives did not inform this discussion. Efficiency, low cost and honesty were the goals to be maximized. These notions carried over to federal deliberations in the next years.

A third idea that shaped the first-wave reform process was that of "political party." Until the 1960s, Canadian democracy had laboured under the fiction that political parties were simply voluntary associations of candidates. This view was a legacy of classical liberal views of democracy, which later came to inform pluralist and elitist visions of society. But such an individualistic interpretation granted little space to parties as national institutions sharing with the state responsibility for the well-being of Canadian democracy. Nor did it pay much attention to how such institutions should operate.

There was at the time no official recognition of the organizational existence of the party in the election. Most important, there was little sense that political parties were central institutions for the maintenance and expansion of democratic participation. The idea that parties might serve as a bridge between individual citizens and the state remained a somewhat foreign concept in federal politics in the 1960s. While political scientists, especially those beholden to structural-functional theoretical approaches, celebrated the integrative potential of political parties, such thinking had not yet percolated into élite or public consciousness. Nor had notions taken root about the role of parties in the education for citizenship. The prevailing popular philosophy, even among the political activists who sat on the Barbeau Committee, was that the crucial relationship was between the individual candidate and the voter.

Obviously this fictitious bond could not be left totally unexamined. Politicians were aware of the importance of party labels for their own success; students of electoral behaviour could cite overwhelming evidence of the importance of party identification for the ways voters perceived politics; and elections were increasingly becoming contests among leaders of parties. Therefore, the Barbeau Committee did recommend forms of recognition for political parties.

This was done most obviously through registration procedures, the addition of party names to the ballot, and procedures for regulating broadcasting and tax credits. Nevertheless, this recognition of parties did not necessarily emerge from any philosophy that the parties were important national institutions, nor did it pay any systematic attention to them as actors with responsibilities for the health of the Canadian polity. Instead, discussions of basic principles of equity and representation tended to focus more on candidates.

The fact that the myth of candidacy remained so prevalent had a number of consequences. It meant that direct funding mechanisms were linked to candidates more than to parties. A second, and even more important consequence, was that direct subsidies (in the form of reimbursements) were confined to "election expenses," the moneys dispersed only at that moment when the nominated candidate and the citizen came into direct contact. Those were considered the only necessary – read legitimate – expenditures. There was little notion that "oppositional" politics or inter-election party work was a public good in itself. Thus the concept of "party financing" became synomonous with "election financing" and the state's oversight of parties was considered as applying primarily to their roles as machines for backing candidates in electoral contests.[21]

Part of the lack of attention arose, of course, out of prevailing Anglo-American depictions of liberal-democratic representation as a relationship among individuals.[22] Further support for the antipathy to recognizing an extended role for political parties came, however, from a particular social theory that had taken root in the postwar years and had been adapted to Canada. It meant that even less thought was given to the responsibility of the state for ensuring that parties acted in ways that contributed to healthy democratic politics. Interventionary state practices, the growth of public bureaucracies, the reinforcement of the power of corporate actors and of organized labour had all contributed to the idea that "bureaucratization" of society was taking place. The supposed power of Big Government, Big Business and Big Labour made some people fearful of further consolidation. Their goal was instead to weaken the power of these actors. Thus, long-standing Canadian conceptions of the state as an actor guaranteeing the collectivity and its values were tempered by fears of the "Big," precisely at this moment of reform. Accordingly, there was support for restricting state as well as corporate and labour intervention in the electoral process. The aim became to disperse among the citizenry the power to act politically. This idea was reflected in the institution of tax credits, which are generated by partisan effort and involve little state regulation, albeit at great state expense.

While this goal of promoting greater citizen participation is an admirable one in general, it did contribute, in the context of that particular time in Canada, to a lack of attention to political parties as national institutions. In countries like Germany, Austria, Sweden or Italy, for example, where the state has been accepted as a counter-force in tripartite relationships, it became legitimate to substitute state support for political parties for that of other powerful actors. This option was much less legitimate in Canada, where hopes for dispersal of power were more centred on individual and small-group action.[23]

One of the unintended consequences of this fear of the "Big" and of bureaucratization was the failure to encourage the growth of parties that could serve as national institutions. While from the perspective of the 1990s we would never argue that state support is the only – even the best – way to encourage such parties, it is important to recognize the continuing legacy of our silence around this matter. For example, where other jurisdictions openly discuss the danger of "petrification" that subsidies might bring – and thereby recognize that innovation in forms and actors is crucial to a healthy party system – Canadian debates still remain silent on the kinds of parties that are desirable. Not having engaged in that discussion explicitly in the first wave of reform, we find it harder, but even more necessary, to undertake it now. Breaking the silence to encourage full consideration of innovative pluralism and equity is one of the most important tasks at the present time.

Fear of the power of "Big" institutions was not the only factor contributing to such silence, however. Also important was the general complacency of the 1960s. The notion had taken hold that the "end of ideology" had arrived. Politics was now to be a process of tidying up the loose ends and maintaining equilibrium. There was very little sense that anything fundamental might change. The important actors and their representatives were assumed to be those who had taken the reins of power after the devastation of the 1930s Depression and the Second World War. A sort of welfare capitalism, managed by these actors, would supposedly provide all the necessary adjustments and innovation in the face of any new circumstances.

This complacency was shattered, of course, by the political protests and turmoil of 1968 and their aftermath in Western Europe. The new social movements appearing in those years mobilized around collective identities that challenged the postwar unity of citizenship based upon an understanding of citizens' contribution to production (Ingelhart 1990). Feminists claimed recognition of sexual difference, in the home as well as at work and in politics. Environmentalists challenged the very goal of industrial production and economic growth. Students, feminists and movements for national and regional autonomy demanded a democratization of society and reallocation of power. All of these movements also dramatically challenged the representational focus of the postwar system and demanded space for themselves within it.[24] The ensuing conflicts within political parties brought many organizational transformations. But of even greater importance was the fact that these new social movements gained space within the party system in their own right, as they acceded to parliamentary institutions in many countries.

This whole process was much more truncated here (Brodie and Jenson 1988, chap. 8). New social movements were much less visible actors in Canadian politics in the late 1960s and even through the 1970s, nor did they as frequently seek the autonomous representation that was the hallmark of the identity-based movements in Western Europe.[25] Thus the false sense of security resulting from far fewer public manifestations of women's, youth's and other activists' concerns allowed the first-wave reform process to ignore such issues. Reformers could sustain their belief that postwar cleavage patterns and representational forms were stable and that equilibrium would endure.

Nor were Canadians in those years much given to public introspection about their electoral processes. Only in Quebec, where the Quiet Revolution involved explorations of the contribution of Quebec society and the Québécois to the supposed *grande noirceur* of the postwar years, was there much discussion of the ways in which fundamental democratic practices were created and sustained. In the rest of the country, complacency was the norm. People expected the Barbeau Committee to do little more than identify the minor adjustments inevitably required when technological changes like those in the mass media occurred.

To the extent that there was a nagging concern to disturb the complacency, it centred on the "problem of Quebec." That issue was quickly represented, however, as one affecting federalism more than democratic and party politics. The long saga of the search for an amending formula began, as did the reorganization of federal-provincial relations (Jenson 1989a). In this way, complacency also contributed, as an unintended consequence, to the lack of attention to the role of parties as national institutions and to the place of representative democracy in the political process.[26]

We have lived for the last 25 years with the consequences of this formative moment. The legislation for public funding that was ultimately passed was founded upon a set of assumptions, some of them quite unexamined. Assumptions that the party system was threatened by too much pluralism, that spending money counted most, that candidates were the central actors and that party financing equalled election financing gave clear shape to the practices of the next years. But of equivalent importance were the meanings reinforced by the legislation: that fundamental questions of equity for new groups and actors would not arise; that innovative adjustments to social change would not pose any problem; and that mechanisms already existed for responding to citizens' concerns about democratizing society and political pluralism. In the context of the mid-1960s, moreover, there was a great deal of concern to be "serious."

How the "Serious" Shut the Door on the "Simply Frivolous"

A familiar critique of our electoral system is that the first-past-the-post decision favours existing parties with already established nation-wide coverage or regionally concentrated smaller parties.[27] A less familiar observation is that the current public funding regime reinforces the position of the major parties and treats less fairly new or smaller political parties.[28] There is no doubt that the current Canadian election-finance legislation based on the registration of political parties and reimbursement for campaign and media expenses strengthens the position of those already "on the inside" and creates severe hindrances to the introduction of new parties or the expansion of small ones. It thereby makes it less likely that a level playing field will be achieved and interferes, therefore, with fair practices of representation.

The requirement that a party have 12 seats in the outgoing House of Commons in order to register obviously constitutes a limit on new political parties. This requirement has been met by only the three major parties.[29] Indeed, the bar suddenly appeared very high in the run-up to the 1984 election when the New Democratic Party (NDP) began to fear that its sliding popularity might lead to its inability to register according to this first criterion.

The *Canada Elections Act* provides an alternative route to registration, of course. With 50 bona fide candidates a party can be registered. Yet this also constitutes a high threshold. It is easy to imagine the effects of such limits on certain kinds of parties. The current legislation obviously makes the situation of regionally based parties very difficult. A party demanding redress for the Atlantic provinces as a region would not be able to reach the 50-seat threshold, even if it fielded candidates in all Atlantic constituencies. Similarly, a "Prairie party" could not be registered. A "western party" might be, but only if it could find candidates for virtually all of the constituencies of the four provinces west of the Ontario-Manitoba border.

Two ideas provided the rationale for the registration procedures. The first was to regulate expenditures and sources of funds. The second was to identify "serious" participants. Registration is based on the notion that there must be some way to accomplish simultaneously two tasks: establish the responsible agent for both spending moneys and receiving them from private and public sources. A primary concern motivating attention to spending, in addition to overcoming corrupt practices, was control of expenditures and the appropriate procedures for identifying contributors (Boyer 1983, 11). This concern would affect, for the most part, those political parties already established, with a reliable constituency, and able to solicit contributions from supporters, whether individuals or groups. Therefore, a registration procedure recognizing their "establishment" seemed quite appropriate and provided the motive in the federal legislation.

There is, nevertheless, another important concern beyond that of regulation of political party activities to guarantee honesty. There is also the issue of equality of opportunity. This means that those with fewer resources – including among these visibility, past electoral popularity, and ability to solicit contributions – must not be discouraged from presenting themselves to the voters. The high-threshold requirements for registration constitute such a discouragement, and therefore in practical terms they limit the space for pluralism and wide-ranging debate in Canada's liberal democracy.

Despite this high threshold, however, several parties beyond the main three have managed to register since 1974. Therefore, while registration procedures should be made more liberal in order to increase fairness, they do not in themselves constitute the greatest blockage. That comes from the procedures for funding. It is there that the impact of the self-interest of the already established is easiest to see.

In the first legislation, a high threshold – 15 percent – for candidates to receive state funds was enacted. A minuscule number of candidates not representing one of the three front-running parties have benefited from reimbursement. Indeed, in the first election in which the Act was fully tested, only half of the New Democrats running reached the 15 percent threshold. That percentage was approximately the same in 1988.[30] Of all candidates running in the last two elections, virtually the same proportion (46 percent in 1984; 47 percent in 1988) reached the threshold. Thus, the subsidy system as it now operates benefits the two largest parties the most, because they rarely fall below the 15 percent threshold in any constituency. The other beneficiary is the NDP, which receives a substantial amount of funding.

In 1983 a set of important amendments to the election expense legislation altered the system, in some ways quite substantially. One important change was in the way reimbursement was calculated. Parties and candidates were rewarded for spending more. Between 1974 and 1980, candidates received a flat rate determined by a formula based on postage rates and the number of electors in the constituency (Seidle and Paltiel 1981, 234). In 1983 the calculation changed: instead of being a fixed amount, reimbursements were available for up to 50 percent of real campaign expenses, the upper limit being 50 percent of allowable expenses. This change was made because of the fear that the cost of postage (to which funding was pegged) was rising faster than other costs and increasing reimbursements at too great a rate (Paltiel 1988, 141–42). Instead of keeping the rates of reimbursement down by simply changing the formula, however, the government adopted a change in principle of some import. After 1983, the more candidates spent, the more they could claim (up to the limit). Previously, the principle of allocation had been based on the number of electors; after 1983 it was based on the number of dollars spent. This change then would benefit those parties able to raise more money and therefore able to spend closer to the limit.

A similar path was followed in revising the regulations for reimbursing parties in 1983. This change also advantaged the "big spenders" while closing off access to public moneys for those who spent less. The formula for reimbursing parties was changed: any party that *spent at least 10 percent of its limit* would be reimbursed for 22.5 percent of its expenses.[31]

As has been well documented, however, all three major federal parties in the 1980s substantially expanded their sources of funding and the amounts solicited, in large part as a result of the advantages of the tax credit provided by the *Canada Elections Act* (Paltiel 1989, 69ff.). Therefore, while the subsidies do have the real benefits often cited (including creating some independence of local constituencies and enhancing grassroots democracy), the program is sometimes like icing on an already rich cake for the three major parties.

All observers agree that the reimbursement moneys are an important element stabilizing the practices of elected members of Parliament (MPs) both during and between election campaigns. They provide, according to some MPs, the means not only to finance their elections but even to be better members of Parliament.[32] Yet these are benefits available only to sitting members and to established parties. MPs obtaining public funds demonstrate a singular lack of interest in extending such benefits to others. For example, Benno Friesen, Conservative MP, told the Ontario Commission on Election Contributions and Expenses in 1982: "You have to preserve free access for everybody to run, but I don't think that the 'nuts' ought to be able to run *and* have the cost of elections mushrooming. There has to be a weeding out so that the democratic process can function unhindered. I think you have to earn your right to be heard and only if you have a substantial following should you be able to get that kind of subsidy" (quoted in Ontario, Commission on Election Contributions 1982, 20).

This statement, in fact, captures quite well the conflicting ideas about democracy, subsidies and election expenses. It is obviously true that elections are expensive and that there probably should be some limit on public subsidization to them. Yet, it is precisely those candidates with the fewest resources who most benefit from the provision of funds.

For them the subsidy is not simply a pleasant gift from the government that allows them to do more than they might have. For candidates from small and new parties, a subsidy of basic election expenses permits them to *be* serious candidates, enabling them to present a program to their constituency and to disseminate that program. Mr. Friesen's notion that one is either a "nut" or lacking a substantial following if one does not receive at least 15 percent of the vote flies in the face not only of basic democratic principles but of long-standing experience with Canada's multi-party system.[33]

The notion of "seriousness," deeply embedded in the practices of the machinery regulating public funding, reflects not only the ideas of its originators but also the self-interest of the actors already on the scene, who have never been compelled to be other than stingy with recognition of what is "serious." Subsidies for federal candidates were proposed, of course, by the Barbeau Committee on Election Expenses, which stated: "The Committee therefore considers it desirable that certain basic necessities of a minimal election campaign receive public support so that all serious candidates may be provided with an opportunity to present their views and policies to the electorate" (quoted in Paltiel 1970, 139).

Subsequently there has been a continuing – indeed intensifying – practice of using periodic reforms of the legislation to strengthen the hand of the three main parties. In writing Bill C-169 the newly empowered political parties used their positions as *interlocuteurs valables* to shape the system of party financing even more in their favour. After the passage of the Bill, K.Z. Paltiel (1988, 140–41), describing the Committee that prepared the Bill, wrote: [It was an] "Ad Hoc Committee composed of representatives of the chief electoral officer and the political parties represented in the House of Commons." This body, an extralegal administrative creation, consisting largely of non-elected, paid, full-time party professionals, has been the source of the bulk of the legislative amendments and administrative practices affecting the *Election Expenses Act* of 1974. It should occasion no surprise, therefore, that its suggestions tend to benefit established parties already represented in Parliament rather than challengers from outside.

This process was the no doubt unintended consequence of the mechanism selected by the chief electoral officer to review the operation of the law on party and election financing.[34] But the result was that the institutions thereby created had few, if any, mechanisms for accommodating change and encouraging pluralism. They reinforced the power of those already *in* the system and gave little encouragement to those who might challenge. Moreover, they inserted the principle of rewarding fund-raising and spending into the regime even more than had been the case.

This study contends that "serious" candidates representing the necessary ideas and support for innovation in any democratic party system may not receive the 15 percent vote currently necessary to define their "seriousness." Moreover, failure to recognize and welcome innovative pluralism may itself constitute a threat to the representative capacity and legitimacy of the electoral and partisan process. In other words, hindering the access of challengers has risks attached to it, including among them that the Canadian population may cease to take their representative institutions "seriously." Second, the perversion of the equity principles by the overwhelming stress on spending money has called into question the extent to which the system remains a fair one for all concerned.

Diminishing Legitimacy for National Parties

One of the clearest indicators of the weakened representative capacity of the party system comes from attitudinal and behavioural data collected from the Canadian population. There is evidence that the attitudinal disaffection with elected officials and political parties has translated into less participation in the more demanding forms of electoral behaviour. While there is no systematic evidence of a decline in the most simple of electoral activities – voting – there is some possibility that investment of time in other electoral activities may be less likely.[35] At the same time, however, Canadians do continue to discuss politics and try to get things done. The rates of non-electoral political participation remain high or are even on the rise. Moreover, Canadians grant such non-electoral activities legitimacy (Mishler and Clarke 1990, 163).

While these data cannot provide a definitive picture of the participatory patterns of Canadians, they are indicative of a process that has been observed via other types of analysis as well. There has been a diversion of representative energy from the electoral and party system to other sites, including, in particular, state bureaucracies, federal-provincial institutions and interest-group politics (Meisel 1985, 100–104; Clarke et al. 1991, 10–13).

One effect of this diversion of representative capacity is the decline of political parties as national institutions. Parties are less – indeed no longer – recognized as national actors capable of generating projects of interest to and representative of all Canadians. Now provincial governments in dialogue with the federal government perform many of the tasks of interest representation and mediation that previously (and according to liberal-democratic principles) belonged to the political parties. Parties now appear as relatively impotent actors, and the elections upon which they spend so much time seem diverting but relatively unimportant events. The real power to make decisions lies elsewhere, as the processes by which decisions about constitutional change and other crucial matters have demonstrated in the recent past.

Similar points can be made about interest-group politics and the extent to which they have become substitutes for organizing within parties. In the past decade a number of interest groups representing the new social movements of contemporary Canada found themselves better able to influence results by direct intervention in public debates and mobilization of their own networks.[36] In this they were joined by several organizations of the business community, like the Business Council on National Issues, which set out as their primary goal a reorientation of the public agenda. These groups mobilized for or against the major issues of political and economic change – the 1982 Constitution and free trade – and not surprisingly sought to play an expanded role in the election campaign of 1988.

Such diversion of representational capacity is related to the spaces within the party system for innovation. The debate about "third-party" participation that came to a head in 1988 demonstrates some of the longer-term effects of the party system's failure to encourage political pluralism. Innovation in earlier times had often been associated with the arrival of "third parties" – that is, minor parties – in the party system. By 1988 demands for alternatives unrepresented *within* the party system were being expressed again by "third parties," but this time they were not political parties but interest groups. A gap in the representational capacity of the party system was thereby clearly revealed.

Not all party systems experienced this same crisis, however. Such challenges have been better handled in some countries of Western Europe. Therefore, an examination of the relationship between their support for national parties and principles of equity and innovation is in order.

THE COMPARATIVE CASES

The Federal Republic of Germany

Postwar West Germany provides the best example of a system of public subsidies designed to support parties as national institutions. It pays much less attention to the needs of individual candidates. It is a system that attempts to encourage widening popular involvement in politics, using both tax credits and subsidies to parties to achieve that goal. The Basic Law, which is the postwar Constitution, recognizes parties and assigns them a central role in generating constitutional government.[37]

Article 21 of the Constitution recognizes political parties, mandates a democratic internal order for them and requires parties to account publicly for their income.[38] Efforts to develop legislation to implement the third of these elements has been subject to repeated review by the Federal Constitutional Court, which has utilized a doctrine of equality of opportunity or treatment (*Chancengleichheit*).[39] In addition, in its ruling on a 1959 law granting subsidies to parties for "political education," the Court held that public funds for parties could be paid only for waging election campaigns. These reactions from the highest Court both provoked and guided the 1967 legislation in the Federal Republic of Germany (FRG).

Defining the parties as a "constitutionally necessary part of the free democratic basic order," the law recognized that parties need funds to compensate for the "necessary costs of an appropriate election campaign."[40] The procedures focused on the costs of campaigns. The rationale for public funding was that it was expensive to conduct campaigns and therefore parties needed subsidies. The flat-rate grants were based on the number of electors, with the rate set per elector. Nevertheless, a very broad reading of the campaign process grounded the legislation. Funds were actually made available throughout the inter-election period. A sliding scale was instituted for distributing funds over four years.[41] The notion was that political mobilization and discussion of policies were never confined simply to the campaign; parties' contributions to the electoral process and democratic politics depended upon their ability to speak to the voters constantly and consistently.

Originally the law set the threshold to qualify for the subsidies at 2.5 percent of the vote. A 1968 decision by the Federal Constitutional Court found a limitation of this sort excessive and suggested a threshold of 0.5 percent, which the Bundestag accepted.[42] When the Europarliamentary elections began in 1979, the funding procedures were extended to them as well, and many state governments enacted similar provisions. Free radio and television time was provided, based on performance in past elections but also recognizing the need to allocate time to new or previously unsuccessful parties.[43]

The legislation never assumed that public moneys would be the only source of campaign funds. The 1967 legislation, as modified after court challenges, included a change in the income tax law to include deductions for contributions to a political party by individuals, couples and corporations. The reporting procedures for party funds mandated a separate list identifying large donors, whether individuals or corporations, but this requirement was not considered an inhibition on widespread public participation.[44] Rather, the provisions were included precisely to encourage such participation, nurturing the link between citizens and parties.

The most unusual aspect of party finance in the FRG, and one that clearly indicates the commitment to parties as being much more than simple electoral machines, is the public funding of party foundations. Set up as part of efforts to decentralize political activity and recognize its complexity, some foundations were established before public funding was instituted. Others, however, were created after subsidies for political education were separated, at the Court's insistence, from support for campaign costs. The foundations are designed to play an important role in public education and mobilization of popular energies in Germany and abroad by raising public knowledge, concern and attention to politics, in the broadest sense.[45] They are supposed to provide a wide range of general educational programs to the public and also service the parties with their research activities. Although enjoying considerable autonomy from the party organization, the foundations are an adjunct to them.[46]

One rationale for such foundations is the idea that a healthy democracy needs institutions that respond to a changing environment more coherently than by lurching from electoral contest to electoral contest. Foundations, for example, may be more responsive to the appearance of new issues, new concerns and even newly mobilized segments of the population. With resources for both research and publicity, they may direct attention to matters that candidates or even party organizations attuned to electioneering may not sufficiently address. The interactive relationship with the parties prevents them, however, from becoming too "academic" or losing sight of the reasons for their creation.

The 1967 legislation did not work as well as had been hoped. The parties found themselves underfunded and forced to turn more and more to donations to make up the difference.[47] An independent commission reported in 1983 that overspending and excessive borrowing as well as illegal acts lay at the root of the problem. A revised law was passed in December 1983. Its constitutionality was challenged by the Green Party, with the Court decision coming in 1986. Most of the new legislation altered the tax structure to encourage private donations and discourage illegal, "creative" financing methods. While the details of the tax-credit system need not detain us, the principles against which the Constitutional Court tested the law are important (Gunlicks 1988, 42–44; Schneider 1989).

One goal of the law was to increase the parties' reliance on citizen support by encouraging donations by individuals, couples and corporations. Nevertheless, the legislators and the Court recognized that all parties did not have the same chance of gaining private support. Therefore, the principle of equality of opportunity was preserved in the revised legislation via the institution of equalization measures (*Chancenausgleich*). These applied again to any party that received 0.5 percent of the vote:

> All contributions and party dues received by the parties for the year are multiplied by 40 percent, the result of which is assumed to be the value of the tax expenditure of the federal government. This sum is then divided by the number of votes received in the last national election. The party that has the highest index score becomes the standard against which the others are measured, and the "deficit" parties then receive equalization funds, thus following the constitutional principle of equality of opportunity among the parties. (Gunlicks 1988, 43)

An upper limit for campaign reimbursements also ensured that such transfers would not exceed income from other sources.

This legislation affects each party differently. Membership dues and contributions are an important source of income for the Social Democrats and Christian Democrats, the major parties. Public funding is, however, absolutely crucial for the Free Democratic Party (FDP) and the *Grünen* (Green Party), the two smaller parties. In 1987, 56 percent of the *Grünen's* income was from public funds, while the figure for the FDP was 49 percent (Doublet 1990, 38).

One result of the public funding regime begun in the 1960s and its subsequent alteration was that the West German party system adapted relatively smoothly and quickly to the introduction of issues like feminism, ecology and new styles of politics. In part it was the monetary support mandated by the larger parties to their smaller competitors – under pressure from the Court, to be sure – that helped to account for this. Given the low threshold for recognition, the relatively generous funding and the hegemony of the principle of equal opportunity, the two largest parties were never able to monopolize the representational terrain. They also had to face, in the *Grünen*, a new party that challenged the very discourse of postwar politics and, coming out of the New Left, particularly threatened the constituency of the Social Democrats. They also had had to face the Free Democrats, who gained new-found autonomy with public funding and in 1966 could risk abandoning their Christian Democratic alliance partner. In this way, the two major parties incurred costs for their "generosity," but they refused to be completely short-sighted and self-interested in the reform process.

An additional result was that the energy that fuelled the protests of the 1960s and also led to the downfall of the German Democratic Republic in 1989–90 was relatively quickly translated into partisan politics in the FRG. Consequential debates about Germany's future continued to be channelled into the party system and conflict shaped by electoral contests. Despite the intensity of conflict over such political and geographical restructuring, the well-being of the party system is not an issue. "The new forms of participation, the further development of pluralism, and the increased competition of ideas make it a democracy governed essentially by parliamentary parties yet more responsive to extraparliamentary forces" (Schoomaker 1988, 49). Levels of popular satisfaction with the ways in which West German democracy functioned were highest among the six countries of the European Community in the years 1973–86 (Ingelhart 1990, fig. A-1, 435). The contrast to Canada could not be more striking.

Other Countries that Support National Parties

Several European countries have followed the route pioneered by the FRG. They also instituted regimes for public funding of the parties, providing support for a range of party activities beyond direct election expenses. These cases, of which Sweden, Austria and Italy are the best examples, all place a high value on the parties as mobilizers of democratic activity in general.[48]

Austria followed quickly on the heels of the FRG, establishing mechanisms for public funding in 1963. Rather than reimbursing election expenses, however, the Austrian practice follows the original German intent – set out before the Federal Constitutional Court overturned the legislation – and focuses more directly on party organization, both inside and outside the legislature. Costs of publicity and maintaining the organization, as well as party academies, are partially met by these procedures. Each party receives the same basic amount and then additional moneys according to the size of its parliamentary delegation. The national party headquarters receive the bulk of the subsidies (Nassmacher 1989, table 1, 242). But in addition there are salaries for legislators and money for parliamentary parties, including supplementary funds for their publicity work. Party academies also receive a basic grant and a sliding one, the amount set according to the number of parliamentary seats held.[49] The Austrian Broadcasting Corporation also provides free air time. Finally, substantial public subsidies support the party press for purposes of civic education (United States, Library of Congress 1979, 3–9). Tax benefits for contributions to political parties are not available in Austria.

Because the Austrian process depends so heavily on parliamentary representation, there was a fear that the system would penalize parties not already inside the system. A special subsidy was made available for parties that ran and did not gain seats (with the threshold set at 1 percent of the vote). These funds could be claimed only in election years.

In Sweden, subsidies began in 1965 as a result of concerns about high costs, especially for the party press (Doublet 1990, 96). The goals were to eliminate corruption, limit costs and reduce unequal advantages to those parties with access to superior financial resources (United States, Library of Congress 1979, 71). The first subsidy program was designed as a substitute for public funding of the party press, but by 1969 a separate payment to the press, and therefore including the party press, was also instituted. By the late 1960s local authorities took over major responsibility for subsidizing party activities. Free time for broadcasting was also available, and extra time could not be purchased.

As in Austria the funds in Sweden are intended to meet the costs of general party organization. One part is directed toward general organizational expenses; another covers the costs of the secretariat. Parties are subsidized in proportion to seats held, but a standard grant also meets certain basic and relatively invariable organizational costs. Additionally, a 50 percent bonus is paid to parties in opposition.

Sweden has contributed its own innovation to the story of public funding by distributing it to regional and local party organizations, through the provincial and municipal authorities (Doublet 1990, 99–100). The rationale for this procedure is to reduce the effects of the very centralized political process that characterizes postwar Swedish politics.

Once again, as in Austria, no reimbursements for campaign expenses exist. In part, this decision not to reimburse campaign costs directly can be explained by strong public opposition to granting state support to any individual seeking elective office, as well as to an understanding of society in corporate terms (United States, Library of Congress 1979, 67). Nevertheless, there is also a recognition that an exclusive focus on parliamentary representation as a measure of "significant support in the electorate" may be too narrow.[50] Therefore, there are subsidies for parties that gain the support of 2.5 percent of the electorate.

Italy is the only case of these four that is a truly multi-party system. Its programs for public funding have even greater effects for minor parties because of that. The Italian procedures fall somewhere between those of Austria and Sweden on the one hand and those of the FRG on the other. Public financing emerged relatively late and in response to concerns about corruption more than about rising costs and equity. In 1974, public funding of electoral expenses as well as ongoing organizational costs began. The legislation was confirmed, albeit narrowly, in a 1978 referendum (Ciaurro 1989).

Public funding in Italy exists for regional, national and European elections. While the thresholds differ by type of election, they are relatively low. For elections to the National Chamber and Senate, parties are eligible for funding if they present candidates in two-thirds of the constitutencies and win one seat or no less than 2 percent of the national vote. Account is also taken of regional concentrations, however, and there are measures to protect the South Tyrolese and Valdostan ethnolinguistic minority parties (Doublet 1990, 76). The funds are dispersed in two ways. A basic grant to all parties takes 20 percent of the total allocation and the remaining 80 percent is proportional to votes obtained.

Payments to parliamentary groups are also divided into basic and proportional components. The legislators may retain 10 percent of the subsidy for their own work and must present 90 percent to their party headquarters in order to help defray its costs. As in Sweden and Austria, the bulk of public subsidies go to maintaining party organizations (Nassmacher 1989, table 1, 242–43; Doublet 1990, 76–77). Broadcast and press subsidies also exist in Italy.

In Italy, Sweden and Austria, we see certain similarities, despite the differences of detail. Moreover, in underlying principles this group of countries is quite close to the case of the FRG. The goal is quite explicitly to use state funds to meet many of the costs of party organization, precisely because these institutions are considered crucial to a healthy democratic polity. Three of the four cases (the FRG, Sweden and Austria) are countries whose political practices in general tend toward corporatism. Therefore they all share the notion that the well-being of the polity depends on strong and healthy intermediary institutions, not only in the electoral realm.

But beyond the concern for strong national parties is also a recognition of the value of political pluralism and electoral competition. In the FRG the principle of equality of opportunity is well established and the threshold for access to subsidies is very low. One result is that the *Grünen* were able to enter the party system, undertaking "party building by public subsidy."[51]

In Italy as well the small parties, associated with new social movements and other constituencies, have relied extensively on public funding to sustain themselves and make their voices heard. Only for the Christian Democrats, Communists and Socialists in Italy does public funding constitute less than 50 percent of party revenue. For all other formations, only the subsidies allow them to participate fully. The example of the Radical Party is instructive here. That small party, sixth in overall votes for the Chamber in 1979, played a role in the 1970s that its size belies. In several campaigns, especially for reform of the divorce and abortion laws, it served as a conduit into the legislative arena for feminists' and other movements' demands when the traditional parties refused to take them up (Jenson 1982; Boggs 1986, 12). This representational task was crucial, not only for achieving reform but also for legitimating the "constitutional arch" in the turbulence of Italian politics during the 1970s. These small parties served as a route to power for new actors, including rather than excluding them from constitutional and electoral activities, while isolating the proponents of violent extra-parliamentary action. Throughout the last half of the 1970s and the 1980s, the Radicals depended on subsidies for no less than three-fifths of their revenues and at crucial moments, like 1981 when the abortion referendum was on the agenda, for as much as 94 percent. The situation of all the other small parties was similar (Ciaurro 1989, 160). In Sweden, too, the smallest parties depend on public subsidies, which are particularly important both for the Swedish Communists, who have reincarnated themselves as a progressive, ecological and feminist party, and for the Swedish Greens.[52]

The impact of public funding is not only on small, new parties seeking a place inside the system. Even large and traditional parties benefit. The positive effects for the largest Austrian parties have been no less important than for the Italian Radicals. Public funding has freed the Social Democrats and Christian Democrats from their earlier dependence on the large interest groups that have privileged status in that corporatist polity. Thus even the largest parties in Austria depend on subsidies for their autonomy. Another advantage of subsidies for generating party autonomy is seen in the FRG, where the Free Democratic Party (FDP) can now act more easily as an independent actor, choosing whether to align with the Social Democrats or Christian Democrats. In the 1960s the FDP's corporate supporters threatened to abandon it if it "put the Socialists in power." The FDP could change its position more easily after public funding ensured that so doing would no longer be equivalent to committing financial suicide. A political outcome in the opposite direction occurred in Sweden, where the Centre Party was emboldened to break from its long-standing coalition with the Social Democratic Party (SDP), thus facilitating the process that broke the SDP's 40-year hold on power.[53]

In all these cases, then, we see that public commitment to parties more than to candidates and to covering organizational costs more than campaign expenditures correlates with party systems open to an innovative pluralism of actors and issues as well as autonomy and strategic responsiveness for traditional parties. The existing parties have not used their positions of strength to block innovators. Instead the parties have ensured that equality of opportunity is part of the regulatory package. Moreover, in the use of basic grants as well as sliding scales in these cases, there is recognition that there are certain irreducible costs to "being" a party. The funding programs should acknowledge this rather than being strictly proportional to seats or votes. Overall, then, the intent is to strengthen the polity and the party system within it.

The experience of the next two countries examined – France and the United Kingdom – may also be assessed in light of this correlation. Their reforms have focused less on support for parties and the party system, and they demonstrate some of the characteristics of "petrification" feared by students of party finance and reform.

France

It was only in 1958, with Article 4 of the Constitution of the Fifth Republic, that French law recognized the specific characteristics of political parties.[54] Despite many claims at the time of the Liberation of France that the country's weaknesses in the Third Republic and defeat in 1940 were linked to the disorganization and poor functioning of its parties, agreement could not be reached about entrenching certain goals for parties and electoral competition in the Constitution of the Fourth Republic. Indeed, opposition to some proposals for state regulation of revenues and expenditures, as well as fears that there would be no space for independent candidates, led to the defeat of the proposals in 1944–45 (Kheitmi 1964, 283–86).

Discussions in the 1950s and 1960s about improving the status of political parties were directed toward a number of goals. The first was to guarantee democracy, both among and within parties. One argument made was that democracy would only be on a strong footing when parties organized the parliamentary process. As André Philip, an advocate of reform in 1945 as well as later, wrote: "A real democracy only exists ... when the voters make a choice, not between the men into whose hands we give up power, but between parties"[translation] (quoted in Kheitmi 1964, 287). A second goal was to ensure that no French party was subordinate to foreign influences, a concern that applied most to the Communist Party at the height of the cold war. Regulation of the finances of parties formed an important topic in these discussions.

These two principles of legal recognition of parties and their regulation by the state remained highly contested, however. The experience of the Fourth Republic, in which partisan formations came and went with great rapidity and a party might be little more than an individual and "his friends," meant that there was a tendency to attach greater importance to individual candidacies than to party organization. Moreover, General de Gaulle, the first and highly influential president of the Fifth Republic, was not fond of political parties or party democracy.[55] Therefore only a few voices were raised demanding regularization of the status of parties in law and recognizing them as crucial societal actors (del Castillo Vera 1985, 78). The result of this impasse was that financing was unregulated because it was unreported.[56]

The subsidies that did exist went simply to candidates (Doublet 1990, 57–61). The first subsidies were given in 1946, as a minor reimbursement for paper, printing, etc. The threshold for reimbursement was set at 5 percent, and that bar remained through subsequent decades and the next Republic for designating "serious" candidates in elections to the National Assembly. Thus a 1966 law provided for underwriting the costs of paper and printing ballots, posters and circulars for candidates who met the 5 percent criterion. For the Senate, too, subsidies focused on printing.[57]

In both 1988 and 1990 new legislation was passed. Since 1988 parties have acquired a new legal status allowing them to receive the public subsidies now available (Doublet 1990, 59–60). Funding of parties – both for parliamentary work and extra-parliamentary activities – is based on their numbers in the National Assembly, which means that existing parties benefit more than do new ones (ibid., 20). Additional funding is also provided for candidates, even though election spending is limited.

The subsidy and financial regulations for presidential elections are quite different. Since 1981 a petition system has been in place. Candidates must be endorsed publicly by 500 elected officials from at least 30 departments. There are approximately 40 000 such officials in the country (Toinet 1988, 14). This threshold is a high one, and some candidacies depend on a certain amount of jockeying by parties other than the candidate's own.[58] Once any candidate is accepted, however, her or his campaign costs will be reimbursed. This means that public subsidies can suddenly become available to a theretofore marginal candidate.

The experience of the *Verts* (Green Party) with the system of reimbursement is very suggestive here and marks a great contrast with the case of the FRG. Reimbursement for parliamentary and European elections come only once a candidate has crossed the high threshold of 5 percent. When the *Verts* began running in the 1970s, they did not achieve the magic number of 5 percent, and candidacies and campaigns always depended on the contributions of individual candidates and militants. Then a chance ordering of elections between spring 1988 and June 1989 worked to maximize the benefits of public funding for the party, as well as to demonstrate just how much the 5 percent had been an impediment. The five elections in the 15-month period included all types of electoral systems. As luck would have it, though, the series started with a presidential election, in which the candidate of a minor political formation could establish some credibility in the first round and thereby accumulate resources for subsequent elections.

The *Verts* had become a party in 1984, and therefore the funds accruing to the party's candidate in 1988 went directly to an organization rather than to an ad hoc campaign committee. Indeed a strong motive for founding the party in 1984 was to overcome the serious limitations of an *association biodégradable*, which had to be created for each campaign and which could not organize and manage inter-campaign activities and funds. But the party founded in 1984 had no money. Only after Antoine Waecheter's "profitable" presidential run in 1986 brought a huge infusion of funds could the *Verts* afford to hire full-time national staff for the first time and begin organization-maintenance tasks.[59]

It was largely a concern about funds that convinced the *Verts* not to run in the 1988 legislative elections, but money was available to promote the municipal campaigns in March 1989. The unique order of elections (after the *Verts'* crucial decision not to contest in June 1988) meant therefore that for once the electoral institutions did not overwhelm the ecologists. By June 1989 the party had passed the threshold for the Europarliamentary election by gaining 11 percent of the vote and becoming the fourth party in France.[60] Once the party had elected officials, another form of subsidy became available: Europarliamentarians began to pay a large proportion of their salaries into the party coffers.[61]

The corruption associated with the system of reimbursement of printing and other expenses, as well as the blockage in the system to new parties and their supporters, has had at least two consequences in France. The first is a plummeting public opinion: there is little to celebrate in party politics racked by scandal. A second consequence is the reform of the law on election financing finally passed in January 1990. It is obviously too soon to evaluate its effects, but the law does change the rules in ways that should bring an improvement.[62]

We see in France prior to 1990, however, much to confirm the proposition of this study that recognition of and support for parties as organizations contribute more to the popular legitimacy of the democratic polity than do individualistic politics of personal candidacies and efforts to discourage mobilization of new partisan formations. Few really new popularly based actors have penetrated the party system in a meaningful way for years.[63] The French party system, locked into a competition among the traditional four big parties through the 1970s, did little to adapt to the new social movement politics of those years. Moreover, the individualizing politics of internal jockeying, fuelled by the notion that several parties are little more than vehicles for candidates and their "friends," meant that parties never acquired legitimacy as crucial societal actors.[64] Public opinion has been profoundly critical of this kind of politics, giving very little approval to politics and politicians and exhibiting many signs of increasing distrust and disinterest.

Public funding for political parties will never alone change these long-standing practices, but improvements in financing might contribute to increased commitment to equity and innovation for new societal – as opposed to individual – voices in the political system.[65]

The United Kingdom

The story of public funding for election or party expenses in the United Kingdom is not a long one. No direct payments or reimbursements are made to parties, although the state does provide some other subsidies, most of which date in principle from 1918. These involve support for mailings and meetings and provision of broadcast time. These all constitute a type of subsidy in kind (Ewing 1987, 104–109, 117ff.; Fiori 1988).

In the 1970s costs began to rise, as the parties had to contest referenda and the Europarliamentary elections. Therefore in 1974 the government appointed a special committee, chaired by Lord Houghton, a former Labour cabinet minister. The committee report in 1976 did not gain bipartisan support: the Conservatives and several Labour MPs were opposed. Therefore, the suggestion that the state modestly subsidize the parties went nowhere; it was not even discussed in the House (Seidle 1980, 81ff.; Doublet 1990, 87).

Several reasons have been brought forward to account for the lack of success of the committee's proposals. One was an ideological objection to public spending, made by the Conservatives (Seidle 1980, 83). Another was the difficulty of increasing state expenditures when the International Monetary Fund was at the door (Doublet 1990, 87). Yet a third was the fear of subsidizing the National Front (Seidle 1980, 83).[66] The debate resurfaced after the 1983 election, when both the Alliance and the Labour Party advocated public subsidies. Nevertheless, no new forms of support were forthcoming, and the Conservatives used legislation regulating trade unions to force reorganization of Labour Party funding (Pinto-Duschinsky 1989).

The British story continues to be, then, one in which the most important subsidies remain those for broadcasting, and that process favours the major parties. After loud complaints, some minor parties gained access to the electronic media during the electoral period, but time for important inter-election broadcasts (the party political broadcasts) remains more difficult to obtain. Indeed, the 1977 Committee on the Future of Broadcasting (Annan) "gave no serious consideration in its report to the problem of minority representation," and case law has built up to rationalize the exclusion (Ewing 1987, 113ff.).

In all of this, we see little evidence of a concern for the equity principle or for encouraging innovative pluralism in the representational system. The assumption underpinning the (lack of) arrangements for public support of the parties in the United Kingdom is that the state has little responsibility for fostering a healthy climate of democratic pluralism.

As in France, there has been a prevailing notion in Britain that the state and the system of representation are clearly demarcated and autonomous. The so-called "private sector" of party competition is supposed to generate innovation and guarantee equity of representation. But the cases of the FRG, Austria, Italy and Sweden demonstrate that there is another way to think about the matter. In those countries, representation is not taken for granted. Rather, it is clearly understood that the state shares an oversight responsibility with the parties for guaranteeing the institutions of representation. Moreover, in these countries one measure of the health of their institutions is a lively pluralism of position, which can come only if parties are autonomous of other powerful social interests and if new issues and new identities can gain access to the electoral arena. If the state must spend money as a way of meeting its responsibilities for the system of national parties, then it will do so. Finally, the commitment of all actors to these principles prevents the parties themselves from perverting the regulatory system completely to their own advantage.

IMPLICATIONS AND OPTIONS FOR CANADA

Some Basic Principles

Public funding of political parties provides an avenue for the state to represent society to itself. Access and fairness have been central goals since the first steps toward public funding. Not only the Barbeau Committee but also almost all countries that established legislation to regulate and influence party and electoral financing presented such motives for action. Implementing these goals has involved finding ways to open up partisan and electoral processes. Thus, reform efforts have focused on widening candidates' and parties' ability to participate.

In these ways, public funding allows the state to make a statement about the forms of political debate and activity and the political actors that it values. When a state attempts, through its funding activities, to alter existing power relations in the direction of greater equality of access – thereby intervening in the name of equity – it provides an important statement about the shared understandings of power in that society. Moreover, when any state chooses to identify political parties as crucial national institutions of intermediation between the state and society, it contributes to a representation of liberal-democratic society in which certain collective values are being pursued alongside individualistic ones.

Public funding has been identified in almost all countries as one of the means of encouraging pluralistic participation. Nevertheless, despite widespread agreement on this broad goal, specific mechanisms diverge. Each country has selected the modalities it considers will put fundamental principles into practice.

The first choice that must be made involves identifying the types of parties to be recognized as contributors to pluralistic and fair debate among alternatives. In Western Europe, commitment to equitable access has translated into funding mechanisms that discriminate against or discourage small parties less than Canadian ones do. In essence, this has been achieved by setting low thresholds for access to public money.

A second choice concerns the basis for allocation of public funds. In Western Europe, the tendency has usually been to make distribution dependent upon success among the voters. Either the number of votes received or the number of legislative seats won forms the basis of the allocation rule for access to public funds (Doublet 1990, 18–19). Moreover, there is general agreement that a system using votes rather than seats is more equitable. Canada, in contrast, now rewards spending more than vote-getting by reimbursing expenses on the basis of "ability to spend."

A third choice about public funding involves deciding whether to provide support only for elections or for inter-electoral activities as well. Funding only for elections suggests that they are the privileged moment of liberal democracy: "politics" equals elections. In contrast, funding that lasts longer indicates a belief that representation in liberal democracies is an ongoing process, requiring nurturing and care at all times.

The final principle over which differences exist involves recognition of actors. Most Western European countries pay little attention to candidates, preferring to acknowledge ongoing partisan institutions' fundamental contribution to the polity. Some countries do – and Canada is among them – bypass the parties somewhat by providing substantial public funding to candidates, however.

These four matters all involve choices. The selection made results in a variable combination of mechanisms that together operate as a system to either encourage or discourage the primary goals of fairness of access and broadened participation. The choice made depends, as has been argued here, on the universe of political discourse of each country, a universe that is mapped in part by the broader political culture and in part by the institutionalization of past practices.

In Canada the regime of public funding has worked in accordance with a specific set of decisions made about these principles. Access to public funding is difficult, with high thresholds set to discourage "frivolous" candidates. This section of the study makes proposals to change this standard by lowering the thresholds in the name of fairness.

The expenditure limits – for which there is a great deal of enthusiasm – have been accompanied by *reimbursements* of election expenses. With the decision to reimburse (rather than to make allocations on other possible grounds), the federal system has embedded the notion of "spending" at the heart of the funding regime. Moreover, in 1983 there was a reinforcement of the spending principle with the decision to reimburse actual expenditures rather than to pay a flat grant.

It is argued here that such a commitment to spending (i.e., to reimbursements) is not necessarily a logical consequence of setting spending limits. Such limits can continue to exist, even as other principles and mechanisms of funding are altered to reflect more democratic and more equitable principles. Therefore, proposals are made to fund parties on the basis of their national vote totals rather than on the amount of money they spend.

The reimbursement procedures in the Canadian regime assign strong emphasis to the electoral moment. While tax credits, at least those issued by parties, recognize the importance of activity throughout the electoral cycle, reliance on reimbursements as the form of direct public funding favours elections.

This section of the study argues both for new registration procedures and for new funding formulae that would weight the balance more in the direction of inter-election public support.

Finally, mechanisms of direct public funding in Canada support candidates more than parties. Money for reimbursement of election expenses goes disproportionately to the candidates. This section argues for a reallocation of such funds between the candidates and the parties.

These four proposals follow from lessons gleaned from analysis of the Western European cases detailed above, as well as consideration of some of the provincial regimes within Canada, which have made other choices from the menu of mechanisms. In summary form, the proposals made here are based on the claim that the goals of equality of access, fairness and therefore innovation are better met by choices that (1) accept the legitimacy of new and even small voices representing alternative positions rather than branding them "frivolous"; (2) reward vote-getting rather than spending; (3) do not privilege the electoral moment; and (4) acknowledge the importance of parties more than candidates.

A second analytic element generating the proposals made in this section of the study derives from the approach to representation developed in this paper. If the practices of representation involve society's representation of itself as much as they involve representation of competing interests, it is important for the regime of public funding to express the commitment to the collectivity – and to political parties and the state as guardians of that collectivity – that has characterized Canadian political culture (Christian and Campbell 1983). The current regime institutionalizes the idea that the state has a responsibility for the health of Canadian democracy, including the political parties through which so much representation passes. The decision to institute tax credits and reimbursements reflected that commitment: the state spent money to meet its responsibility. This responsibility continues.

There are, however, ways of undertaking that task that highlight the contribution of the state and ways that hide it. A system of direct public funding does the first, because it is a visible transfer of funds from the state to candidates and parties in order to support their activities. Tax credits, on the other hand, partially disguise the fact that the state is spending money. Tax expenditures, whether they are supposed to promote economic growth or democratic institutions, are not as visible to the public. They are real, and costly, to the taxpayer, to be sure. Yet tax expenditures often appear to be more "private," to involve less state activity. In the case of tax credits for political contributions, they highlight the link between the citizen and the party, with the state's involvement appearing to be more distant, even invisible.

The argument made in this section is that if the Canadian state continues to assume a responsibility for the health of our democratic institutions by spending or forgoing substantial amounts of money, it should continue to do so in ways that make its expenditure apparent. Such a visible representation of state responsibility requires a regime that retains a combination of tax expenditures and direct public funding.

The latter cannot disappear completely; nor should it be much down-played.

With these principles in mind, several options for reform of the mechanisms of public funding are presented below.

Registration and Funding

There is no doubt that current Canadian practices, especially the thresholds for access to public funds, do nothing to welcome parties representing perspectives different from those of the existing three main participants. Registration is difficult. A high threshold for receiving funds makes it unlikely small but significant voices will be heard. The formulae for reimbursement reinforce existing resources rather than serve as mechanisms to boost the weaker parties.

Thus, the principle of equality of opportunity – or the so-called level playing field – does not appear to have provided inspiration for the present mechanisms of public funding, no matter how much a belief in the need for equity-generating state actions suffused the original reform. As the first part of this study has described, some mechanisms were intentionally designed to be discouraging in order to deter the so-called "frivolous" candidates, as well as to dampen any tendencies toward fragmentation of the party system. Others (particularly the 1983 move toward rewarding spending) may have perhaps been the unintended consequences of a regulatory process in which the existing parties played a decisive role.

Nevertheless, no matter what the root, the message communicated is one of a system dominated by those already "on the inside." The weakness of mechanisms to encourage fair access, as well as the absence of any equity-generating provisions directed toward new and small parties, contributes to this image. Among the costs of communicating these messages about the fairness of the system may be declining legitimacy for the representational process as a whole.

There are a number of ways in which this message might be altered to become one placing greater stress on pluralism and access. Altering the mechanisms of registration and public funding is one step in that direction. While there can never be any guarantee that the result will be greater enthusiasm for Canadian democracy and improved representation of innovative alternatives, the chances of such a result are increased thereby.

Registration

The greatest need is for reform of the funding procedures. However, alteration of procedures for registration would create few negative consequences and several potentially positive ones. Registration of parties exists in order to regularize the procedures by which they receive and spend funds. In other words, it is intended and designed to address primarily the "agency" element of party finance. There is, therefore, little justification for registration procedures that serve as a barrier to the efforts of groups to name themselves as a collectivity and present themselves to the electorate.

Currently there are two registration procedures. One requires parties to nominate 50 candidates in order to register officially. The second recognizes parties that have at least 12 seats in the House of Commons.

The first procedure is the one with the greatest potential impact on actors attempting to get into the system. It is unnecessarily restrictive. Moreover, it provides yet another message that the only party activity that really "counts" is fighting elections. There are, however, other ways in which a party may demonstrate its "seriousness" of purpose as well as its ability to garner popular support.

A procedure of *registration by petition*, similar to that present in the Ontario and Quebec legislation, provides for such demonstrations.[67] In Ontario a party may register by nominating candidates in 50 percent of the electoral districts *or* by collecting 10 000 signatures from eligible voters who endorse the registration of the party. In Quebec an authorized party is one that "undertakes, through its leader, to present official candidates in at least ten electoral divisions at any general election" (*Election Act* S.Q. 1989, c.1, s.47) and that can provide a petition supporting authorization from at least 1 000 electors. If such a party fails to nominate the 10 candidates once the election is called, the chief electoral officer may withdraw authorization.

These different provincial routes to registration permit some emphasis on a new party's ability to convincingly mobilize public attitudes around its positions in the inter-electoral period as well as during the campaign. They send a message not only that the party system welcomes pluralism but that politics itself may involve more than election campaigns. Nevertheless, these registration procedures vary in the height of the barrier they set. Ontario's is remarkably high, requiring a greater absolute number of candidates than is necessary for registration at the federal level (65), or written support of one of every 630 voters. Quebec's arrangements are more liberal: a party need field candidates in only 8 percent of the constituencies and get the written support of one person for every 4 600 voters.

The recommendation made here is for a registration rate less demanding than that of Ontario yet requiring a substantial effort on the part of any new party to indicate its commitment to the electoral process. A procedure for registration by petition of *10 000 eligible voters* would require any party to seek support from one person for every 1 800 voters. Such a petition could emanate from any single province – all of which have more than 10 000 eligible voters – but it would discourage single-province parties by making the threshold in any province higher than that currently in place for Ontario's provincial elections. Thus, while not blocking parties that might wish to concentrate on one province, it does send a clear message that a wider representational range is desirable.

Registration by petition has several advantages. It sends a message of welcome by providing an alternative route, simultaneously emphasizing the inter-electoral period. One disadvantage, however, is that it provides no obvious way to "clear the books" of registered parties that are no longer active. Therefore, the model provided by Quebec, which couples a petition with a requirement of nomination, would overcome this problem, *if the required number of candidates is reduced.* Currently, the 50-candidate requirement means that a party must nominate candidates in one-sixth of the ridings. Quebec asks for candidates in almost exactly half that number of ridings, that is, 10 of 125.

The recommendation made here is that the federal threshold be lowered to 25 seats for parties that use the petition route to registration. Thus, a party could gain official status by having 12 seats in the House of Commons, by nominating 50 candidates or by petitioning and nominating 25 candidates for the next election. Any party that petitioned but failed to field 25 people would lose status.

In any inter-election period, parties would face the same menu of choices. They could choose to re-petition and field only 25 candidates. If they did not re-petition, they would then have to come up with 50 candidates. In other words, they would have to demonstrate that they had "grown" over time. If they had not grown in this way, they would be compelled to demonstrate again that public support for the cause existed.

This procedure has an additional advantage to the ones already mentioned. It might discourage parties from fielding an excessive number of candidates, simply in order to be able to run any. All such candidates have to be monitored by the electoral officer, which is a costly task. Moreover, if changes with regard to reimbursing more parties are adopted, there would be advantages to discouraging parties from fielding candidates simply in order to be registered. A leaner and trimmer party of 25 would cost less, even if the thresholds for public funds are also reduced. Nevertheless, maintaining the 50-candidate option as a way to avoid having to re-petition also sends the message that "more is better."

Direct Funding – Thresholds and Mechanisms of Allocation (Options 1 and 2)

The whole thrust of this research based on comparative analysis is to stress the advantages present in systems of party financing that maintain low thresholds for public funding. Not surprisingly, then, this section of the study will explore the ways in which the thresholds might be lowered in Canada and the possible consequences. It will also examine the effects of removing the "spending" element from direct funding and replacing it with an allocation principle based on votes received.

At present, the Canadian regime operates according to two basic principles, reflecting the choices made as to how public funding should be implemented.[68] The first principle is that only "serious" candidates deserve to receive the taxpayers' money – and to be serious, one must receive 15 percent of the vote. This is the basis of the reimbursement procedure for candidates.

The second principle, reinforced since 1983, is to reward those who can spend more. For parties to receive any direct subsidies at all, they must be able to spend at least 10 percent of their limit. The same principle applies to candidates who receive more if they spend more, up to the 50 percent limit. In other words, those who have more resources to spend, and therefore spend more, are entitled to more public funding.

This practice means that we have chosen to reward parties' ability to raise and spend money more than their ability to gain public support, despite the fact that it is generally assumed that the primary test for any party is its ability to generate support, measured by votes.

Neither of these principles encourages access to the institutions of representation. In this sense there is no commitment by the state to political pluralism, a commitment that in other countries has involved taking steps to expand the space for alternative viewpoints. By reinforcing the strong and ignoring the new and the weak, the principles do not project fairness.

These two principles can also be seen as challenging a basic notion of what's fair, or equitable, in another way. By rewarding spending rather than vote-getting, current practices represent a somewhat peculiar vision of democracy as being more about money than about popular support. Thus, a shift toward allocating public funds based on success in the electorate might provide a better representation of the state's view of Canada's liberal democratic system.

It is important to note, in this context, that the emphasis on reimbursement – and later on actual spending – follows from the context in which the Barbeau Committee did its work. Since the impetus for setting up the Committee was escalating costs of elections, it is not surprising that the mechanisms of public funding addressed expenditure needs. The original legislation provided for these needs with a flat grant, reflecting the notion that candidates faced real costs of "being" candidates (and thus the postage rate was used as a standard). The 1983 change, however, shifted that principle to one of spending per se. Only real expenditures were to be reimbursed: and the more you spent (up to the limit), the more you got back. Therefore, as in all systems of conditional grants, there was an incentive to spend.

We see in this history two things. The first is the historical specificity of the mechanisms. Therefore, when needs and concerns change, it is also appropriate to think about better ways of meeting such needs. In the 1990s the re-legitimization of electoral politics is much more pressing than it was in the 1970s, and has provided part of the motivation for this Royal Commission. Therefore public funding mechanisms should try to meet that need by finding new ways of expressing a commitment to equity. The second message is the variabilty of procedures. The ones we now have are less than a decade old and by no means written in stone.

There are, then, two options for generating a more equitable system. One option is simply to lower the threshold but continue to reward spending; a second is to alter both principles by lowering the threshold and allocating public funds on the basis of support in the electorate. Each of these options will now be examined here.

The first option maintains the concept of rewarding those who can spend more while lowering the threshold for being reimbursed. Tables 3.1 and 3.2 show the results of altering the threshold and then reimbursing parties at the rate of 22.5 percent of their reported expenses and funding candidates at 50 percent.

These tables show the effects of this minimalist position. They demonstrate, first, that change would be effected only by eliminating the threshold, or reducing it to a very low level. Any decision to lower the threshold to even 5 percent would have a greater effect on the three main parties than it would on the smaller ones. Thus, if the goal is to send a message that pluralistic debate is welcome, the example of countries like the Federal Republic of Germany, with very low thresholds for funding, would be most reasonable.

Second, it is evident that making this change raises the price of public funding. The cost rises because the second principle remains unchanged; parties are still rewarded for spending more. While the increase for 1988 would have been relatively small, and could probably be considered a reasonable amount for the state to invest in promoting democracy, it is also probable that such a change would generate

Table 3.1
Reimbursement to parties: option 1

Party	Variable thresholds	
	Existing threshold[a]	No threshold[b]
Progressive Conservative	1 782 391	1 782 391
Liberal	1 538 972	1 538 972
NDP	1 588 627	1 588 627
Christian Heritage	48 906	48 906
Social Credit	—	779
Communist	—	8 325
Libertarian	—	36 890
Rhinoceros	—	1 289
Green	—	418
Confederation of Regions Western Party	—	1 545
Commonwealth	—	12 391
Reform	—	25 283
Total	4 958 896	5 045 816

Source: Canada, Elections Canada (1988b, 2-1).

[a]22.5 percent reimbursed if at least 10 percent of allowable limit spent.

[b]22.5 percent of reported expenses.

higher costs in the future. Once small parties realize the additional benefits of fund-raising and spending (that partially matching funds were being generated), then greater effort on their part to raise and spend money could be expected.

Such a change, in and of itself, might be a public good. Fund-raising by parties, particularly when done as it is in Canada by focusing on small donations, does generate benefits by increasing political awareness and commitment to party politics. This effect should never be minimized. Nevertheless, the cost to the treasury could become significantly larger if this option is adopted. This is its major disadvantage.

The second option is somewhat more radical. It involves altering both principles simultaneously. Option two shifts the basis for funding from spending to vote-getting. The activity explicitly rewarded is the winning of support in the election. This constitutes a move away from

Table 3.2
Reimbursement to candidates: option 1

Party	Variable thresholds, reimburse at existing rates		
	15 percent threshold	5 percent threshold	No threshold
Progressive Conservative	293	295	295
Liberal	264	294	294
NDP	170	292	295
Christian Heritage	—	11	63
Social Credit	—	—	9
Communist	—	—	52
Libertarian	—	1	88
Rhinoceros	—	1	74
Green	—	—	68
Confederation of Regions Western Party	—	7	52
Commonwealth	—	—	61
Reform	11	39	72
Independents	1	2	154
Total	739	942	1 577
Reimbursements	$13 734 568	$15 744 471	$17 132 278

Source: Data provided by Royal Commission on Electoral Reform and Party Financing.

the notion of "reimbursement for expenses" and a move back toward the idea that funding is intended to meet the costs of "being" a party.

This principle of proportional funding is used in most of the countries of Western Europe discussed earlier as well as in provinces like Quebec, New Brunswick and Prince Edward Island, which support parties' organizational costs. Nevertheless, the funding is never strictly proportional.[69] Basic grants are then "topped-up" by proportional funding. In this way, two principles – equity and rewarding strength – are combined.

The proposals made here for this second option also involve another change in the mechanisms for public funding. The proposal is to provide a fixed pool of money, which would then be distributed among the parties. There are several advantages to thinking in terms of a pool.

A first advantage is to the state itself. When real expenses are reimbursed, costs to the state are unpredictable, albeit within a limited range (since they can be no higher than 50 percent of 50 percent of the expenditure limits, etc.). There is no way to know in advance how much candidates or parties will spend or how many will qualify. Use of a fixed pool means that the state's costs are both known and limited in advance.

A second advantage is for the election system itself. Since there is evidence that some candidates spend up to the limit, because they are spending 50-cent dollars, there is a built-in escalator pushing up election expenses overall. Similarly, even small parties have an incentive to get to 10 percent. With a fixed pool of money and the knowledge that spending per se will not bring more money, any tendencies to be profligate might be tempered.

Use of a pool has advantages over the flat-rate system too. One criticism of the flat-rate system is that it may become too expensive if tied to an item whose cost is rising. This is what happened in Canada between 1974 and 1983. More common, however, is the problem of finding a reasonable rate that is not too expensive and will keep up with parties' real costs. For example, some commentators have pointed to the lack of flexibility in the West German flat rate as an explanation for the "creative financing" techniques developed by parties in that country. Moreover, constant needs to readjust the rates, which are usually set in "round numbers" by legislation, risk turning party finance into a political football. A fixed pool, indexed to the consumer price index (CPI), avoids such problems.

The major advantage of using a pool, however, is the ease of translating a commitment to fairness into public funding. When real expenses are reimbursed or when a flat-rate payment is used, there is pressure for keeping thresholds high in order to keep costs down. As tables 3.1 and 3.2 show, admitting more parties to a regime based on reimbursements immediately pushes costs up. Similarly, if flat-rate grants are to be made to the current 12 registered parties, costs would explode. Therefore, the provinces that use flat-rate grants, as well as those with reimbursement procedures, tend to set high thresholds. If the goal is to institute a regime of public funding that appears more welcoming – and fairer – then the use of a pool of money has real advantages.

Tables 3.3 and 3.4 show the effects of taking up the option of rewarding vote-getting rather than spending, using the 1988 levels of public funding to create a pool of money. Once again, it is only by eliminating thresholds that any substantial effect is obtained for the small parties. Moreover, as table 3.5 clearly demonstrates, the effect would be similar to that in Western Europe. In 1988 the Canadian Green Party, for

Table 3.3
Direct public funding of parties: option 2

Party	Allocation by national votes received, variable thresholds, no increase in funding pool			
	1988 public funding[a]	5 percent threshold[b]	2 percent threshold[b]	No threshold[b]
Progressive Conservative	1 782 391	2 236 462	2 191 832	2 142 243
Liberal	1 538 972	1 661 230	1 626 518	1 586 847
NDP	1 588 627	1 061 204	1 036 409	1 016 574
Christian Heritage	48 906	—	—	38 679
Social Credit	—	—	—	1 488
Communist	—	—	—	2 479
Libertarian	—	—	—	12 397
Rhinoceros	—	—	—	19 340
Green	—	—	—	17 852
Confederation of Regions Western Party	—	—	—	15 375
Commonwealth	—	—	—	3 479
Reform	—	—	104 137	104 337
Total pool[c]	4 958 896	4 958 896	4 958 896	4 958 896

[a]Reimbursement under the *Canada Elections Act. Source:* Canada, Elections Canada (1988b, p. 2-1).

[b]Calculation based on "percent of fundable vote" for each threshold. This excludes the votes received by any party or candidate *not* eligible for funding under the scheme. *Source:* Canada, Elections Canada (1988a, table 5, 19).

[c]Because of rounding, the total of the allocation in each column may not be equal to the total pool.

example, would have received substantially more money than they spent. More important, however, all the other parties would have received some funding in recognition of the fact that they had gained some electoral support.

Table 3.6 shows the redistribution of the pool of money now allocated to parties (1988 = $4 958 896) by implementing an absolutely essential element of the Western European systems: the mix of basic grants and proportional funding. Two levels of basic grant are indicated: $30 000 and $50 000. The table allocates all parties a basic grant. Those parties whose share of the pool of public funds comes to less than the basic grant, based on national vote alone (column 4 of table 3.3),

Table 3.4
Direct public funding of candidates: option 2

Party	Allocation by votes received, variable thresholds,[a] no increase in funding pool			
	1988 public funding	5 percent threshold[b]	2 percent threshold[b]	No threshold[c]
Progressive Conservative	6 055 597	6 198 411	6 065 185	5 908 611
Liberal	4 655 526	4 599 707	4 500 818	4 384 074
NDP	2 839 253	2 936 451	2 873 272	2 799 105
Christian Heritage	—	—	—	107 130
Social Credit	—	—	—	4 120
Communist	—	—	—	6 867
Libertarian	—	—	—	34 336
Rhinoceros	—	—	—	54 938
Green	—	—	—	49 444
Confederation of Regions Western Party	—	—	—	42 577
Commonwealth	—	—	—	8 241
Reform	162 122	—	295 293	287 052
Independent	22 122	—	—	23 349
None	—	—	—	26 096
Total pool[d]	13 734 568	13 734 568	13 734 568	13 734 568

Source: Calculated from data in Canada, Elections Canada (1988a, table 5, 19; 1988b, 3–339).

[a]Calculation based on each party's national vote.

[b]Calculation based on "percent of fundable vote," for each threshold. This excludes the votes received by any party or candidate *not* eligible for funding under the scheme.

[c]Calculated as percentage of valid votes received.

[d]Because of rounding, the total of the allocation in each column may not be equal to the total pool.

receive no more. All other parties receive a share (proportional to their vote in the election) of the pool that remains, once the basic grants have been subtracted. These moneys would be paid by the state upon receipt of statements of party expenses. Thus, parties would have to demonstrate that they were indeed active and capable of spending the money, although allowable expenses would not be only those for elections. Other types of party costs would be acceptable.

Table 3.5
Comparison of election expenses and public funding based on national vote: option 2

Party	Expenses reported, candidates and parties 1988[a]	Expenses reimbursed 1988[a]	Sum of candidate and party funding based on percent of vote received[b]
Progressive Conservative	19 785 977	7 837 988	8 050 854
(%)		39.6	40.7
Liberal	16 516 871	6 194 498	7 557 768
(%)		37.5	45.8
NDP	14 366 977	4 427 880	3 815 679
(%)		30.8	26.6
Christian Heritage	1 125 761	48 906	145 809
Social Credit	3 600	—	5 608
Communist	92 533	—	9 346
Libertarian	208 610	—	46 733
Rhinoceros	22 024	—	74 278
Green	33 973	—	67 296
Confederation of Regions Western Party	163 639	—	57 952
Commonwealth	59 861	—	11 720
Reform	1 108 062	162 122	391 389

[a]Canada, Elections Canada (1988b, 2-1, 3 – 339).

[b]Sum of column 4 in table 3.3 and in table 3.4.

This use of public funds would recognize the costs of "being" a party and provide a fair distribution of public funds based on electoral success.

Implementing a funding regime based on vote totals rather than spending would have substantial, and positive, implications. It would increase the revenue of new parties, allowing them to make their voices heard, thereby contributing to a pluralism of debate. It would reward *all* parties for the basic activity of liberal democracy – winning support for one's position – while downplaying the notion that the primary activity of parties is spending money. Finally, the shift could be made without necessarily building higher costs into the process. All calculations in tables 3.3–3.6 are based on treating the pool of money available in 1988 as fixed. With a set pool, then, the percentage of voting support received becomes the allocation rule.

Table 3.6
Public funding of parties: option 2

Party	Basic grant: allocation based on national vote totals,[a] no increase in funding pool[b]	
	Basic grant = $30 000	Basic grant = $50 000
Progressive Conservative	2 044 316	1 976 632
Liberal	1 524 641	1 479 718
NDP	981 971	961 009
Christian Heritage	66 791	50 000
Social Credit	30 000	50 000
Communist	30 000	50 000
Libertarian	30 000	50 000
Rhinoceros	30 000	50 000
Green	30 000	50 000
Confederation of Regions Western Party	30 000	50 000
Commonwealth	30 000	50 000
Reform	126 577	141 537
Total pool[c]	4 958 896	4 958 896

[a]Calculation based on "percent of fundable vote." This excludes the votes received by any party *not* eligible for funds in addition to the basic grant, at each level.

[b]The pool is the $4.96 million allocated to the parties in 1988.

[c]Because of rounding, the total of the allocation in each column may not be equal to the total pool.

Support for Parties as National Institutions

One of clearest lessons to emerge from the experience of Western Europe was that there was an advantage to giving public recognition to political parties by designating them institutions that are vitally necessary to the relationship between the state and the citizens. Constitutional entrenchment was often an expression of this public recognition, but even without it, there has been a notion that political parties reside in a sort of para-public realm, being not only autonomous institutions but also ones with responsibilities toward the citizenry, the state and the democratic regime in general. Moreover, behind the public funding was the idea that popular mobilization and political pluralism were never confined solely to the campaign: parties' contributions to representational success depended upon their ability to speak to the voters constantly and consistently.

Beginning from the assumption that one way to regenerate some enthusiasm for Canadian democracy is to attempt to strengthen the political parties as national institutions and to encourage their efforts to do more than lurch from electoral competition to electoral competition, three options emerge. The motive behind each of them is to provide inducements – and the resources – for political parties of all kinds to broaden their representational repertoire.

In Canada, there was a partial move in the direction of expressing this view of parties in the first wave of reform, with one of the major innovations of the *Election Expenses Act* in 1974 being the expanded recognition of political parties (the party name was put on the ballot by 1970 legislation). This recognition was accompanied by practical mechanisms, like the tax credit and the reimbursement of parties' election expenses. Nevertheless, the reform retained two long-standing traditional themes: that elections were the privileged moment of party activity and that the basic relationship was between candidates for office and voters. Thus, rather than "funding" parties, the state undertook "reimbursement" of campaign expenses. The only direct state subsidies were for election expenses, at the same time that reimbursement went disproportionately to candidates. Moreover, tax credits, which have become increasingly important to parties, were a form of funding that made the role of the state almost invisible – not only to the average citizen but even to the parties – because it took the form of a tax expenditure.

It is time to rethink these assumptions and to consider choices confronting those establishing any regime of public funding: whom to fund, and when to fund them.

The current situation is described in table 3.7, which maps a number of patterns. The first is that more public funding goes to election-year activities, despite the fact that parties do gain substantial inter-electoral benefits from tax credits. Thus, of total state support for parties and candidates between 1985 and 1988 ($66.66 million), 56 percent was provided in a single year, that of the election. Moreover, of the direct subsidies, 100 percent ($18.69 million) was paid for election expenses, and of that, only 27 percent ($4.96 million) went to the political parties. The options considered below will vary this distribution across actors and across time.

Fund Only the Parties (Option 3)

Strong arguments exist for weakening the emphasis on the "fictitious bond" between candidate and voter and identifying the one that

Table 3.7
Public funding: some characteristics

	$
Inter-election tax credits (1985–87)	29 116 000[a]
Election-year tax credits (1988)	18 848 000[a]
Election expense reimbursement (1988)	18 693 464[b]
Total public funding (1985–88)	66 657 464
Election-year funding as a percentage of total public funding	56%
Funding of parties as a percentage of direct subsidies	27%

[a] Data provided by the Royal Commission on Electoral Reform and Party Financing.
[b] See Tables 3. 1 and 3. 2.

better corresponds to contemporary realities, that between the party and the voters. One such argument involves treating the parties as more than a string of local candidates and encouraging them to perform as national institutions with responsibility for designing a slate of candidates that expresses a commitment to equitable representation.

An intriguing method for doing this is simply to give all tax credits and all public funds to the parties, which would then redistribute them to their candidates. This is the model of the continental European cases, with the exception of France. The major advantage of this change is that it recognizes the reality that elections are fought among parties. A parliamentary system and new technologies make this increasingly the case. Moreover, such a change would allow parties to determine the needs of candidates and to allocate available funds in creative and differential ways. Such tailoring of funding to "need" might encourage candidacies of currently disadvantaged groups for whom the existing formally egalitarian allocation of the election expenses legislation remains insufficient. Parties could choose to give more to candidates who had fewer personal resources, as well as using money more strategically. Thus, in addition to strengthening the parties' role in representation, this option has the potential for increasing equality for groups currently disadvantaged in seeking to be candidates.

A disadvantage is that it puts a great deal of power in the hands of the parties and depends upon their good will – or responsiveness to pressure – to guarantee that running for office is not limited to certain categories of people. Evidence from Western Europe shows that centralized parties have been at least as open to the demands of disadvantaged groups for representation as has the Canadian system,[70] suggesting this preferential treatment of candidates may be a minor risk. Nevertheless, it does continue to be worrisome, in the absence of any other inducements that might make parties pay closer attention to this matter.[71] Such inducements – for example higher rates of funding when they run more women or visible minority candidates – would help dispel such fears.

Reallocate the Pool (Option 4)

A less dramatic change but one moving in the same direction would take the pool of public funds available and split it between parties and candidates equally. Under the current regime, candidates are well funded and tend to run large surpluses. Therefore, an argument for redistribution can be made. Moreover, a shift in principle from "reimbursement" to public funding based on vote totals might encourage candidates to be less jealous of "their" funds and less desirous of hanging on to them to meet all contingencies. Once the notion disappears that they are being paid back for their expenses, then it might become easier for them to imagine that they and the party are all "in it together." Nevertheless, a reallocation of this sort would probably necessitate a change in tax credit arrangements, so that local constituencies could anticipate being able to raise more money by being permitted to issue tax credits for an extended period of time.

Based on the 1988 pool, such a 50–50 split would mean that parties would receive $9.34 million – an increase of $4.38 million, or almost a doubling of funds.

The decision of which parties would receive these funds again raises the issue of thresholds. Table 3.8 delineates the distributional differences of allocating this pool when thresholds are varied and when allocation is based on national vote totals. It assumes that vote-getting is again the grounds for allocation. A similar pattern to that of table 3.3 emerges: only when the threshold is eliminated is there any impact on the number of parties receiving public funds.

In table 3.9 the same 50–50 reallocation is made, but the notion of basic grants is reintroduced. This table shows the distributional patterns of varying four factors simultaneously: eliminating thresholds, funding on the basis of national vote totals, instituting basic grants and redistributing money from candidates to parties.

Table 3.8
Public funding of parties – 50% of pool: option 4a

Party	Variable thresholds, no increase in funding pool[a]		
	15 percent threshold	2 percent threshold	No threshold
Progressive Conservative	4 215 376	4 131 256	4 037 788
Liberal	3 131 155	3 065 728	2 990 954
NDP	2 000 201	1 953 467	1 916 080
Christian Heritage	—	—	74 774
Social Credit	—	—	2 804
Communist	—	—	4 673
Libertarian	—	—	28 040
Rhinoceros	—	—	37 387
Green	—	—	32 648
Confederation of Regions Western Party	—	—	28 040
Commonwealth	—	—	5 608
Reform	—	196 281	196 281
Total pool[b]	9 346 732	9 346 732	9 346 732

[a]The pool is created by taking half of the reimbursements allocated to candidates and parties in 1988.

[b]Because of rounding, the total of the allocation for each column may not be equal to the total pool.

Reallocate across the Electoral Cycle (Option 5)

If parties as institutions are to receive a greater share of direct public funds, the increase should not be simply designated a windfall to cover election expenses. It would be advisable to establish a mechanism to send an even stronger signal that parties' representational activities are ongoing than the one presently given by the fact that 56 percent of state funding goes to parties in one year of the four-year electoral cycle (table 3.7). This message needs to be strengthened, because the percentage of state funds being expended in the election year increased between 1984 (50 percent) and 1988 (56 percent), despite the fact that tax credits in the inter-election years of the last electoral cycle were higher than in the previous one.

Table 3.9
Public funding of parties – 50% of pool: option 4b

Party	Basic grant: allocation based on national vote total,[a] no increase in funding pool[b]	
	Basic grant = $30 000	Basic grant = $50 000
Progressive Conservative	3 966 189	3 916 056
Liberal	2 950 688	2 918 928
NDP	1 890 254	1 878 067
Christian Heritage	101 894	50 000
Social Credit	30 000	50 000
Communist	30 000	50 000
Libertarian	30 000	50 000
Rhinoceros	30 000	50 000
Green	30 000	50 000
Confederation of Regions Western Party	30 000	50 000
Commonwealth	30 000	50 000
Reform	218 721	233 681
Total pool[c]	9 346 732	9 346 732

[a]Calculation based on "percent of fundable vote." This excludes the votes received by any party *not* eligible for funds in addition to the basic grant, at each level.

[b]The pool is created by taking half of the reimbursements allocated to candidates and parties in 1988.

[c]Because of rounding, the total of the allocation for each column may not be equal to the total pool.

To send this signal, a staggered payment system, similar to that of the FRG, could be used. If 40 percent ($3.74 million) is paid in the year after the election, the parties would receive almost as much as they now do. However, the payment of the remaining 60 percent – at the rate of $1.87 million – over the next four years could be used to encourage the parties to use the money for other representational tasks, such as providing consultations with the population, educating the public by holding meetings and doing research, for example. Thus, the parties could become present among the citizens for much more time than simply in the few weeks of the campaign.

Obviously, the actual distribution of these funds would depend on the choices made about other mechanisms discussed under options 1–4.

CONCLUSION

While healthy democratic politics can only be generated by citizens and not by the state, the latter does have a role to play in removing barriers and providing inducements to certain kinds of behaviours. One important way to do that is through expanding access. The options presented here could be expected to move Canada in the direction of one of the major goals set out in the Barbeau Committee and reaffirmed by this Royal Commission, that of equity. These options, confined to the topic of state funding for parties and elections, can never provide complete consideration of the equity principle. That must be addressed more broadly, with a whole series of reforms. Nevertheless, some of the options discussed here would increase the equity-generating quality of federal politics and would be likely, then, to contribute to an expanded political pluralism and healthy debate.

All of these options for altering the provisions of public funding – which affect not only small and new parties but also the major actors in the present party system – are put forward as suggestions for incorporating into the Canadian federal party system lessons learned from the Western European experience. While it is obvious that Canada differs from those countries in several ways, it is also true that the parliamentary system depends upon strong parties.

The Canadian state has had – and should continue to maintain – a commitment to improving liberal democracy by supporting the political party as an institution. Such a commitment draws Canada closer to the experience of Western Europe than to that of the United States. The experience of those countries, not only in reinforcing parties but also in recognizing the importance of encouraging pluralistic debate and acceptance of difference in party politics, merits the attention of Canadians as we face up to the current limitations in our liberal democracy. Only by doing so can we imagine ways to reach the goal of further strengthening Canadian democracy as we move into the 21st century.

NOTES

1. Not only academics are concerned. The population as a whole is very discouraged and dissatisfied with parties, leaders and candidates (Clarke et al. 1991, chap. 2; Mishler and Clarke 1990). Public-opinion polls also turn up a huge change in only a decade in the public's perceptions of politicians. Over the decade 1980–90, many more Canadians learned to think of their politicians as unprincipled (57 percent in 1990 vs. 28 percent in 1980), concerned with money (81 percent vs. 53 percent) and incompetent (65

percent vs. 33 percent), while far fewer considered them to be principled (40 percent vs. 63 percent), concerned with people (16 percent vs. 37 percent) and competent (32 percent vs. 57 percent). Decima Research polls from March 1980 and March 1990, reported in the *Globe and Mail*, 1 October 1990.

2. Such cross-national comparison is implicit in the classic article on the "decline of party" written in the 1970s by John Meisel (1985). His account mixes peculiarly Canadian elements with those common to most advanced industrial societies at the time.

3. Lipset and Rokkan (1967) proposed the concept of "frozen" party systems. This notion had extraordinary influence on political sociologists studying the party systems of Western Europe, and the hegemony of the analysis into the early 1970s accounts for many of the difficulties observers initially faced in making sense of post-1968 conditions.

4. The question of how to categorize these party systems is not well addressed in the literature. Some authors make a simple dichotomy between "North America" and "Europe" (Nassmacher 1989, 237). This geographical distinction fails to recognize that several provinces (Quebec, New Brunswick, Prince Edward Island) in Canada do provide direct subsidies to support the organizational costs of parties, while the federal government provides an indirect subsidy for inter-election expenses through the tax credit. A better distinction is one between candidate orientation and party orientation. This interpretation should not be used, however, to obscure the distinction between forms of government (parliamentary/presidential) and forms of subsidy. Alexander (1980, 338ff.) makes this error.

5. For a discussion of some of these alternatives, see Paltiel (1980).

6. On party labels as means of reducing information costs, see Jenson (1975).

7. However, Canada is not at variance with the United Kingdom on this matter. Indeed, probably another legacy of our long-standing ties to that country has been the transmission of its relatively underexamined notions of the role of political parties in a democratic polity. The second part of this study argues that the United Kingdom is no more the appropriate model (because of the negative consequences of this silence about state-party relations) than is the United States, with its very different party system.

8. On such visions of society, see Berger (1981). On the changes that the political, social and economic events of the last two decades have worked in such visions, see Maier (1987), especially articles by Charles Maier and Claus Offe.

9. These varied visions exist within Canada too. The legacies of Catholicism and Toryism, as well as the famous social-democratic tinge, have set limits to the hegemony of liberal thinking (Christian and Campbell 1983). Thus, the more collectivist goal of "peace, order and good government" exists alongside – and sometimes in uneasy relation to – liberalism's notions

of order, which look to self-regulation by market forces and electoral competition.

10. The goal of autonomy provided an early motive for reform. A major push toward state subsidies for parties came with the fear on the part of the parties themselves that they might be captured by other powerful interests. Thus in the FRG it was the Christian Democrats who sought to free themselves from powerful corporations via public funding. Their fear of the corporations was greater than their fear of the state (Leonard 1979, 43–44). The Social Democrats were not initially enthusiastic about intensifying the link between the party and the state, because they feared a loss of autonomy. Despite the differences in perspective, each reaction indicates the importance of the discourse of autonomous representation by parties.

11. On the importance of language in politics, see Jenson (1986) and Bell (1990, 138–39).

12. For a description of its founding, see Canada, Committee (1966) and Paltiel (1970, chap. 9).

13. For these differences, see Brodie and Jenson (1988, chap. 7).

14. See, inter alia, Regenstrief (1964).

15. Between 1957 and 1968 the Liberals were reduced to one or two seats, if not closed out all together, in Manitoba, Saskatchewan and Alberta, while the Tories' precipitious decline in Quebec began again in 1962.

16. Prior to 1957 the last minority government had been in 1925.

17. The Committee was concerned about candidates from smaller parties and independents, so it proposed a free mailing for all candidates. Seidle (1985, 115–16) provides an overview of the Barbeau Committee's recommendations.

18. While not totally divorced from the issue of corrupt practices, it was true that Quebec elections had long been more expensive than elsewhere (Angell 1966, 281–84).

19. The first head of the federal committee, François Nobert, was also linked to the Quebec model. He was a former president of the Quebec Liberal party. When he died, Barbeau replaced him (Paltiel 1970, 135).

20. The three-fifths rule could be met by having nominated that number in the previous election or by having reached three-fifths before nominations closed.

21. This result contradicts somewhat the argument made previously that Quebec served as a model for the federal legislation. In amendments to Quebec legislation, political parties were already emerging as acknowledged, even valued, organizations. By 1965 a recognized party could be reimbursed for the expense involved in maintaining a permanent office

in Montreal and Quebec City. Later, bloc funding intended to cover general organizational costs became available in Quebec.

22. On this point see Macpherson (1977). For a discussion of its impact in Canada, see Brodie and Jenson (1989).

23. In this context it is important to contrast the practices in Quebec to those at the federal level. Tripartite mechanisms were much more frequently constructed and utilized in Quebec throughout the 1960s and 1970s than they were in the rest of Canada, especially at the federal level.

24. See, inter alia, Kitschelt (1989) and Jenson (1991).

25. There was also much less political protest and violence in Canada than elsewhere (Mishler and Clarke 1990, 164).

26. It should be noted that not everyone shared this complacency, of course. Leftist critics struggled to have their own prescriptions taken seriously, including discussions of the problems of the party system. For example, advocates of "creative politics" developed an alternative vision of representation, which had little effect, even within their own organizations (Bradford 1989).

27. For the classic analysis of this relationship, see Cairns (1968).

28. For a recent discussion of precisely this issue, see Paltiel (1989).

29. Special dispensation was given the Créditistes when they fell below the threshold, and a loud claim was made by the Bloc Québécois in the fall of 1990. The Speaker agreed to give that formation special consideration under the rules of the House, but it will have to meet the registration requirements for campaign reimbursement, etc., in any future elections.

30. Indeed, the statistic has been steady, hovering around 50 percent (Seidle and Paltiel 1981, 272).

31. The purpose in this change was to address an objection to the 1974 legislation, that its provisions favoured the electronic media (Seidle 1985, 125). While broadening the types of expenses covered, a substantial blockage for small parties' access to public funds was introduced.

32. As Nelson Riis, New Democratic Party MP, told the Ontario Commission on Election Contributions: "By having some money left over to call meetings and do a variety of other things, you maintain interest in politics ... The money is going to come anyway so we ought as well [sic] use it now. It has enabled me, as a Member of the House, to actually do a better job and provide better service" (quoted in Ontario, Commission on Election Contributions 1982, 17).

33. In fact, Mr. Friesen would have preferred the limit for subsidies to be set at 20 percent (Ontario, Commission on Election Contributions 1982, 20).

34. For a complete description of the working of the ad hoc committee, see Seidle (1985, 123–25).

35. Mishler and Clarke (1990, 160–62) discuss Canada's middling performance on the official turnout records, as well as the patterns since 1945.

36. Some such groups do not act through the parties because of a commitment to autonomous politics linked to the standard strategic position of new social movements. But another important reason is that such groups have had much more success achieving reactions from the state than from the political parties (Cameron 1989). The experience of the women's movement is exemplary here. In the late 1960s, women's mobilization received more attention from state officials (establishment of the Royal Commission on the Status of Women and the Secretary of State's responsibility for gender equality, for example) than from the political parties. This lesson was not lost on activists through the 1980s. For a discussion of the women's movement's experience with the state, see Findlay (1987). Clarke et al. (1991, 11–12) consider this process in terms of party politics.

37. This postwar stress on the constitutional entrenchment of parties arose from analyses about the contribution of a weak and disorganized party system to the turbulent politics of the interwar period. The emphasis on maximizing wide-ranging popular involvement came from similar arguments about excessive centralization in the Third Reich. Italy also recognized the constitutional right of citizens to organize for democratic purposes in its 1947 Constitution. Doublet (1990, 7–9) provides an overview of constitutional entrenchment in several countries.

38. These requirements for parties are set out in section 1 of Article 21. Later sections forbid anti-democratic parties and provide the constitutional grounds for exclusion of certain categories of activists from public service, including from the system of higher education.

39. For example, in 1957 the Court overturned a tax deduction for contributions to political parties that required a party to have at least one parliamentary seat in order to qualify. Then "in 1958 it ruled that tax deductions for political parties, whether represented in parliament or not, are unconstitutional violations of the principle of equality of opportunity or equality of treatment ... The Court argued that some parties, for example pro-business middle-class parties and their higher income supporters, would benefit more from such tax provisions" (Gunlicks 1988, 32).

40. The law also regulated accounting procedures and the internal organization of parties. This description of the 1967 law is drawn primarily from Gunlicks (1988). See also Leonard (1979) and Nassmacher (1989).

41. Forty percent was paid immediately after the election, with the rest distributed over the other years (Leonard 1979, 45–46; Doublet 1990, 34).

42. It is important to note the distinction between the low threshold for public funding (0.5 percent) and the relatively high threshold for gaining access to the legislature (5 percent). The latter was intended to prevent fragmentation of the parliamentary system, while the former was designed to maximize political pluralism and equality of opportunity.

43. Other forms of direct subsidies, provided on a continuing basis, have included prominent public space for posters and allocation of part of legislators' state-paid salaries to their parties.

44. The original legislation required a separate listing for individuals or couples contributing more than DM20 000 and corporations giving more than DM200 000. The Court's 1968 ruling, which provoked a revision of the law in 1969, lowered the limit to DM20 000 for all types of contributors.

45. In the mid-1980s, four of the five major parties had foundations. All were named after historic party leaders (Gunlicks 1988, 34–35). Von Nordheim (1980, 376–78) provides a good description of the activities of such foundations. He was the Washington-based director of the Christian Democrats' Konrad Adenauer Foundation.

46. The German foundations are controversial institutions. For a quite critical review see, for example, Pinto-Duschinsky (1991). Evaluation of them depends not only upon the criteria used but also upon the hopes for overcoming certain structural tendencies toward centralization, not to mention the power of wealth.

47. Part of the reason for the problem was that the subsidy amount was fixed by legislation, so it could not respond to inflation or other changes in cost structures.

48. Much of the information for this section, unless otherwise indicated, is from Nassmacher (1989).

49. Neither Sweden nor Italy funds party foundations. The Dutch system does provide support for research institutes while giving no direct subsidies, out of fear of freezing the status quo (Koole 1989, 210).

50. The criterion of "significant support," measured by winning parliamentary seats, was from the beginning a basic principle of subsidization.

51. This term is used by Nassmacher (1989, 248). For example, in 1979 the *Grünen* spent DM300 000 in the Europarliamentary campaign, received 3.2 percent of the votes, and collected DM4.5 million in public funds. This money allowed them to begin to build a party organization and mobilize for subsequent national, regional and local elections (Hoffmann-Martinot, 1990). The different situation of the French *Verts* will become apparent further on.

52. In 1972 the threshold in the Swedish legislation was lowered to 2.5 percent to help the Communists remain one of the five parties (Leonard 1979, 56).

53. Crude pressure exerted on the FDP provided one of the motives for commencing the reform process in the 1960s in the FRG (Paltiel 1980, 358).

54. Before 1958, the law of 1 July 1901 grouped political parties with other associations that were *désintéressés*. But this law was an inadequate basis for the recognition of parties, which were thereby deprived of a meaningful juridical existence (Kheitmi 1964).

55. As he said in an interview in 1965, "I proposed the Constitution of 1958 to the country ... with the intention of ending the rule of parties" (quoted in Toinet 1988, 12).

56. The Left candidate for president, François Mitterrand, and several other Socialists did propose reforms of party and election financing in these years (del Castillo Vera 1985, 78). However, it took until 1990, fully nine years after Mitterrand had been elected, to sort through the mess that the existing system had created and settle the question of illegal behaviour on all sides (Doublet 1990, 61).

57. The method of reimbursement of printing and other costs led to a great deal of corruption rather than limiting expenses as initially hoped. One way that parties have raised money involved the presentation of spurious invoices (*fausses factures*) to the state. See one discussion in "L'Election présidentielle: 26 avril–10 mai 1981," *Le Monde: Dossiers et Documents*, May 1981, 61–62. It was the problem of the *fausses factures* and amnesty provisions that made the reform process so controversial in 1989–90.

58. "In 1981 it was said that Brice Lalonde, candidate of the Greens, would never have been able to get the necessary legal endorsements without the help of the UDF and especially the Social Democratic Center (CDS) and the Radical Party, which hoped that Lalonde would win some support away from the left" (Toinet 1988, 12).

59. Interviews with both the staff of the *Verts* and long-time militants continually stressed that the money available during and after the presidential election was an absolutely crucial factor explaining the *Verts'* successes in subsequent elections in 1988–89. The French ecologists often did no worse than the *Grünen* in the elections of the 1970s, but only the latter were able to begin constructing an organization immediately, because of the campaign financing laws. For example, when their 3.2 percent of the Europarliamentary vote in 1979 gave the *Grünen* DM4.5 million, the *Verts'* 3.4 percent in 1984 gave them no public money whatsoever.

60. Obviously one would not want to attribute all the *Verts'* success in 1989 to public funds. Other factors were clearly important (Jenson 1989b). Yet there is a dramatic difference between what a party can do when it can afford to pay staff, organize its propaganda and run meetings and what

it can do when it depends exclusively on the good will and money of its activists. For one thing, it does not have to be a party of the wealthy or middle class, because funds can be made available to subsidize the costs of less affluent activists.

61. This long-standing practice is an important source of funds for many small and Left parties.

62. Finances and certain kinds of campaigning techniques are now regulated, expenditure limits exist and larger public subsidies and tax credits have been created. The 5 percent threshold has been eliminated. This law of 15 January 1990 does not apply to municipal elections and cantonal elections where there are fewer than 9 000 inhabitants (Doublet 1990, 68ff.).

63. The last was the *Parti Socialiste Unifié* (PSU), born in the 1960s out of the energies of the French New Left. While party names change very frequently in France, the new formations rarely represent a new organizational initiative. They are much more likely to be a regrouping of old formations around a new candidate and his (and now sometimes her) "friends."

64. Even the *Parti Socialiste*, founded only in 1971, was not a new party but one made up of the remnants of the old Socialist party and several other currents grouped around leaders. These *tendances* were constitutionally recognized by the Socialist party and have provided the focus for conflict – and interest – since then. Debate over issues is encoded in disputes over who will succeed Mitterrand. The Communist party is obviously an exception to this personalized form of politics.

65. An even more important change would involve altering the electoral system. The two-round system now effectively closes out any small formation not able to make an alliance. The *Verts* stand very little chance of winning legislative seats because of their refusal to make coalitions and other agreements for reciprocal standing down on the second round. Similarly, the *Front National* is closed out as long as other formations maintain a common front against it. The introduction of proportional representation for one legislative election in 1986 demonstrated the rapidity with which the composition of the National Assembly might change. In 1986 the *Front National* gained 35 seats, with 9.8 percent of the votes. In 1988, after the return to the original system, 8.8 percent of the vote brought one seat.

66. The use of election finance legislation rather than constitutional and political practices to block unacceptable parties is particularly pernicious. Several countries, like the FRG, use a constitutional inhibition against undemocratic parties. This is a much less blunt instrument than financing legislation, as was done in the United Kingdom, or manipulation of the electoral law, as was done in France.

67. Alberta also uses a procedure for registration by petition, modelled on that of Ontario.

68. Obviously, the tax credit system operates according to the more equitable principle of "existence." This means that registration or nomination gives a party or candidate access to public funding.

69. The clear exception is the FRG, which uses flat-rate subsidies for election expenses. The original German legislation, struck down by the Constitutional Court, would have provided proportional funding.

70. Indeed, many – like the Scandinavian parties – have been very much more responsive than in Canada.

71. Of course, this matter also depends, therefore, on what might be done to promote access in other ways. The systemic character of the reform process is clear here.

REFERENCES

Adamany, D.W., and G.E. Agree. 1980. *Political Money: A Strategy for Campaign Financing in America.* Baltimore: Johns Hopkins University Press.

Alexander, H.E. 1980. "Political Finance Regulation in International Perspective." In *Parties, Interest Groups and Campaign Finance Laws,* ed. M.J. Malbin. Washington, DC: American Enterprise Institute for Public Policy Research.

———. 1989. "Money and Politics: A Conceptual Framework." In *Comparative Political Finance in the 1980s,* ed. H.E. Alexander. Cambridge: Cambridge University Press.

Angell, H.M. 1966. "The Evolution and Application of Quebec Election Expense Legislation, 1960–66." In Canada, Committee on Election Expenses, 1966. *Report.* Ottawa: Queen's Printer.

Beck, J. Murray. 1968. *Pendulum of Power: Canada's Federal Elections.* Scarborough: Prentice-Hall.

Bell, D.V. 1990. "Political Culture in Canada." In *Canadian Politics in the 1990s,* ed. M.S. Whittington and G. Williams. Scarborough: Nelson Canada.

Berger, Suzanne. 1981. *Organizing Interests in Western Europe.* Cambridge: Cambridge University Press.

Boggs, Carl. 1986. *Social Movements and Political Power: Emerging Forms of Radicalism in the West.* Philadelphia: Temple University Press.

Boyer, J.P. 1983. *Money and Message: The Law Governing Election Financing, Advertising, Broadcasting and Campaigning in Canada.* Toronto: Butterworths.

Bradford, Neil. 1989. "Ideas, Intellectuals and Social Democracy in Canada." In *Canadian Parties in Transition: Discourse, Organization, and Representation*, ed. A.G. Gagnon and A.B. Tanguay. Scarborough: Nelson Canada.

Brodie, Janine, and Jane Jenson. 1988. *Crisis, Challenge and Change: Party and Class in Canada Revisited*. Ottawa: Carleton University Press.

———. 1989. "Piercing the Smokescreen: Brokerage Politics and Class Politics in Canada." In *Canadian Parties in Transition: Discourse, Organization, and Representation*, ed. A.G. Gagnon and A.B. Tanguay. Scarborough: Nelson Canada.

Cairns, Alan. 1968. "The Electoral System and the Party System in Canada, 1921–65." *Canadian Journal of Political Science* 1:55–80.

Cameron, Duncan. 1989. "Political Discourse in the 1980s." In *Canadian Parties in Transition: Discourse, Organization, and Representation*, ed. A.G. Gagnon and A.B. Tanguay. Scarborough: Nelson Canada.

Canada. Committee on Election Expenses. 1966. *Report*. Ottawa: Queen's Printer.

Canada. Elections Canada. 1988a. *Report of the Chief Electoral Officer, Thirty-Fourth General Election, Appendices*. Ottawa: Minister of Supply and Services Canada.

———. 1988b. *Report of the Chief Electoral Officer Respecting Election Expenses, Thirty-Fourth General Election 1988*. Ottawa: Minister of Supply and Services Canada.

Christian, William, and Colin Campbell. 1983. *Political Parties and Ideologies in Canada*. 2d ed. Toronto: McGraw-Hill.

Ciaurro, G. F. 1989. "Public Financing of Parties in Italy." In *Comparative Political Finance in the 1980s*, ed. H.E. Alexander. Cambridge: Cambridge University Press.

Clarke, H., J. Jenson, L. LeDuc and J. Pammett. 1979. *Political Choice in Canada*. Toronto: McGraw-Hill.

———. 1991. *Absent Mandate: Interpreting Change in Canadian Politics*. 2d ed. Toronto: Gage.

del Castillo Vera, Pilar. 1985. *La Financiación de partidos y candidatos en las democracias occidentales*. Madrid: Siglo Vientiuno.

Doublet, Y.-M. 1990. *Le Financement de la vie politique*. Paris: Seuil.

Ewing, Keith. 1987. *The Funding of Political Parties in Britain*. Cambridge: Cambridge University Press.

Findlay, Sue. 1987. "Facing the State: The Politics of the Women's Movement Reconsidered." In *Feminism and Political Economy*, ed. H.J. Maroney and Meg Luxton. Toronto: Methuen.

Fiori, R.S. 1988. "A Comparative Analysis of English and American Campaign Finance Law." *Hastings International and Comparative Law Review* 11.

Gunlicks, A.B. 1988. "Campaign and Party Finance in the West German 'Party State'." *Review of Politics* 50 (1): 30–48.

Hoffmann-Martinot, Vincent. 1990. "Grüne et Verts: deux faces de l'écologisme européen."

Ingelhart, Ronald. 1990. *Culture Shift in Advanced Industrial Society.* Princeton: Princeton University Press.

Jenson, Jane. 1975. "Party Loyalty in Canada: The Question of Party Identification." *Canadian Journal of Political Science* 8:543–53.

———. 1982. "The Modern Women's Movements in Italy, France and Great Britain." In *Comparative Social Research*, ed. R.F. Tomassen. Greenwich: JAI.

———. 1986. "Gender and Reproduction: Or, Babies and the State." *Studies in Political Economy* 20 (Summer): 9–46.

———. 1989a. "'Different' but not 'Exceptional': Canada's Permeable Fordism." *Canadian Review of Sociology and Anthropology* 26:69–94.

———. 1989b. "From *baba cool* to a *vote utile*: The Trajectory of the French Verts." *French Politics and Society* 6(4).

———. 1991. "All the World's a Stage: Ideas, Time and Space in Canadian Political Economy." *Studies in Political Economy* 36 (Fall 1991).

Kheitmi, M.R. 1964. *Les Partis politiques et le droit positif français.* Paris: Pichon et Durand-Auzias.

Kitschelt, Herbert. 1989. *The Logics of Party Competition.* Ithaca: Cornell University Press.

Koole, Rude. 1989. "The 'Modesty' of Dutch Party Finance." In *Comparative Political Finance in the 1980s*, ed. H.E. Alexander. Cambridge: Cambridge University Press.

Leonard, Dick. 1979. "Contrasts in Selected Western Democracies: Germany, Sweden, and Britain." In *Political Finance*, ed. H.E. Alexander. Beverly Hills: Sage.

Lipset, S.M., and S. Rokkan. 1967. *Party Systems and Voter Alignments.* Princeton: Princeton University Press.

Macpherson, C.B. 1977. *The Life and Times of Liberal Democracy.* London: Oxford University Press.

Maier, Charles. 1987. *Changing Boundaries of the Political.* Cambridge: Cambridge University Press.

Meisel, John. 1985. "The Decline of Party in Canada." In *Party Politics in Canada,* 5th ed., ed. H.G. Thorburn. Scarborough: Prentice-Hall.

Mishler, William, and Harold Clarke. 1990. "Political Participation in Canada." In *Canadian Politics in the 1990s,* ed. M.S. Whittington and G. Williams. Scarborough: Nelson Canada.

Nassmacher, K.-H. 1989. "Structure and Impact of Public Subsidies to Political Parties in Europe: The Examples of Austria, Italy, Sweden and West Germany." In *Comparative Political Finance in the 1980s,* ed. H.E. Alexander. Cambridge: Cambridge University Press.

Ontario. Commission on Election Contributions and Expenses. 1982. *Canadian Election Reform: Dialogue on Issues and Effects.* Toronto: The Commission.

Paltiel, K.Z. 1970. *Political Party Financing in Canada.* Toronto: McGraw-Hill.

———. 1980. "Public Financing Abroad: Contrasts and Effects." In *Parties, Interest Groups, and Campaign Finance Laws,* ed. M.J. Malbin. Washington, DC: American Enterprise Institute for Public Policy Research.

———. 1988. "The 1984 Federal Election and Developments in Canadian Party Finance." In *Canada at the Polls 1984,* ed. Howard Penniman. Durham: Duke University Press.

———. 1989. "Canadian Election Expense Legislation, 1963–85: A Critical Appraisal or Was the Effort Worth It?" In *Comparative Political Finance in the 1980s,* ed. H. E. Alexander. Cambridge: Cambridge University Press.

Pinto-Duschinsky, Michael. 1989. "Trends in British Political Funding, 1979–84." In *Comparative Political Finance in the 1980s,* ed. H.E. Alexander. Cambridge: Cambridge University Press.

———. 1991. "The Party Foundations and Political Finance in Germany." In *Comparative Issues in Party and Election Finance.* Vol. 4 of the research studies of the Royal Commission on Electoral Reform and Party Financing. Ottawa and Toronto: RCERPF/Dundurn.

Regenstrief, Peter. 1964. *The Diefenbaker Interlude.* New York: Longmans.

Schneider, H.-P. 1989. "The New German System of Party Funding." In *Comparative Political Finance in the 1980s,* ed. H.E. Alexander. Cambridge: Cambridge University Press.

Schoomaker, Donald. 1988. "The Changing Party Scene in West Germany and the Consequences for Stable Democracy." *Review of Politics* 50:49–70.

Seidle, F.L. 1980. "State Aid for Political Parties." *The Parliamentarian* 61 (April): 79–86.

———. 1985. "The Election Expenses Act: The House of Commons and the Parties." In *The Canadian House of Commons: Essays in Honour of Norman Ward,* ed. J.C. Courtney. Calgary: University of Calgary Press.

Seidle, F.L., and K.Z. Paltiel. 1981. "Party Finance, the Election Expenses Act, and Campaign Spending in 1979 and 1980." In *Canada at the Polls 1979 and 1980,* ed. H.R. Penniman. Washington, DC: American Enterprise Institute for Public Policy Research.

Toinet, M.F. 1988. "The Elections of 1981: Political Background and Legal Setting." In *France at the Polls, 1981 and 1986,* ed. H.R. Penniman. Durham: Duke University Press.

United States. Library of Congress. 1979. *Government Financing of National Elections.* Washington, DC: Library of Congress.

von Nordheim, Manfred. 1980. "Commentaries." In *Parties, Interest Groups, and Campaign Finance Law,* ed. M.J. Malbin. Washington, DC: American Enterprise Institute for Public Policy Research.

4

THE PARTY FOUNDATIONS AND POLITICAL FINANCE IN GERMANY

Michael Pinto-Duschinsky

Money MAY BE used to secure political influence in many ways and through a variety of channels. If especially stringent regulations are applied to control candidates' election expenses and party funding, there will be a natural tendency for politicians and their supporters to develop other methods of political financing using organizations that are not called "parties" – and, therefore, are not subject to the same restrictions – but actually perform similar functions.

The German political foundations (*Stiftungen*) are the prime example of bodies that legally are independent of political parties but in practice are involved in electoral and party politics.

To understand the legislation that governs political funding in Germany, it is therefore vital to take account of the fact that the national, regional and local organizations of the political parties are only one part of a larger party system. It has the following three major components:

- extraparliamentary party organizations;
- parliamentary party organizations and legislators' personal staffs; and
- political foundations (*Stiftungen*).[1]

Studies of political funding in Germany often concentrate on the parties. This is partly because the political foundations have frequently been secretive about their operations (Forrester 1985). By contrast, this study will explore the activities of the political foundations – particularly their domestic activities – and will discuss whether these bodies provide ways in which constitutional restrictions on political parties can be evaded.

Apart from their interest as possible devices whereby restrictions on party funding may be circumvented, the German political foundations are also significant because, as argued by their domestic and foreign admirers, they have valuable democracy-building functions in addition to those normally carried out by party organizations. According to one British Labour member of Parliament, the party foundations are a political "miracle" on a par with the West German economic miracle: "German democracy, as much alive and just as effective as our own, is the real miracle of postwar Europe ... The state-financed foundations – small-scale universities, each mainly serving one of the political parties – have now, at long last, given Germany thinking political parties, trained officials, mutually fruitful international links and increasingly educated memberships ... I know that the firm, vigorous democracy that now exists in the Federal Republic of Germany would not be in so healthy a state had it not been for these foundations" (Fletcher 1978). The main political foundations are:

- The Konrad Adenauer Foundation (KAS), linked with the Christian Democratic Union;
- The Friedrich Ebert Foundation (FES), linked with the Social Democratic Party;
- The Friedrich Naumann Foundation (FNS), linked with the Free Democratic Party;
- The Hanns Seidel Foundation (HSS), linked with the Christian Social Union.

There are additional political foundations in some of the *Länder* (states). Their connections are with political party organizations at the state level. (See Vieregge 1977, especially chap. 2.) There is also a set of foundations linked with the Green Party (*Die Grünen*), the decentralized Rainbow (*Regenbogen*) Foundation. This group will not be considered in the paper because its activities are on a relatively small scale. The public subsidies for the Rainbow Foundation, introduced before the 1990 elections to the Bundestag (House of Representatives), were due to increase over a period of years to the levels enjoyed by the Naumann (FDP) and Seidel (CSU) foundations. The poor performance of the Green Party in the elections and its failure (except in the *Länder* of the former DDR) to surmount the 5 percent barrier needed to secure representation in the Bundestag put in doubt the future of grants to the Rainbow Foundation.

The study will summarize the historical background of the main *Stiftungen;* it will then analyse their funding and organization and their relationships to the extraparliamentary party organizations and to such governmental bodies as the Chancellor's Office; finally it will evaluate the regulations relating to political funding in Germany. This last section will consider the funding of the party system as a whole, including both the extraparliamentary party organizations and the *Stiftungen.*

The study was prepared at a time when the unification of the Federal German Republic and the German Democratic Republic was taking place. The party foundations responded quickly to the political changes in East Germany in 1989–90, and they are currently being further affected by the unification process and by the recent decision to adopt Berlin as the capital. The foundations' role in the process of German unification will be summarized.

HISTORICAL BACKGROUND

When the German Federal Republic was created and the Basic Law enacted in 1949, the constitution-makers and the occupying powers were determined to encourage the development of pluralist democratic institutions such as parties and trade unions. Since free political organizations had been banned under the Nazis, their revival was to be fostered by programs of governmental action. There was also a desire to avoid a repetition of what were seen as the weaknesses of the Weimar Constitution (in particular, the proliferation of small political parties in the legislature).

These aims affected the political institutions and programs introduced during the early years of the new republic. In the first place, the Basic Law included provisions specifying a strong role for political parties and an "equality of chances" for them (Tsatsos and Morlok 1982). The extent to which political parties are mentioned in Article 21 of the Basic Law is a distinctive feature of the West German constitutional system. It has meant that legislation regarding parties and party financing has been repeatedly challenged before the Constitutional Court in Karlsruhe.

Second, from 1953 the right to seats in the Bundestag was restricted to parties gaining at least 5 percent of the national vote. This "exclusion clause" was intended to limit the number of political parties and thereby to promote political stability and avoid extremism. Later, laws relating to public funding for political parties were intended to discriminate against splinter parties, though the rights of these small parties were sometimes protected by the Constitutional Court.

Third, there were active programs of civic education. Starting in 1945, German prisoners of war held in Britain who were classified as anti-Nazi were invited to attend political education courses at Wilton Park. The courses were intended to reintroduce them to habits of free discussion and political participation. A former prisoner of war who later became a senior official at the federal development ministry (BMZ) and was influential in promoting the system of federal grants for the party foundations described his experience as a German member of staff at Wilton Park as a "date with freedom."

"Education for democracy" became a major feature of German life under Allied occupation in the late 1940s.[2] The newly created West German authorities encouraged similar programs in the 1950s. One significant institution was the "free academy" at Loccum in Lower Saxony. The need to counter the ideological offensive of the rival Communist regime in East Germany and to reply to propaganda funded by the Soviet bloc provided a further motive for offering government funds for civic education. Subsidies for propaganda went to organizations representing groups of immigrants ("expellees") who had previously lived in territories beyond the Oder-Neisse line, which came under Polish rule in 1945.

In 1952, a federally funded organization for political education was created. Originally named the Bundeszentrale für Heimatdienst, it later became the federal political education centre or Bundeszentrale für politische Bildung. It was funded by the interior ministry (BMI). Parallel organizations at the state level were set up to subsidize political education courses and publications. Political education institutions existed earlier, both at the time of the Weimar Republic (the Reichszentrale für Heimatdienst) and, notoriously, under the Nazis. Indeed, a major objective of the institution created in the 1950s was to counteract the legacy of Goebbels (Bundeszentrale für politische Bildung 1988, 9, and 1990, 9).

Partly under the sponsorship of the Bundeszentrale für politische Bildung, a whole range of institutions, including religious organizations and trade unions, arranged lectures, residential courses lasting for a weekend or for a few days, discussion groups and other forms of education in democratic citizenship.[3] The political parties also became active in the enterprise.

Some political education was organized by the party organizations themselves. Special political academies, linked with the parties but with their own distinct identities, were set up during the 1950s. The oldest of these political *Stiftungen* was the Friedrich Ebert Foundation. It had been founded in 1925, shortly after the death of Ebert, the first president of the Weimar Republic and its leading Social Democratic politician. His political followers in the Social Democratic Party solicited contributions to form a memorial fund by requesting money in lieu of flowers for his funeral. The proceeds were used to provide bursaries for "talented proletarian youths." By the time the Ebert Foundation was formally banned by the Nazis in 1933, it had provided 295 such bursaries.

In 1947, following a resolution by the German Federation of Socialist Students, the Friedrich Ebert Foundation was re-established (Friedrich-Ebert-Stiftung 1989). It later received compensation for the confiscation of its assets by the Nazi regime.[4]

This funding helped the foundation to build a new program of activities as a part of the Social Democratic Party's network. In 1956, the *Stiftung* expanded its work and inaugurated the first of several residential centres for political education courses and discussions. These institutions are known as *Heimvolkshochschulen*. The building opened in 1956 was situated at Bergneustadt near Cologne. The foundation again started to offer a limited number of scholarships to students and acted in the late 1950s as a channel for occasional international political projects funded by the foreign ministry (Auswärtiges Amt) (see Pinto-Duschinsky 1991).

Supporters of the ruling Christian Democratic party (CDU) soon set up a counterpart to the Ebert Foundation. In 1956, they established a "political academy" at Eichholz, a castle near Bonn. This institution became operational in 1958 and formed the basis of what was in 1964 to become the Konrad Adenauer Foundation. The Free Democrats followed suit in 1958 with the Friedrich Naumann Foundation, named in memory of a Liberal leader who had set up a short-lived political school after the First World War. In these early years, the political foundations operated on a small scale compared with their size in later years. However, they soon became significant components of their parent parties, involving themselves in research and publication as well as in "education for democracy."

The *Stiftungen* developed steadily in the 1960s. This was partly because of important changes concerning the funding of the party organizations themselves. The foundations benefited from a series of decisions by the Constitutional Court about party finance, since the judgements restricted both private and public payments to political parties. Thus, the foundations were increasingly used as substitute channels of political funding.

While the Social Democratic Party (SPD) financed itself in the 1950s largely through the subscriptions of its members and through a series of party enterprises, the CDU and FDP received heavy backing from associations of business sponsors (Heidenheimer 1957; Duebber and Braunthal 1963; Heidenheimer and Langdon 1968). The extensive business contributions to the parties of the centre and the right were a reflection of the re-establishment and prosperity of some of Germany's main banks and industrial enterprises.

In addition to business money, party campaigning and propaganda – especially on behalf of the ruling CDU – received considerable support from public funds during the 1950s. It is almost impossible to provide an accurate picture of these early state subsidies, as many of them were secret and others were dispersed or disguised.

During the period of postwar occupation, assistance had come from Allied military governments and from funds related to the Marshall Aid program for a variety of "democracy-building" projects. The United States Central Intelligence Agency was involved in a number of payments for German politics in the early years of the new republic, while political aid for the far left came from the Soviet bloc.

By the 1950s, Konrad Adenauer had re-established a secret discretionary fund financed by German taxpayers. He could draw on this fund in his capacity as chancellor. Some of the money from this Chancellor fund (popularly known as the "reptile fund") was reportedly used to assist the cause of the CDU during the election campaign of 1957. According to Uwe Kitzinger, "It was generally admitted that Government funds were used on a large scale before and during the election to propagate the Government's foreign, military, and domestic policies among the electorate. The Chancellor's fund of 11 million DM per annum was one of the chief sources of finance for such activity, the Press and Information Office with its annual budget of 20 million DM ... and the information budgets of the various ministries, particularly that of the Ministry of Defence, which amounted to 6 million DM per annum were also used ... for ... activity of this kind" (Kitzinger 1960, 311).

The 1957 election produced the third successive defeat for the Social Democrats. Though the party had 600 000 members, compared with the CDU's total of 250 000, business contributions made the CDU considerably richer and able easily to outspend the SPD in campaigns. There followed a challenge in the Constitutional Court. In 1958 the Court declared that it was unconstitutional to grant tax exemptions for business donations to political parties (Heidenheimer and Langdon 1968). The judgement threatened to damage the fund-raising advantages enjoyed by the governing party, the CDU.

In 1959, the Christian Democrats responded by introducing an annual DM5 million subsidy in the federal budget "for the promotion of political education by the parties" (Schleth and Pinto-Duschinsky 1970, 43). Public subsidies could be expected to compensate for the shortfall in corporate political payments as part of the coalition bargaining. An additional DM15 million was granted in 1962 as "special funds for the tasks of political parties according to Article 21 of the Constitution." In 1964, the total federal government subsidy to the main parties was raised to DM38 million.

From 1960 onward, a number of governments at the state level followed Lower Saxony's lead in introducing their own party subsidies.

Besides the direct payments by the federal and state governments to party organizations, further public funding went to the party foundations. By the early 1960s, the *Stiftungen* were already receiving small-scale support for particular projects from state and federal authorities. In 1962, a committee of the Bundestag voted narrowly to allocate funds to the *Stiftungen* for projects involving political education in developing countries from the budget of the recently created federal development ministry (BMZ). This source of public finance was to mushroom, from DM130 000 in 1962 to over DM45 million by 1970. Though these funds were earmarked for overseas work, the resulting increase in the budgets of the *Stiftungen* and in their headquarters staffs was of indirect benefit to their domestic activities.

Though the Constitutional Court's judgement of 1958 had helped the SPD opposition by removing corporations' rights to tax deductions for their contributions to political parties, some SPD politicians remained unhappy about the escalation of public subsidies for the parties from 1959 onward. The latter arguably compensated the Christian Democrats for their relatively small number of members and their insignificant income from membership subscriptions (Duebber and Braunthal 1963, 779). The SPD government in the state of Hesse mounted a constitutional challenge against the subsidies. Fringe parties such as the National Democratic Party joined the case, claiming that the subsidies contravened the Basic Law's requirement of "equality of chances" for political parties, since it handicapped new and small parties.

The challenge proved successful. In 1966, "The Court ... ruled that the Constitution calls for a 'free and open process of opinion and will formation leading from the people to the organs of the state, not in the reverse direction' ... The judges declared the federal subsidization practice a threat to these principles. They declared the then existing public subsidies program unconstitutional because it would have turned the continuous financial support of the parties into an obligation of the state. However, the court's opinion indicated that reimbursement of the 'necessary costs of an appropriate *election campaign*' from public funds would be admissible if this were extended to smaller parties as well" (Schleth and Pinto-Duschinsky 1970, 45).

In response to this judgement, a Parties Law was enacted in 1967. Under the revised system, the only public subsidy to extraparliamentary party organizations was to be for campaign expenditure in Bundestag elections. In 1979, federal campaign reimbursements were extended to include elections to the European Parliament, and the rates of reimbursement for German federal elections were raised by the Parties Law of 1983. From 1967, *Länder* governments introduced their own schemes to subsidize parties on account of *Länder* elections.

The intent of the Constitutional Court was nevertheless evaded by the Bundestag from 1967 onward in two important ways. First, the Parties Law of 1967 stretched the definition of "campaign" expenditure. It was argued that party organizations must prepare for an election campaign over a period of years. Thus, expenditures that may have appeared to be routine actually needed to be categorized as campaign items. The "campaign only" provisions were expanded on these grounds to include considerable payments for party organization between elections, with 60 percent of the new federal grants payable in years prior to the election (Wildenmann 1987, 96).

Second, the Bundestag introduced a new form of federal political subsidy. It would not be paid to parties, but rather to the political foundations. An annual block grant (*Globalzuschuss*) was to be paid from the budget of the interior ministry for the benefit of a foundation linked with each party represented in the Bundestag. Since these *Stiftungen* were legally independent entities, their activities were not subject to the Constitutional Court's recent judgement. Moreover, the political foundations did not have to account for their use of the subsidy on a project by project basis.

The use of party foundations not only circumvented the 1966 Constitutional Court ruling in making possible a continuation of public subsidies for non-campaign purposes, it served the interests of the established parties in another way, too. Whereas the campaign subsidies to parties, introduced in 1967, were available – following the Constitutional Court's decision mandating "equality of chances" – to all parties gaining at least 0.5 percent of the national vote, the new "global subsidy" for the party foundations was restricted to *Stiftungen* associated with parties with at least 5 percent of the vote.

From 1967 onward, the party foundations thus benefited not only from ever-growing federal grants for foreign political projects (from the development ministry), but also from the interior ministry's new block grants for their domestic activities. They also obtained smaller, but nevertheless substantial, payments from a number of other federal ministries and from state governments.

Until 1967, there were foundations attached to the CDU, SPD and FDP. In order to take advantage of the global subsidy from the interior ministry, the CDU's coalition partner, the Bavarian Christian Social Union (CSU), created a political foundation of its own in that year, though it was not until 1976 that the new *Stiftung*, the Hanns Seidel Foundation, received grants from the development ministry for foreign projects.

The status of the *Stiftungen* was conveniently ambiguous. To qualify for the interior ministry's global subsidy, each foundation was required to be attached to one of the political parties represented in the Bundestag. This rule avoided the need to give a share of the interior ministry's subsidy to parties that had failed to gain 5 percent of the vote in a national election (and therefore failed to qualify for seats in the Bundestag) or to nonpolitical organizations. At the same time, the foundations had to be formally distinct from parties to escape from the restrictions imposed by the Constitutional Court's decisions of 1958 and 1966. The political foundations were thus referred to by a technical term, *parteinahe*, i.e., "near" to a party. In other words, they could be treated either as party or nonparty organs according to need.[5]

The legal separation between party and *Stiftung* had a further advantage for the major parties. Following the Constitutional Court's ruling of 1958, corporate donations to political parties failed to qualify for tax exceptions. By contrast, business payments to the political foundations remained tax exempt. It was therefore tax efficient to conduct as many political functions as possible through the foundations, for example, policy research and opinion polling. Because of their privileged status, the *Stiftungen* were able to supplement their income from public subsidies with donations, though the lion's share of their income came from the state.

To sustain a separate legal identity, the *Stiftungen* had their own governing boards; to assure the party link, the members of the boards were leading party politicians, ministers, legislators or public figures who were active in party circles (see table 4.4).

By the 1970s, the escalating subsidies made the party foundations an increasingly significant force in West German politics. The established parties had a strong collective interest in safeguarding their benefits under the system against public criticism and against complaints from fringe parties, which were excluded from it. A leading official of one foundation referred in an interview to the regular meetings between senior officials of the *Stiftungen* linked with the rival political parties as gatherings of members of a "club." An official of another *Stiftung* expressed the view, "We're more than a club, we're a mafia."

The growth of the party foundations emerges clearly from an examination of the totals received in grants from the federal government, their main but not their only source of revenue. Payments from the development ministry to the *Stiftungen* for projects in Third World countries grew from DM0.13 million in 1962 and DM28.7 million in 1969 to DM91.2 million in 1975, DM155.5 million in 1980 and DM218.7 million in 1985. The interior ministry's "global" grants for the foundations' domestic activities started at a total rate of DM9.0 million a year in 1967 and DM10.0 million in 1969 and then increased to DM42.5 million in 1975, DM72.6 million in 1980, DM99.3 million in 1985 and no less than DM184.9 million in 1990 (see table 4.2).

The escalation of public funding for the foundations is also demonstrated by the actual totals received from the federal treasury. The totals include subsidies from a variety of budget categories ("titles") and from a number of federal ministries, including the BMZ and BMI. Overall federal government payments to the *Stiftungen* increased from DM74.3 million in 1970 and DM160.6 million in 1975 to DM270.9 million in 1980, DM381.5 million in 1985 and over DM500 million in 1990 (see table 4.3).

By the early 1980s, the role of the party foundations had become one of a set of concerns about political financing in the Federal German Republic. A particular worry was about the effects of the inconsistency that meant that large donations directly to the parties were subject to the payments of income taxes whereas donations to the party foundations were not. This provided an incentive for donors and parties to direct political payments to the foundations on the understanding that the money would then be transferred to their associated parties. (However, it should be noted that the foundations were not the only or the main devices for laundering donations to the parties.)

In March 1982, the Federal President, Professor Dr. Karl Carstens, set up a cross-party committee of experts to study and to report on the issues relating to party finance. The committee recommended, among other things, that payments by the *Stiftungen* to the parties should be impermissible, that the foundations' accounts should be more intensively audited and that both parties and *Stiftungen* should have separate chairmen and treasurers at the national level. The committee based some of its recommendations on the premise "that it is inappropriate for a free democracy to discriminate in terms of tax laws against political parties in relation to other organizations" (Schneider 1989, 226).

Following the committee's report, a new Parties Law was enacted in 1983. It incorporated only some of the recommendations. The law was challenged in the Constitutional Court by the Greens. The case was occasioned not only by the new law itself but also by scandals that had filled the press since 1981. The "Flick affair" was by far the most important, but by no means the only one. According to Erhard Blankenburg, the widespread nature of the abuses relating to political contributions was illustrated by the fact that between 1982 and 1988, preliminary proceedings had been opened in more than 1 800 cases, involving all major parties (except the Greens) and a good part of Germany's corporate élite. Few of the cases were taken to court, however, "as most of them were either dismissed or settled by fines in a plea-bargaining fashion" (Blankenburg et al. 1989, 920–21).

There is no need here to describe the revelations and allegations relating to the Flick concern's remarkable political donations, which amounted to DM26 million between 1969 and 1980 (Alemann 1989, 865). It is enough to point out that the Flick affair developed into one of West Germany's most serious corruption scandals. It was suggested that in return for extensive political payments, the Flick concern had obtained massive tax concessions as a result of discretionary government decisions. The charge was not proved in court, though two former federal economics ministers, Hans Friderichs and Otto Graf Lambsdorff, were fined in 1987 for their role in illegally channelling corporate donations (Blankenburg et al. 1989, 926).

The fact that the Flick concern had given payments amounting to DM4.4 million to the party foundations raised questions about their roles as channels for tax-free payments to political parties (Forrester 1985, 44). The Ebert Foundation received DM2.76 million between 1975 and 1980; the Naumann Foundation, DM1.35 million, the Seidel Foundation DM280 000 and the Adenauer Foundation, DM10 000.

Other questionable practices relating to the *Stiftungen* emerged. The Friedrich Naumann Foundation lost its tax-privileged status for the years 1978–82 when it was discovered that it had, in effect, provided services for the Free Democratic Party by giving its own staffers time to work for the party, by making cars available for party purposes, by subsidizing party literature through its block subscriptions and in other ways (Wewer 1988b and information from the Naumann Foundation).

In their case before the Constitutional Court, the Greens argued that the public grants to the foundations effectively constituted payments for the benefit of the parties linked with the foundations. The payments were therefore unconstitutional, argued the Greens, since the system excluded fringe parties from its largesse and thus was contrary to the "equality of chances" guaranteed by the Basic Law. The

Constitutional Court's decision, delivered in 1986, failed to implement the Greens' aim, resulting instead in their incorporation into the system. The new party obtained the right to receive federal grants for a foundation of its own. With some misgivings, the Greens accepted their new right to public money and established the decentralized Rainbow Foundation. While confirming the constitutionality of federal subsidies to party foundations, the 1986 Court ruling nevertheless attacked some practices of the *Stiftungen*. A recent report of the federal audit office has also criticized them.

As a result of these recent scandals, a stricter boundary line has been drawn between the funding of *Stiftungen* and of their related political parties. Nonetheless, as will be argued later, even if the foundations no longer serve as channels for private payments to the West German parties, it is not practicable to establish clear distinctions between some of the operations of the parties and of the party foundations. They still carry out work that is of benefit to their related parties.

FUNDING AND ORGANIZATION

Public Funding of the Political Foundations

A useful introduction to the functions of the party foundations is provided by a review of their finances. One useful source of financial information and organization is found in the annual reports of the *Stiftungen*. These reports are nevertheless not presented in a format that permits comparison between foundations. They do not give a clear picture of private donations and, in the past, they have probably omitted some special funds. Moreover, the accounts do not permit the reader to make an accurate breakdown of spending for domestic and for foreign purposes. This is because some items, such as administration, may cover both home and overseas projects.

Official reports are a second source. The problem here is that most categories ("titles") in the published federal budgets include money given both to the *Stiftungen* and to other organizations. It is often impossible to derive the totals given to the foundations alone. Breakdowns of spending under certain headings are given in special documents presented to the relevant Bundestag committees, but these are sometimes confidential documents. Some of the most precise and comprehensive information about federal grants to the party foundations was included in an answer to a set of parliamentary questions put by the Greens in 1986 (Drucksache 10/5281). This answer includes details of federal grants to the *Stiftungen* under different categories (titles) from 1970 to 1986.

Assuming that the party foundations' published accounts include all special funds and private contributions (not always a safe assumption in the past), the vast bulk of their income is from the federal budget. For example, these federal subsidies accounted for over 90 percent of the Adenauer Foundation's budget in each year between 1980 and 1986, ranging from a low of 91.3 percent of the total in 1980 to 98.4 percent in 1981 (Schürmann 1989, 49).

According to the budgets of the Adenauer and Naumann foundations for 1989 and for the Ebert and Seidel foundations for 1988, sources of the combined incomes of the four organizations (net of loans and fees for courses) were as follows:

- federal government subsidies 95 percent;
- other public subsidies (mainly from state governments) 2 percent;
- donations 1 percent; and
- other 2 percent.

The growth in total federal government subsidies to the *Stiftungen* from 1970 is given in table 4.1, which is derived from Drucksache (10/5281, 2). The statistics include grants for both domestic and foreign purposes.

The major categories of federal government grants to the *Stiftungen* (figures from 1985 in millions of DM) are as follows:

A. *Grants for domestic purposes*

Bundesministerium des Inneren
(Interior Ministry – BMI)
    Global subsidy   99.3

Bundesministerium für Bildung und Wissenschaft
(Education Ministry – BMBW)
    Scholarships and grants for German students   23.0

Bundesministerium für innerdeutsche Beziehungen
(Ministry for Inner-German Relations – BMiB)
    Events and visits to West Berlin   4.3

B. *Grants for foreign purposes*

Bundesministerium für wirtschaftliche Zusammenarbeit
(Ministry for Economic Cooperation – BMZ)
    Projects in developing countries   218.7

Table 4.1
Total grants to the political foundations by the federal government, 1970–86
(in thousands of DM)

Year	Friedrich-Naumann-Stiftung	Friedrich-Ebert-Stiftung	Hanns-Seidel-Stiftung	Konrad-Adenauer-Stiftung	Totals
1970	12 210	32 806	1 606	27 684	74 306
1971	11 650	44 613	1 653	35 982	93 898
1972	15 442	52 345	2 361	38 386	108 534
1973	15 917	50 380	3 193	41 224	110 714
1974	22 671	71 146	4 667	48 982	147 466
1975	23 927	71 873	6 178	58 587	160 565
1976	25 658	66 402	6 079	56 229	154 368
1977	29 355	78 082	9 712	65 054	182 203
1978	33 685	90 185	13 794	73 496	211 160
1979	40 175	104 453	16 611	84 569	245 808
1980	44 035	114 996	23 615	88 252	270 898
1981	48 975	118 457	31 903	105 655	304 990
1982	49 976	120 765	37 432	109 091	317 264
1983	51 426	122 382	42 527	114 855	331 190
1984	53 782	124 753	46 614	117 971	343 120
1985	56 444	139 684	58 152	127 267	381 547
1986	61 296	136 177	59 979	134 983	392 435

Source: Deutscher Bundestag, Drucksache 10/5281, 04.04.86, Antwort der Bundesregierung
auf die Kleine Anfrage der Abgeordneten Schily, Suhr und der Fraktion DIE GRÜNEN —
Drucksache 10/4652. (German Federal Parliament, Publication 10/5281, 04.04.86, response of the
federal government to the question of the members Schily and Suhr and the Green Party caucus
— Publication 10/4652.)

> Auswärtiges Amt
> (Foreign Ministry – AA)
>   Scholarships for foreign students and for
>   *Stiftungen* in industrialized countries   21.8

Payments for domestic purposes accounted for 28 percent of the federal government's various subsidies to the *Stiftungen* in 1970. The proportion rose to 35 percent in 1980 and in 1985. In 1989, about 40 percent of the money granted to the foundations from public coffers was for domestic purposes. As will be evident from these statistics, overseas political projects constituted the largest area of activity of the party foundations. These foreign undertakings will be covered only briefly in this study.

The growth of the federal interior ministry's "global subsidy" to the foundations is shown in table 4.2. This grant is the main source of money for the foundations' programs within Germany.

The federal education ministry's payments since 1970 are given in table 4.3. The money is mainly for scholarships to German students, which are awarded by the *Stiftungen*.

Organizational Structure

In view of their large budgets, it is not surprising that the party foundations maintain extensive offices both within the Federal German Republic and abroad. The Friedrich Ebert Foundation's red brick complex in Bonn, situated close to the Social Democratic Party's headquarters, is being considerably extended. In addition, the foundation maintains Karl Marx's house in Trier, a meeting centre for its scholarship holders in Bonn-Venusberg, six branch offices in West Germany and eight residential education centres (Annual Report 1989).

The Adenauer Foundation's headquarters, which the weekly magazine *Der Spiegel* jokingly likened to an insurance company office, is in Sankt Augustin, a modern suburb of Bonn, several miles away from the Christian Democratic Union's headquarters. The foundation has a residential centre and offices at Schloss Eichholz and, by 1990, had 14 other centres in different parts of Germany (Konrad-Adenauer-Stiftung 1990b, 35).

Until 1984, the Friedrich Naumann Foundation shared its headquarters building with its associated political party, the FDP. The foundation then moved into separate premises several miles away. Its main office is now in the picturesque Margarethenhof, a converted resort hotel and conference centre in the hills above Königswinter, near Bonn.[6] The foundation also rents premises in Berlin and has political education centres in attractive surroundings in Saarbrücken and Konstanz. Further centres are planned in Lauenburg, near Hamburg, and at two sites in the former German Democratic Republic.

The Hanns Seidel Foundation's headquarters is in a converted apartment building in Munich. The *Stiftung* operates two major educational centres in Bavaria and an office in Bonn.

The Friedrich Ebert Foundation's full-time staff numbered 754 in 1989. The total included 399 at the headquarters, 220 at the foundation's

Table 4.2

Global subsidies (Globalzuschüsse) to political foundations from federal interior ministry (BMI), 1967–86

(in thousands of DM)

Year	Friedrich-Naumann-Stiftung	Friedrich-Ebert-Stiftung	Hanns-Seidel-Stiftung	Konrad-Adenauer-Stiftung	Stiftungs-verband Regenbogen	Totals (rounded)
1967	1 000	3 500	1 000	3 500	0	9 000
1968	1 000	3 500	1 000	3 500	0	9 000
1969	1 100	3 900	1 100	3 900	0	10 000
1970	2 888	5 944	1 600	5 566	0	16 000
1971	2 888	5 944	1 600	5 566	0	16 000
1972	4 388	8 694	2 321	8 095	0	23 500
1973	5 721	10 861	3 154	9 761	0	29 500
1974	6 443	12 556	4 543	11 456	0	35 000
1975	7 971	14 778	6 070	13 679	0	42 500
1976	8 071	15 522	5 893	14 281	0	42 333
1977	8 917	19 959	8 660	18 132	0	55 670
1978	9 973	22 886	9 973	20 715	0	63 549
1979	10 694	25 877	10 694	23 292	0	70 358
1980	11 046	26 673	11 046	23 879	0	72 645
1981	12 097	30 421	12 097	27 212	0	81 829
1982	12 476	31 734	12 476	28 272	0	84 960
1983	12 759	32 642	12 778	29 047	0	87 226
1984	12 861	32 998	12 919	29 405	0	88 183
1985	13 964	36 067	15 274	34 033	0	99 340
1986	15 562	36 311	15 562	36 311	0	103 747
1987	18 189	41 743	19 339	44 994	0	124 265
1988	20 134	51 735	22 765	48 804	0	143 438
1989	24 277	52 882	23 547	46 526	4 181	151 413
1990	25 881	65 633	24 011	59 933	9 467	184 925

Sources: 1967–69: Vieregge (1977, 46); 1970–85 Drucksache 10/5281; 1986–90: Information from BMI (supplied by the Friedrich Naumann Foundation).

Notes: 1986–90 include grants earmarked for construction and repair of foundation buildings.

Totals are in some cases slightly inconsistent with the sum of columns.

Table 4.3
Grants by federal education ministry to political foundations, 1970–86
(in thousands of DM)

Year	Friedrich-Naumann-Stiftung	Friedrich-Ebert-Stiftung	Hanns-Seidel-Stiftung	Konrad-Adenauer-Stiftung	Totals
1970		1 557		1 113	2 670
1971		2 544		2 061	4 606
1972		3 765		2 748	6 512
1973	60	4 394		3 348	7 803
1974	229	5 048		3 811	9 087
1975	400	5 502		4 740	10 641
1976	515	5 454		4 684	10 652
1977	636	6 074		5 676	12 386
1978	971	6 594		6 246	13 811
1979	1 582	6 708		6 394	14 684
1980	1 774	7 048		6 919	15 742
1981	1 731	6 555		6 296	14 574
1982	1 984	7 450	70	7 066	16 570
1983	2 073	7 935	287	6 842	17 136
1984	2 385	8 782	855	7 516	19 538
1985	2 918	9 769	1 840	8 505	23 043
1986	3 203	10 205	2 593	9 640	25 641

Source: Drucksache 10/5281.

Note: Totals are in some cases slightly inconsistent with the sum of columns.

education centres and regional offices and 135 overseas representatives (Annual Report 1989). The figures do not include secretarial and other staff employed locally in the foundation's overseas offices.[7]

The Adenauer Foundation employed a total of 432 within Germany in 1987 and 80 field representatives stationed abroad. Many hundreds more were employed in foreign countries in connection with the foundation's overseas projects. According to Deussen (1979, 108), the number employed locally by the foundation's overseas offices and projects had reached 1 500 by 1979.

The Naumann Foundation's staff within Germany numbered 191 in 1989. There were 50 overseas representatives, as well as locally employed foreign staff.

The Seidel Foundation's payroll in 1988 included 241 within Germany, 53 overseas representatives and some 500 employed abroad.

Of the approximately 1 500 employees of the foundations within Germany, most work in the domestic programs. A precise breakdown of numbers employed in connection with domestic and foreign projects is unavailable, since several departments (dealing with finance and administration, for example) are responsible for both areas of activity.

The four political foundations have broadly similar administrative structures. Their main departments are responsible for political education, research, student grants and international activities. The *Stiftungen* also house the archives of their related parties and have active publication programs.

Formal control of the *Stiftungen* is in the hands of a set of boards of several dozen members (*Mitglieder*), of smaller executive boards and of boards of trustees. (There are slight variations between the foundations. For details, see Vieregge 1977.) The board of each foundation consists largely of senior politicians from its associated party. For example, Dr. Helmut Kohl, the Federal Chancellor, is an active member of the Adenauer Foundation's board.[8] According to Veronica Forrester's analysis in 1985, 80 percent of the Adenauer Foundation's board consisted of "leading CDU politicians," and two-thirds of the Ebert Foundation's board were SPD politicians, state premiers including three current or former state premiers, the party leader and the party general secretary.

The board included, in addition, leading trade unionists and directors of companies such as Daimler-Benz (normally card-carrying members of the party associated with each foundation). Similarly, 77 percent of the Seidel Foundation's board were CSU politicians, including the party leader, Franz-Josef Strauss. The Naumann Foundation's board of directors was chaired by Ralf Dahrendorf, and 54 percent of the board of trustees were FDP politicians, such as former Federal President Walter Scheel and Count Lambsdorff (Forrester 1985, 43).

The pattern of interlocking directorates between *Stiftungen* and parties is shown in Kress (1985). This is reproduced as table 4.4.

The party affiliations of members of the current boards of the political foundations are discussed later.

ACTIVITIES

Political Education

As already outlined, "political education" was the original function of the foundations. Their operations are in accord with the 1967 Parties Law,

Table 4.4
Party connections of board members of political foundations, 1982–84
(in percentages)

	Friedrich-Naumann-Stiftung	Friedrich-Ebert-Stiftung	Hanns-Seidel-Stiftung	Konrad-Adenauer-Stiftung
Members of the federal or state governments	23	25	28	27.5
Members of the federal or state legislatures	32	28	36	57.5
Members of organizations linked with the party associated with the Stiftung	5	31	16	10
Other	41	16	20	5
	100	100	100	100

Sources: Annual reports of the foundations, cited in Kress (1985, 26).

Note: Includes former ministers and legislators. Statistics for the Friedrich Naumann Foundation are for the Kuratorium (board of trustees). Percentages do not add to 100 because of rounding.

which assigned to them the function of "inspiring and furthering political education" (Nicolls 1984, 198). Today, the *Stiftungen* operate a whole series of residential and nonresidential facilities.

In addition to its original *Heimvolkshochschule* at Bergneustadt near Cologne, the Ebert Foundation has added seven residential educational centres in other parts of the country. The smallest, at Bad Münstereifel near Bonn, contains 35 beds in single and double rooms, while the Gustav-Heinemann-Akademie in Freudenberg, opened in 1974, caters for up to 93 people and has 49 bedrooms. The eight residential centres can accommodate a total of 495 residents, and each centre is equipped with one or more seminar rooms and with other educational and social facilities. The emphasis on residential facilities located in attractive country retreats is based on the assumption that overnight courses provide opportunities for informal discussions between participants and provide a more intensive experience than is otherwise possible.

Six regional offices of the FES provide educational facilities but have no accommodation. Ebert also has a special centre for students receiving scholarships from the *Stiftung*. Another program involves 34 regional FES discussion circles.

The Adenauer Foundation's political education activities have their headquarters at Schloss Eichholz in Wesseling, which is situated between Bonn and Cologne. Modern buildings have been added near the castle. There are 14 regional educational programs, but Schloss Eichholz is so far the foundation's only residential centre. (Another is to be built in the former DDR in Erfurt or Magdeburg.) Residential courses run by the regional educational programs use hotels or rented *Heimvolkshochschulen.*

The Hanns Seidel Foundation operates its residential seminars from two handsome buildings at opposite ends of Bavaria, one of them a converted castle and the other a former monastery (Kloster Banz and Wildbad Kreuth).

The Friedrich Naumann Foundation's main educational centre, the Theodor-Heuss-Akademie, which houses the Archive of German Liberalism, is situated at Gummersbach near Cologne, and there are "European meeting centres" in the Saarland and in West Berlin. Meetings are organized at the political club at the headquarters of the *Stiftung* at the Margarethenhof, which as already mentioned is a converted hotel in the Siebengebirge hills near Königswinter. There is another residential centre at Waldhaus Jakob near Konstanz.

The foundations' annual reports include statistics about the conferences, seminars and courses offered at these attractive locations. A summary of numbers attending such courses and events in 1982 is given by Kress. This information is reproduced as table 4.5.

According to the most recent annual report of the Friedrich Ebert Foundation, a total of 53 579 people attended political education events in 1989. The foundation held 2 152 courses and meetings.

An internal Konrad Adenauer Foundation report (1990a) gave a total attendance of 60 218 at 1 427 political education meetings and courses. This total does not include the smaller numbers attending conferences organized by other departments such as the political academy and the research department. The political academy organizes functions each year for some 2 000 German and European "experts."

The Friedrich Naumann Foundation's annual report for 1989 records an attendance of 8 410 at its three main political education centres. (The statistics exclude the numbers attending the foundation's centres in Berlin and Konstanz.)

The Bavaria-based Hanns Seidel Foundation's annual report for 1988 reported 504 political education seminars with a total attendance of 18 231 and an additional 44 meetings sponsored by its political academy and attended by 6 410 people.

The statistics include events of varying duration. For example, of the 504 seminars held in 1988 by the Seidel Foundation, 183

Table 4.5

Number of political education events organized by political foundations and numbers attending, 1982

	Number of meetings	Total attending
Friedrich Naumann Foundation		
Theodor-Heuss-Akademie	80–100	about 10 000
Other	99	about 10 000
Friedrich Ebert Foundation		
Political education	1 317	33 817
Sociopolitical information	727	18 700
Hanns Seidel Foundation		
Political education	364	about 20 750
Political academy	49	2 600
Konrad Adenauer Foundation		
Political education	1 310	44 000
Political academy		1 800

Source: Kress (1985, 33–34).

Note: The Friedrich Ebert Foundation's category for "Sociopolitical information" refers to nonresidential activities.

(36 percent) lasted for a week, 146 (29 percent) for three days, 30 (6 percent) for two days and 145 (29 percent) for one day. In 1980, 10 percent of the Adenauer Foundation's 1 082 political education meetings lasted at least 3.5 days, 36 percent for 2.5 days, 22 percent for 1.5 days, 15 percent for one day and 16 percent for an afternoon. Each meeting normally involves 20 to 30 participants.

In their early years, the party foundations provided both the travel and accommodation costs of participants. More recently, small charges have been introduced, though they are sometimes waived. For instance, the Friedrich Naumann Foundation charges DM60 for a weekend (two-and-a-half-day) residential conference, including board and lodging. This usually represents less than one-fifth of the cost of such a meeting. The Adenauer Foundation charges between DM10 and DM100 for courses in what was West Germany and more for courses held in Berlin. Travel is sometimes subsidized. As with the Naumann Foundation, the Adenauer reckons to charge fees amounting to one-fifth of the cost of courses.

"Political education" includes a variety of activities aimed at a range of audiences. The courses aim to encourage political participation by bringing groups of citizens together for more or less structured discussions about aspects of public issues. There are occasional relatively high-level meetings for academics, technical experts and senior politicians. Other seminars are designed to appeal to students, women, trade unionists or other special groups. There are even events for schoolchildren. Most meetings are devoted to the discussion of an area of policy, but there are also training sessions in such political skills as public speaking. "Political education" has also taken the form of study tours to what was East Germany or to other countries.

The party foundations report that those attending the general political education courses tend to be middle-level activists and office holders in local party organizations.

Though the activities of the *Stiftungen* follow a broadly similar pattern, there are some differences of style and content. The Friedrich Ebert Foundation organizes some of its courses in cooperation with the German trade union federation (the Deutscher Gewerkschaftsbund – DGB) and the white-collar Deutsche Angestellten-Gewerkschaft (DAG). The foundation has recently organized seminars and courses around the main themes of free speech, policies relating to women, relations between East and West Germany or "Deutschlandpolitik" and new technology. Two sections at the foundation's headquarters are responsible for political education. One deals with residential courses and the other with nonresidential political information, events and discussions.

The Adenauer Foundation's political education institute has organized special meetings for teachers, journalists, soldiers, policemen, local government politicians, women, students and young adults. There are special courses for teachers at American and British military bases in Germany. The institute also produces the journal *Eichholz Brief*, which is designed to keep former participants in touch with the foundation and to provide background discussion material of current issues. A separate, small department, the "political academy," organizes gatherings of "experts," including a series of conferences and meetings held for many years for party activists and others from a number of European countries. The political academy, too, produces a series of publications.

The Adenauer Foundation's political education institute makes a broad distinction between meetings and courses held by its regional centres – intended for the general public – and courses held at Schloss Eichholz, geared to specialist groups such as teachers, lawyers, journalists and local politicians, who will then be in a position to influence larger numbers of people in the course of their work.

The institute stresses that its aim is not narrowly party political and that only about one-third of those who attend are CDU members. The aim is to promote political consensus building, though admittedly from a Christian Democrat point of view.

The Hanns Seidel Foundation has developed an extensive political education program, considering that its activities are effectively limited to Bavaria. In 1988, its 504 courses included 14 for 620 policemen, 28 courses in rhetoric, 37 seminars on agrarian issues and 17 Berlin seminars, as well as forums for the "older generation" and seminars for female politicians. The foundation's Akademie für Politik und Zeitgeschehen organizes specialist seminars and has additional responsibilities for research and publications. It produces the journal *Politische Studien*.

The Friedrich Naumann Foundation expresses its commitment to European integration by situating two of its educational centres near the country's western and eastern borders, in the Saarland and in West Berlin. The "European meeting centre" in Saarbrücken "is dedicated to fostering political and cultural dialogue between Liberals in Germany and France, particularly in the regions of Alsace and Lorraine and South-West Germany" (Friedrich Naumann Foundation 1989a). As far as its meetings at the Theodor-Heuss-Akademie are concerned, some of them are relatively academic (for example, seminars on the work of political philosophers John Rawls and Hannah Arendt). In addition, the foundation arranges a series of regional conferences and instruction sessions on practical topics related to local government budgets and planning and on political skills such as public speaking, working with the press, public relations and producing literature designed for young people and schoolchildren.

Although the foundations regularly assess participants' reactions to their courses, there appears to be no reliable measure of the effectiveness of political education as an instrument for recruiting party members or for promoting political activism.[9] The informal judgements of present and former officials of the *Stiftungen* vary. A former staff member taking part in one of the foundations' political education programs characterized it as a waste of time: "When British workers are bored with their jobs, they go on strike; German workers report sick or take educational leave." Most political education, according to this view, is a boondoggle for "groups of garbage disposal workers" and for others like them.

A more optimistic assessment – or expression of hope – came from a Naumann Foundation official. Political education courses organized by the foundation have two significant functions. For the 80 percent of participants who are already FDP members, courses reinforce commitment to the party and some of them specifically provide training in rhetoric and other political skills. For nonmembers, the courses provide sessions that are sufficiently independent of the party to be attractive but which are attuned to basic liberal values (and may thus aid party recruitment).

The strongest claims about the effectiveness of political education came from a member of the political staff in the Chancellor's Office, who asserted that the political education offered by the Adenauer Foundation is part of its program of communication and information that is of fundamental importance for the long-term maintenance of the CDU's support and that it would be "catastrophic" if the party lacked the foundation's assistance.

In an age when the public is heavily influenced by television (which in Germany has come under party influence), it is open to question whether political attitudes and activities are likely to be significantly affected by the occasional exposure of a minority of electors to political education courses. Doubts about the usefulness of such courses are intensified by the fact that it is difficult, if not impossible, to show whether the attitudes and activities of participants have been affected by their attendance. It would nevertheless be wrong, in my view, to write off "political education" altogether. A weekend in a country retreat together with 25 like-minded participants is likely to intensify loyalties more than evenings in front of the television set. Moreover, the approximately 150 000 people attending such meetings each year are drawn from target groups such as party activists and students. Whether it is appropriate for the state to fund such activities for parties, churches and other public organizations is another matter, which will be raised in the last section. Apart from questions about the impact of short residential courses, there is scope for argument as to whether it is more cost-effective for *Stiftungen* to operate their own premises or to hire accommodation when needed. The policies of the foundations vary. The Ebert Foundation has recently decided that its network of purpose-built residential centres is wastefully expensive.

Scholarships

The original purpose of the Friedrich Ebert Foundation, when it was founded in the 1920s, was to provide scholarships for "talented proletarian youths." After the Second World War, the *Stiftung* inaugurated a similar program for German and later for foreign students. The program was expanded, starting in 1962. In 1965, the Adenauer Foundation started a scholarship scheme of its own, in which all four party foundations are now involved.

By the late 1980s, the political foundations were paying for a total of some 3 500 scholarships to German students and about 1 000 scholarships to foreign students. The statistics, derived from the foundations' most recent published annual reports, are set out in table 4.6.

Table 4.6
Number of scholarships granted by political foundations, 1988–89

	Friedrich-Naumann-Stiftung (1988)	Friedrich-Ebert-Stiftung (1989)	Hanns-Seidel-Stiftung (1988)	Konrad-Adenauer-Stiftung (1988)	Totals
German students	nearly 400	1 324	348	1 408	3 480
Foreign students	nearly 200	368	167	306	1 041
Total	nearly 600	1 692	515	1 714	4 521

Sources: Annual foundation reports and information supplied by the Konrad Adenauer Foundation.
Note: Includes students receiving grants in all years of their courses.

A very small proportion of the money for these scholarships comes from special funds raised by the foundations. The bulk comes from the federal education ministry for German students (see table 4.3) and from the foreign ministry for foreign students. (Until 1970, funding for *Stiftung* scholarships for German students came from the interior ministry.)

The political foundations are not alone in receiving federal funds for scholarships. Organizations linked with the main religious denominations, the Catholic and Protestant churches, also receive taxpayers' money for their own scholarships.

Most of the scholarships awarded to German students by the party foundations are for undergraduate courses, especially in law. About a quarter are for graduate studies. Some grants are for periods of overseas study by German students. For example, 10 percent of the Adenauer Foundation's grantees (137) carried out their studies abroad in 1987. The *Stiftung* arranged for its grantees to study at University College, Oxford, Wolfson College, Cambridge, the Bologna Center of the Johns Hopkins University, American University and the School of Foreign Service at Georgetown University.

The current scholarship rates (introduced by all the political foundations in October 1990) are as follows: undergraduates receive a maximum of DM840 a month, depending upon parental income. Graduates receive DM1 200 a month. Married students are entitled to an extra DM300 a month. All grantees receive an additional DM150 a month categorized as "book money." Unlike other parts of the grant, book money is paid to scholarship holders regardless of parental income.[10] Since German students are not required to pay university tuition fees, the scholarships are used for living expenses. Undergraduates receive scholarships for their entire undergraduate courses (four to five years).

Scholarships for postgraduates are for two years and may be extended for one further year.[11]

The scholarship schemes provide a potentially useful source of patronage for the political parties and churches. The system can obviously be used to build party loyalties and consolidate religious attachments among active members of the student generation. The financial value of the scholarship scheme is lessened by the fact that German students have been entitled since the late 1960s to receive maintenance loans (based on parental income) from the federal education ministry (the BAFÖG scheme).[12] Students receiving *Stiftung* scholarships cannot at the same time claim maintenance loans from BAFÖG. The book money, however, is supplementary. According to statistics for the Adenauer Foundation, 52 percent of its scholars received book money alone in 1989 and the rest also received *Stiftung* maintenance grants. Of the Ebert scholars, 78 percent received maintenance grants in 1989 and 22 percent received only book money. The value of *Stiftung* scholarships is enhanced by the fact that they are outright grants whereas BAFÖG awards are loans.

Awards are made on the basis both of academic qualifications and of political criteria. Some of the foundations publish in their annual reports a tabulation of the examination performances of their scholars as a way of stressing the importance of academic standards. However, scholars are also expected to be political adherents (and, in the case of the church organizations, followers of the creed) of the donor body. For instance, the Naumann Foundation specifies in its literature that one requirement for a scholarship is political and social commitment arising from a basic liberal attitude (Friedrich Naumann Foundation 1989b). The Adenauer Foundation states that each applicant for a scholarship "should be aware of his political responsibilities and show political interest. He should be prepared to work and assume responsibility in academic, political and social organizations." Besides giving young people the opportunity to pursue university studies, the scholarship scheme provides beneficiaries "with a modern political education" (Deussen 1979, 91–92).

According to a senior academic member of the Friedrich Ebert Foundation's scholarship selection committee, the choice is based on three criteria: academic ranking (the foundation requires successful applicants to be in the top half of their age group in terms of their academic grades), "personality" and participation in "social activities." These may include party activities but may also consist of other "non-profit" activities in trade unions or in such voluntary bodies as Amnesty International. Though the foundation likes to use the scholarship scheme to promote party membership, only about 40 percent of those applying and being awarded Friedrich Ebert Foundation scholarships are members of the SPD. The proportion of party members among Ebert scholars has apparently fallen during recent years. This is partly a result of the falling level of activity within the SPD's youth movement.

Applicants for Ebert scholarships are screened by one of the foundation's academic advisers (*Vertrauensdozenten*) on each university campus and are then interviewed by a member of the central scholarship committee. About one applicant in three is successful.

The Adenauer Foundation has a more elaborate selection procedure. Applicants first submit a form. They are not specifically asked to record CDU party membership and activities, but it is generally understood that a party background, as well as other manifestations of "social responsibility," such as membership of a student council, are advantageous. There is then a three-stage selection course, which often lasts from Thursday to Saturday. It starts with an intelligence test similar to that of the Federal Army (*Bundeswehr*). Applicants write two essays, one on a political topic, the other on their proposed career. Further stages consist of a group discussion, observed by the three-person selection panel and, finally, an individual interview. One applicant in four is successful.

The political foundations make active efforts to keep in touch with their grantees during their studies. The Konrad Adenauer Foundation makes it compulsory for all students to attend a special 10-day residential orientation course in the first year they receive their scholarships. It includes instruction on the German political system, democratic theory and the Christian Democratic Union's "social market" approach. Additional seminars and foreign study tours are offered to students during the course of their university studies. The seminars include discussions on particular public issues and occasionally on public speaking, and events are organized for alumni who have held scholarships in the past.

The Naumann Foundation presents courses for its incoming grantees that are usually based on the theme of the "Renaissance of Liberalism." In 1988–89 it mounted regular events for its scholars in Berlin. The foundation arranges special vacation "academies" for its grantees at the Theodor-Heuss-Akademie at Gummersbach. "During their summer break, the Foundation's scholarship holders meet at the Academy with secondary-school and university students for such activities as discussing and singing German folk songs or producing and participating in political cabarets" (Friedrich Naumann Foundation 1988, 6).

In 1989 the Ebert Foundation ran 80 seminars and conferences for its scholars and produced a special magazine for them entitled *Stip-in* (a play on *Stipendiaten*, the German term for scholars). Since 1984 the foundation's building at Bonn-Venusberg has been used exclusively as a meeting centre for Ebert scholars.

The *Stiftungen* strengthen their links with their scholars in another way. They arrange for one or more professors at each university where their grantees are studying to act as personal advisers to them. This pastoral system has the incidental function of involving certain professors in work that identifies them as party supporters. The professors are known within the foundations as "contact" or "trusted" professors (the *Vertrauensdozenten* already referred to). They are not paid, but may hope to improve their chances of obtaining travel grants and *Stiftung* research contracts and more generally to benefit from the patronage of the parent party. The *Stiftungen* expect the contact professors to meet their scholars individually about once a month and to arrange group meetings for them on each campus. The Ebert Foundation lists the names and addresses of 200 of these professors in its annual reports.

The foundations hope that their scholars will be recruited as active party members. In order to maintain contacts, meetings are also arranged for past scholars. The Adenauer Foundation claims that a quarter of all its alumni attend reunion meetings every year.

From both Adenauer and Ebert sources, it appears that money is not the only motive for applicants to the *Stiftung* for scholarships. The meetings and particularly the foreign trips arranged for scholars are reportedly such an attractive feature of the scholarship program that some applicants, who have no pressing financial needs, apply for foundation scholarships specifically to enable them to participate. One official responsible for the scholarship program suggested that scholars were keen to become members of what they viewed as a club, to gain status and to take advantage of the foundation's political and academic contacts, both within Germany and abroad.

Some students are anxious to win a political scholarship in order to forge party contacts and thereby to advance their careers. According to one current foundation grantee, her motive for applying was to improve her chances of a political job in the Bundestag after completing her studies and, subsequently, for entry into the diplomatic service.

It is unclear how often students join campus political associations to improve their claims for a *Stiftung* scholarship. Some report that this does happen. The main effect of the scholarship scheme is probably to intensify the political activities of students who are already involved in the party's youth movement. Where there are ideological divisions within a party or within its youth movement (as in the FDP in some past years), members of factions favoured by each *Stiftung* are reportedly more likely to obtain scholarships.[13]

Research

The political foundations all provide facilities for various forms of research on current politics and on significant areas of public policy. Their research departments have functions that may be loosely compared with those of politically oriented think-tanks in the United States.

The Ebert Foundation set up its research agency (later called the research institute) in 1959. It is active in the field of research into modern German history and, in particular, into topics relating to the Social Democratic Party. The department's researchers benefit from their access to confidential papers of the Social Democratic Party and of political leaders.

By 1989, the research institute had grown into a large organization with divisions responsible for foreign policy, policy toward what was East Germany, international technical cooperation, economic policy, labour and social research. It has conducted studies on topics such as regional economic policy and the policy implications of genetic engineering. The institute commissions occasional surveys, especially on topics related to research on problems of social policy. It normally competes with university departments to raise money from private foundations for funding such work. Unlike the Adenauer Foundation, it does not commission systematic research into voting behaviour. It also sponsors a major program of publications.

It is unclear how far the work of the institute influences the policies and programs of the Social Democratic Party. The foundation certainly uses its various residential facilities to host private, high-level meetings at which policy is discussed with senior party figures. The research institute's studies may provide relevant findings on particular issues. However, it has been claimed that the foundation's research department generally has only a limited impact on party policy making. This is because it concentrates on areas of research that have little immediate relevance – for instance, the history of the German labour movement and problems of the Third World.

Other reasons have also been suggested for the apparently small impact of the Friedrich Ebert Foundation's research on the Social Democratic party's programs. As far as labour relations are concerned, the foundation's research department is overshadowed, according to one view from SPD headquarters, by the research department of the German trade union federation, the DGB. Moreover, according to another report, the foundation's influence on policy has also been limited by the fact that it has often represented a more right-wing strand of the party than the headquarters or the leadership. In general, the research department probably has closer working contacts with members and staff of the SPD caucus in the Bundestag than with SPD headquarters. It has a particular influence in areas such as relations with the former German Democratic Republic, since its research programs had brought members of the department into contact with East German social democrats and even more with the communists.

Academic research was sponsored by the Christian Democrats from the early days of the Eichholz Political Academy, the precursor of the Konrad Adenauer Foundation. In 1967, an academic institute, Wissenschaftliches Institut der Konrad-Adenauer-Stiftung (WIKAS), was created at the Adenauer Foundation. The development of this research department in the late 1960s reflected the fact that the foundation had recently started to receive the "global subsidy" from the federal interior ministry. In 1970 it became the "social science research institute."

Under Dr. Werner Kaltefleiter, a political scientist who later took a senior university position in Kiel, the Konrad Adenauer Foundation developed a major unit for research into public opinion, voting behaviour and mass communications. The research institute adopted a panel-survey approach that had been developed at the University of Michigan. The United States findings had been published in *The American Voter* and had been followed by a parallel study on voting behaviour in Britain. *Political Change in Britain* by David Butler and Donald Stokes was published in 1969.

In the same year, the Konrad Adenauer Foundation set up its own computer centre for similar research. By 1971, Dr. Kaltefleiter had assembled a 59-person research team.

Opinion research has continued to be a major institute activity. Some of the studies are eventually published, but they are normally kept private for a period of two years and provide an important source of confidential political advice for the CDU leadership. Others are published and form the basis of discussions at meetings of party activists. For example, the research department completed a study in late 1989 of the Republican party, which was posing a threat to the CDU following its strong showing in the European elections of June 1989. The study was published and repeatedly presented by foundation officials at both national and local CDU meetings.

The Adenauer Foundation's research institute has established a special expertise in strategic and defence policy. One of its former directors, Dr. Hans Rühle, subsequently became a senior adviser to Manfred Wörner, defence minister in a CDU-led government.

Besides research and publications, the research department organizes occasional meetings and conferences and maintains contacts for research institutions in Germany and abroad.

As with the Ebert Foundation, some knowledgeable insiders report that the Adenauer Foundation has had relatively little direct impact on the formulation of Christian Democrat policy over the past 20 years. This is partly because the foundation, under the chairmanship of Dr. Bruno Heck, represented a more right-wing strand than the party headquarters. Also, the CDU leader, Dr. Kohl, has been mainly dependent for policy advice on the governmental machine since he became Federal Chancellor.

It would nevertheless be wrong to discount the Adenauer Foundation's influence, since it enjoys close contacts with Chancellor Kohl (himself a long-standing and active member of its governing board) and with the Chancellor's Office. In 1989 the foundation reportedly took Chancellor Kohl's side in his dispute with the CDU general secretary, Dr. Heiner Geissler. In matters of political strategy, the Adenauer Foundation's research department is a frequent source of advice, as will be described in the section titled "Role of the Political Foundations in the German Party System."

The Friedrich Naumann Foundation's research department is small and of recent origin. In 1990 it had a staff of only six. The department has special responsibility for studies in Liberal history and ideas, for the development of economic policy and empirical social research including polling. Despite its limited size, the research department and the FNS staff in general seem to have a considerable role in Free Democrat policy making. This is because the organization of the *Stiftung* is much larger than those of FDP headquarters and of the Bundestag caucus (*Fraktion*). The FDP's shortages of money have enhanced the importance of the *Stiftung*. The foundation is represented on the Free Democrat commission responsible for party policy and strategy. As with the Social Democrats, the Liberal foundation appears in matters of policy to have a stronger link with the Bundestag caucus than with party headquarters.[14]

The Seidel Foundation does not have a separate research department but, as mentioned earlier, it has a department known as the "political academy," which also carries out some research .

Maintaining Party Archives
Although the present-day German parties are postwar creations, they look back to their roots in pre-Nazi Germany. The preservation of party

archives not only provides a service to researchers but also helps to reinforce feelings of identity and loyalty in the scholarly community and, more broadly, among party adherents. By maintaining collections of party papers and documents, the *Stiftungen* have relieved their related parties of the expense and trouble of fulfilling the task.

The Friedrich Ebert Foundation has a library for students and researchers of 300 000 volumes, and its documents cover 800 metres of shelf space. The exceptional attention paid by the foundation to its archival work and to historical publications reflects the importance attached by the German Social Democrats to their traditions as a source of continuing political loyalty.

The Konrad Adenauer Foundation has a library of about 100 000 volumes and is responsible for the Archive of Christian Democracy. The archives of both *Stiftungen* include papers and documents relevant to their respective parties as well as press cuttings, posters, photographs and collections of the private papers of prominent party politicians. The archive departments also prepare documents for publication. The FNS and HSS maintain archives on a smaller scale. (The FNS purchased the FDP's archives in the late 1960s.)

Overseas Operations

Nearly two-thirds of the expenditure of the foundations is devoted to projects in foreign countries. With the benefit of grants from the development ministry and the foreign ministry, the *Stiftungen* have become a significant international force. They employ some 330 German representatives abroad, supported by local staffs and project staffs totalling thousands. In 1989, the Ebert Foundation alone had offices in 70 countries and was engaged in projects in 100. The administration of these foreign projects is a major responsibility of the central offices of the foundations.

The *Stiftungen* typically give grants to "partner" organizations abroad. These are sometimes foundations related to foreign political parties and trade unions in the same way as those in Germany are related to the German parties – legally independent but closely linked in practice. In many foreign countries political parties have set up foundations for the specific purpose of receiving the German political grants.

It is beyond the scope of this study to detail these extensive and sometimes important foreign operations.[15] However, it is relevant to make the following points about them. First, when foreign governments have attempted to imitate the *Stiftungen*, it has been their foreign rather than their domestic activities in which they have usually been interested. This applies in particular to the United States. The U.S. National Endowment for Democracy and the associated system of four "core grantees" (National Republican Institute for International Affairs, National Democratic Institute for International Affairs, Free Trade Union Institute and Center for International Private Enterprise), established in 1983, were closely modelled on the foreign work of the German party foundations, though the American institutions operate on a far smaller scale than the *Stiftungen*.

There has also been interest within Britain in the foreign political aid projects of the *Stiftungen*. This more recent concentration by other governments on the international activities of the German party foundations contrasts with that prevailing in the 1970s, when the domestic functions of the *Stiftungen* generated most interest abroad, at least in Great Britain (see section on "Policy Implications" below).

Second, the existence of such extensive overseas operations run by party-related organizations has had indirect effects within Germany. Many academics and other experts are drawn into the orbit of the *Stiftungen* as consultants for foreign projects or as field representatives. The party foundations' publications relating to foreign and development issues are affected by their own overseas experience, and it is reasonable to assume that this affects the formulation of policy. The foundations act as hosts to a stream of political leaders and other visitors to Germany from their partner organizations. Above all, the overhead costs of administering foreign projects, provided by the development ministry, permit the party foundations to enlarge their headquarters buildings and staffs.

Other Activities

Besides the sizable departments for internal administration, personnel and financial control, the foundations have staffs for press and public relations, and three of the *Stiftungen*, the FES, KAS and HSS, have special sections for the purpose. The press offices have a responsibility for some of the foundations' brochures and reports. However, publication activities are not centralized. The different departments produce or sponsor popular and academic literature of their own.

All the foundations pay attention to local government issues. Political education programs are frequently intended for local government councillors and party activists. The Adenauer Foundation has a department for local government studies. The department was considered important as a means to build local CDU cadres when the party was in opposition in the 1970s.[16] Besides its research and conferences relating to local government within Germany, it has concentrated on regional issues at the level of the European Community. In 1987, it organized a 700-person conference on local government, held in Luxembourg, in conjunction with the European People's party in the European Parliament (i.e., the Christian Democratic parliamentary party or *Fraktion*).

A further area of occasional activity is in the arts. The Ebert Foundation is particularly prominent in this field, and there is a considerable art gallery at its main office, where there are regular exhibitions, usually consisting of drawings and paintings by contemporary artists. There is an art gallery at the Friedrich Naumann Foundation's headquarters at the Margarethenhof. The Konrad Adenauer Foundation and the Hanns Seidel Foundation present cultural events, including concerts, with the objective of promoting a sense of public involvement.

The Political Foundations and German Unification

In 1990, the Adenauer, Ebert and Naumann foundations played active and varied parts in furthering the process of German unification. The foundations were already experienced in providing training and aid to emerging political parties and trade unions in foreign countries during periods of upheaval. They were credited with providing vital assistance to anti-Communist forces in Portugal and Spain during the 1970s, during these two countries' turbulent transition to democratic government (Pinto-Duschinsky 1991).

The foundations – especially Ebert – had already been used as instruments for building political contacts with East Germany and Eastern Europe. Their large staffs, their status as independent, though federally funded, political organizations and their experience made them ideal instruments for promoting links between the West German parties and the political forces emerging in Communist-ruled East Germany.

The Adenauer Foundation's new chairman, Chancellor Kohl's close colleague Dr. Bernhard Vogel, made it his primary task to assure his organization's support for the Chancellor's drive to secure German unification. He regularly accompanied Kohl during his dramatic visits to the east in the weeks following the breach of the Berlin wall in November 1989. The foundation established a German Democratic Republic "task force," and officials hurried eastward to establish contacts with possible partner parties and factions.

At a later stage, foundation employees were dispatched as advisers to the political leaders in East Germany whom the Christian Democrats wished to aid and to influence. The Adenauer Foundation's local government specialists played a key role in supporting and training local political cadres in the German Democratic Republic, and the political education institute ran special courses for them.

The foundation focused on fostering political organizations at the state level in East Germany. This was in accord with Chancellor Kohl's strategy of building up five new state administrations there to replace the centralized institutions of the Communist regime.

The Adenauer Foundation established East German offices in Leipzig and Rostock and, by the time of unification, was in the process of setting up offices in each of the new states in the territory of the former Communist republic.

The Ebert Foundation played an important role in the SPD's contacts with its East German counterparts; this was a result of work carried out over a period of years, especially by the section of the research institute concerned with inner-German relations. The institute's economic section devoted almost all its energies in 1990 to providing advisers for the SPD's political allies in East Germany and to running courses designed to train East German politicians in the realities of market economics, giving special assistance in the state of Brandenburg, which elected an SPD administration.

The Naumann Foundation also moved rapidly to expand its political education facilities in Berlin and in the "new states." As mentioned, the foundation's research department produced a significant study on the constitutional implications of unification (see note 14).

Of course, the foundations were not the only West German institutions active in 1990 in East Germany. West German state governments flooded neighbouring administrations in the east with staff. West German newspapers produced large editions for distribution in East Germany before the various elections held in 1990. However, the actions taken by the *Stiftungen* were both significant and distinctive in identifying and promoting political groups and individuals as partners of the West German parties. The uncertainties resulting from the rapid pace of change, combined with the fact that many East German politicians had inevitably been involved in the Communist regime, made this an important, yet tricky task.

Costs of Different Activities

The form in which foundation accounts are drawn up does not make it possible to give an accurate and comparable breakdown of expenditures on different categories of activity. This is because some categories shown in the accounts include foreign expenditures, as well as the domestic spending that is the focus of this study, and because the accounts usually lump together overhead and personnel costs without distinguishing those attributable to each kind of activity. Moreover, the published accounts of the Ebert and Seidel foundations give no breakdowns of types of domestic activity.

The breakdown of expenditures given in the Konrad Adenauer Foundation's 1986 annual report is shown in table 4.7.

Apart from overhead costs, the proportions of the Adenauer Foundation's expenditure on different types of activities in 1986 were as follows: foreign activities (overseas projects and scholarships to foreign students) 67 percent; political education within Germany 15 percent; scholarships for German students 9 percent; research and archives 9 percent.

According to the Friedrich Naumann Foundation's annual report for 1988, the breakdown of its expenditures in that year was as given in table 4.8. It should be noted that the expenditures listed as having been made "within Germany" include some items related to overseas projects, for example scholarships for foreign students and the costs of administering such foreign projects.

Table 4.7
Konrad Adenauer Foundation expenditure by type of activity, 1986

	Millions of DM	Percentage of total
Central overhead for domestic and foreign projects	17.7	12.3
Political education:		12.9
Political Academy[a]	2.6	
Institute for Political Education	16.0	
Scholarships for German and foreign students[b]	17.3	12.0
Research Institute	5.1	3.5
Institute for Local Government Studies	2.7	1.9
Archive for Christian Democratic Politics	3.9	2.7
International Institute (overseas projects)	79.1	54.8
Total	144.4	100.0

Source: Konrad Adenauer Stiftung Jahresbericht (Annual Report) '86 (Sankt Augustin 1987).

[a] Though listed under "Political education," the Political Academy also sponsors education and research.

[b] The bulk of the expenditures for scholarships is for German students. According to Drucksache 10/5281, the federal education ministry's grants to the foundation in 1986 for scholarships to German students totalled DM9.6 million and, as mentioned earlier, the total was slightly supplemented by other scholarship funds.

Table 4.8
Friedrich Naumann Foundation expenditure by type of activity, 1988

	Thousands of DM	Percentage of total
Expenditure within Germany		
Political education within Germany	16 579	42.14
Scholarships	6 551	16.65
Research, planning archives	2 234	5.68
Publications, public relations	699	1.78
Head office, technical services, building costs	13 275	33.75
Total	39 338	100.00
Foreign Expenditures		
Adult political education	13 358	35.67
Media education and support	5 556	14.84
Legal and human rights projects	2 795	7.46
Political dialogue meetings	4 628	12.36
Self-help organizations	11 113	29.67
Total	37 450	100.00

Source: *Friedrich-Naumann-Stiftung Jahresbericht* (Annual Report) *1988* (Königswinter 1989).

ROLE OF THE POLITICAL FOUNDATIONS IN THE GERMAN PARTY SYSTEM

It is beyond doubt that the party foundations have established themselves on the scene of political and public life within Germany. The
sheer scale of the subsidies from the federal treasury and the extent of
their activities guarantee this. To give a personal example, I have been
struck by the large proportion of German political science colleagues
who have at one time or another been actively involved in the work of
a political foundation, as employees or overseas field representatives,
as tutors on political education courses, as experts fulfilling research
contracts, as members of boards or committees of the *Stiftungen*, as
authors of their publications or as personal advisers to students holding foundation scholarships.

The impressive size of the foundations' operations is also seen in
their contacts with political élites in foreign countries. Most prominent
British politicians and many academics have been involved in visits,
conferences or meetings sponsored by a German party foundation.
Contacts with some European countries have been even closer, and in
one celebrated case, a foreign political party – the Portuguese Socialist
party – was created at a meeting held in 1973 at Bad Münstereifel, one
of the Friedrich Ebert Foundation's residential centres. Among their
widespread international operations, the *Stiftungen* have forged close
links with Israeli and American institutions. In Washington, several

leading political think tanks, especially in the strategic studies field, have undertaken joint projects with *Stiftungen,* and the list of those participating in conferences not only includes key congressional aides but reads like a *Who's Who* of U.S. politicians. The significance of the political foundations is indicated by the fact that a few embassies in Bonn have specifically assigned diplomats to keep in touch with their work.

Despite the extent of their projects, the political foundations seem to have remained rather mysterious to the general public in Germany. They have been the subject of spurts of press reporting, which in recent years have all too often centred on some alleged scandal. The rambling Flick affair, various revelations in *Der Spiegel* and attacks stimulated by the Greens have all contributed to this publicity.

In general, the press seems to be less interested in the work of the political foundations than in the different party headquarters.

Though the party foundations are clearly an important set of institutions, it is difficult to define their role within the German political system or to gauge the precise effects of their undertakings. Each of the main German political parties may be seen as consisting of several baronies, of which its party foundation is one. The party barons and their forces – the various party bureaucracies – work with each other for their common purpose, electoral victory. But they also safeguard their own political and institutional interests:

- The party general secretary, who heads the extraparliamentary machine, is one such baron.
- The party leaders within the Bundestag are also prominent figures, with control over their own considerable staff.
- In states where the party has won office, the premier – the regional party leader – has his own machine, and this provides a major power base within the national party. (Within the Bavaria-based CSU, politicians with positions in the state government are especially important). To a lesser extent, the opposition leaders in the states also have their own staffs.
- In the national governing party, the Chancellor's Office (together with the neighbouring federal press and information office) is another vital political bureaucracy.
- Within the Free Democratic Party, a relatively small party that has nevertheless participated in a considerable number of government coalitions, ministerial office provides a semi-independent baronial base, especially for the long-serving foreign minister, Hans-Dietrich Genscher.

- The structure of German trade unions and industries ensures that their leaders are influential in party circles.

In practice, the political role of a *Stiftung* depends to a considerable extent on the personality of its chairman and his individual relationships with other party barons. Though probably not as important a position as that of general secretary of the party, the chairmanship of the party foundation is a plum party job for an elder statesman. Each political foundation has a working chairman, usually a leading political figure, and a chief executive, who is normally a career official of the *Stiftung*. Until his death in 1989, Prof. Dr. Bruno Heck, a former CDU secretary-general and a federal minister, was for many years the Konrad Adenauer Foundation's chairman. His successor, Dr. Bernhard Vogel, was previously CDU chairman and premier of the state government of Rhineland Palatinate from 1976 to 1988 and has long known Chancellor Kohl, the previous CDU premier of the state.

The Friedrich Ebert Foundation's chairman, Holger Börner, is another former state premier, having held the position for the SPD in Hesse. He is also a former SPD general secretary. The Hanns Seidel Foundation's chairman, Dr. Fritz Pirkl, is a member of the European Parliament and a former CSU minister in Bavaria. The Friedrich Naumann Foundation's chairman, Wolfgang Mischnick, was until recently the FDP's parliamentary leader.

The party foundations have an identity and character that distinguish them from the headquarters offices of their related parties. Besides the usual bureaucratic rivalries that naturally arise between sister organizations, there may be some envy of the privileged access of the *Stiftungen* to federal government largesse, since the *Stiftungen* have escaped the financial uncertainties and deficits that have affected the party organizations. It is widely claimed by desk officers both of the political foundations and of the parties that they have little regular contact with each other. They exist in mainly separate worlds.

Foundations and parties are distinguished by the fact that much of their work is different, though often complementary. For instance, the party organizations and legislative caucuses have only small international departments, whereas foreign projects are the most extensive and costly of the party foundations' operations. Moreover, there appears to be relatively little movement of employees between the party organizations and their respective foundations, although there is some exchange of staff. A section of the CDU headquarters (responsible for press cuttings and archives) moved at one point to the Konrad Adenauer Foundation.

According to one report, the Friedrich Ebert Foundation does not generally recruit employees from the SPD headquarters, since it does not consider its staff of sufficiently high calibre. According to another unofficial account, talented young people wishing to work in the political field are generally anxious to obtain a government position, i.e., as patronage employees, or failing that, to become members of political staffs in Parliament. Work at party headquarters is less attractive, especially because contracts are usually for short periods.

In some cases, at least, party foundation staff are not party adherents. One former senior Adenauer Foundation official had been offered an identical job with the Ebert Foundation and was uncertain which position to accept. (He now works for a government agency.) In such, admittedly exceptional, cases, the employee regards the job at the *Stiftung* as technical or academic rather than politically oriented.

It nevertheless would be unrealistic to overstate the independence of the political foundations. Not only are they headed by senior party figures, but the members of their boards, as mentioned earlier, include leading party politicians. In particular, the general secretary and treasurer of the allied party have sometimes been members of the governing board of the party foundation. (For the Adenauer Foundation, see Deussen 1979, chap. 4.) For years, the SPD treasurer, Alfred Nau, served at the same time as the Ebert Foundation's chairman while the recent CDU general secretary, Dr. Heiner Geissler, and the treasurer, Walther Kiep, also served on the Konrad Adenauer Foundation's board. As Göttrik Wewer has written, the fact that Dr. Fritz Fliszar, the FDP federal secretary, went on to become the chief official of the Free Democrats' foundation was just one expression of the connections between the FDP and the Naumann Foundation (Wewer 1988a, 12). Indeed, the Naumann Foundation and the FDP shared the same building until 1984. Moreover, it is now evident – and acknowledged informally by party officials – that some of the foundations occasionally acted in past years as conduits for campaign funds to the party organizations.

There was an attempt in the 1980s to erect legal fences to separate parties from their foundations. Recommendations to this effect emerged in 1983 from the committee set up by the federal president, Professor Dr. Carstens, to consider a new system of political funding. Some of the proposals concerning the *Stiftungen* were ignored by the Bundestag, though the 1983 Parties Law included a ban on payments by party foundations to political parties and made it illegal for party chairmen and treasurers simultaneously to hold the same positions on the board of the party foundation. The Constitutional Court's judgement on the 1983 Parties Law, delivered in 1986, again stressed the need for a demarcation between parties and *Stiftungen,* though it upheld the constitutionality of public funding for both.

The party foundations have become more sensitive than before to the need to demonstrate their legal separation from their parent parties. Yet there has been little practical change. The system of interlocking directorships of parties and foundations has survived. The boards of the foundations continue to be dominated by elder party figures.

In 1989, the 45 governing members of the Adenauer Foundation included 15 Christian Democrat members of the Bundestag (of whom 11 were ministers) and five members of the European and state legislatures. Another eight were former holders of senior political offices. Among party officeholders on the board of the Konrad Adenauer Foundation were the federal chancellor, the CDU general secretary and treasurer, the deputy party leader in the Bundestag, and the leader of the party group in the European Parliament. It should be noted that the presence of the party chairman and treasurer on foundation boards continues to be legal, provided that they do not act as chairman and treasurer.

As far as the Friedrich Ebert Foundation and the SPD are concerned, there remains a significant overlap between their respective governing boards. In 1989, two-thirds of the members of the SPD's presidium were also members of various Friedrich Ebert Foundation boards. As shown in table 4.9, Ebert's 10-person board of directors included in 1989 the SPD general secretary, the party vice-chairman (who was also the SPD premier of the largest state), the president of the German trade union confederation, a former party general secretary (another former state premier) and three prominent SPD Bundestag members.

In their operations, too, there is a significant overlap between the political foundations and party organs, despite the provisos that have been made. Some foundation officials are forthright about this. While apparently respecting barriers between parties and *Stiftungen* imposed by the 1983 Parties Law, by the Constitutional Court's 1986 judgement and by the tax laws, the political foundations are adept at finding ways to help their parent parties. As one foundation official put it, little has changed in practice as a result of the Court's judgement, as none of the main parties is interested in attacking the practices of the others. Some academic observers have suggested, however, that parties and foundations have gradually been drifting apart – a reflection of bureaucratization rather than of legal barriers.

A legal adviser of one of the party organizations explained how it is possible to respect the letter of the law – as the party and the foundation interpret it – while permitting the political foundation to assist

Table 4.9
Affiliations of members of Friedrich Ebert Foundation's board of directors, 1989

Chairman	
Holger Börner	Former SPD general secretary and former premier of the State of Hesse
Deputy chairman	
Johannes Rau	SPD vice-chairman and premier of the State of North Rhine Westphalia
Ernst Breit	President of the German Trade Union Confederation (DGB)
Other members	
Egon Bahr MdB	Former SPD federal minister and member of SPD Präsidium
Professor Dr. Horst Ehmke MdB	Former SPD federal minister and former deputy SPD caucus leader in the Bundestag
Anke Fuchs MdB	SPD general secretary and former deputy SPD caucus leader in the Bundestag
Dr. Peter Glotz MdB	Former SPD general secretary
Dr. Günther Grünwald	Former general secretary, Friedrich Ebert Foundation
Fritz Heine	Former director, Friedrich Ebert Foundation and former SPD official
Professor Dr. Peter von Oertzen	Former minister, State of Lower Saxony, SPD chairman, Hanover, and former member of the SPD Präsidium

Source: Friedrich-Ebert-Stiftung (1989, 27).

Note: MdB = *Mitglied des Bundestages* (Member of Federal Parliament).

the party. For instance, it is permissible for the *Stiftung* to give party officials access to its confidential opinion surveys, provided the survey results are eventually published. Delayed publication means that party strategists are able to take advantage of such results, which remain confidential during the time they are operationally useful. To give another example, though a foundation may not finance a training course that is formally restricted to party members or activists, it may make arrangements that ensure that in practice, those signing up are preponderantly party activists.

Since the limits of the law are untested, the different parties vary on their policies concerning the relationship between *Stiftung* and party. A general conclusion from a number of interviews is that there is currently less cooperation between the SPD headquarters and the neighbouring Friedrich Ebert campus than in the case of the other parties and foundations. It was not possible to establish whether this interview information corresponds to reality.

An Ebert official suggested that his foundation was obliged to maintain a more substantial barrier between itself and the SPD than those created by the parties and foundations of the governing Christian

Democrat–Free Democrat coalition. Foundations are more likely to face legal action, he argued, while their parent parties are in opposition. This view is open to question, since the *Stiftungen* have, in practice, protected each other from legal challenges.

Another reason for the Ebert Foundation's apparent caution during recent years, cited by the same official, is that the foundation's former general secretary was threatened throughout the late 1980s with prosecution, as a result of the donations made to the foundation by the Flick concern. The foundation's new chairman, Holger Börner, and general secretary, Dr. Jürgen Burckhardt, are, according to this interpretation, likely to be less inhibited in their dealings with the SPD.

Alternative explanations of the reported decline in the Ebert Foundation's participation in party life were also suggested. According to another senior official, the foundation has been affected by the ravages of Parkinson's Law: as its buildings and staff have expanded, their influence has diminished. Another complaint, expressed at the headquarters both of the *Stiftung* and the SPD, was that the party's candidate for the office of chancellor in the 1990 election campaign, Oskar Lafontaine, Premier of the Saarland, relied excessively on his political staff. The distance between party and *Stiftung* was part of a more extensive lack of coordination that also affected dealings between the candidate and party headquarters.

A further interpretation is possible. The Ebert Foundation's relative caution about acknowledging its party links – largely a consequence of its experience relating to the prolonged Flick affair – may possibly disguise a closer, though less apparent working relationship.

Some Naumann and Adenauer foundation officials are less cautious about describing their party connections. For instance, the overlap between the polling activities of the Naumann Foundation and the FDP has already been noted (see note 14).

Many of the most interesting questions about linkage relate to the Chancellor, his office, his party organization and the Adenauer Foundation. As mentioned earlier, the foundation reportedly has a relatively small impact on the formal CDU program, since this is a party responsibility and staff work is carried out at party headquarters. The foundation is nevertheless a significant source of advice on political strategy and an arm of the Chancellor's power.

In order to understand the foundation's role, it is important to appreciate that it is a hybrid between a governmental and a party body. Indeed, the boundary between state and party organs in Germany is unclear, as will be discussed in a later section. The working relationships between *Stiftung*, party headquarters, the Chancellor's Office

(*Kanzleramt*) and the federal press and information office will be illustrated by three examples.

1. Private opinion polling. There is a distinction in theory and to an extent in practice between the long-term, academic opinion surveys commissioned and analysed by the Konrad Adenauer Foundation and the short-term, operational polls carried out for the party headquarters and for party organizations in the individual states. However, the various surveys are often coordinated.

   In 1990, the polling operations on behalf of Chancellor Kohl and his party were reportedly as follows: The Adenauer Foundation continued its program of surveys into long-term trends in voting behaviour and the effects of lifestyles in both West and East Germany. The foundation normally commissions two or three major surveys a year. These are particularly significant in the run-up to the election campaign, when strategy is being formulated. The foundation is additionally responsible for collating and analysing results on the night after the poll and for a postelection survey. Normally the *Stiftung* does not commission polls during the actual campaign, though it did conduct some small-scale telephone surveys in the 1990 campaign as follow-ups to earlier surveys. The findings of the Adenauer Foundation's polls are distributed to CDU headquarters and to the Chancellor's Office.

   CDU headquarters apparently did not carry out regular polls in 1990. Instead, polls were reportedly conducted by the state organizations of the party. At the national level, the main tactical opinion surveys for the Kohl team were those of the federal press and information office. It commissioned weekly surveys from three different opinion research organizations: Infas, Emnid and the Institut für Demoskopie at Allensbach. There were special Infas surveys relating to opinion in East and West Germany on German unification. Further surveys were commissioned by various federal ministries.

   This system would appear to reduce the pressure on the party headquarters to pay for opinion research, since much of the long-term work is carried out by the party foundation, and surveys of short-term trends are commissioned by the federal press and information office.

   In 1990, senior officials of the Chancellor's Office, the federal press and information office, the party headquarters and the Adenauer Foundation were in regular contact, and their respective poll findings were circulated among each other. The main officials involved were Baldur Wagner, the head of the department of social and political analysis in the Chancellor's Office, Professor Bergsdorff, the head of the federal press and information office's department of internal affairs (a former Kohl aide at party headquarters), Peter Radunski, the chief executive at party headquarters and Dr. Hans-Joachim Veen, the head of the Adenauer Foundation's research department.

The fact that senior Christian Democrats wear several hats makes coordination easy. For example, the Chancellor and the party general secretary are both members of the Adenauer Foundation's board. Professor Elisabeth Noelle-Neumann is not only one of the Chancellor's closest personal advisers on public opinion, she is also the major figure in the Allensbach institute (which carries out private polls for the federal press and information office) and a member of the Adenauer Foundation's senior board (*Vorstand*).

2. Konrad Adenauer Foundation publications. In the case of studies relating to sensitive areas of policy, decisions about publication are subject to scrutiny and, in exceptional cases, to intervention by the Chancellor himself. During the crucial weeks following the breach of the Berlin wall, the foundation's DDR task force found that even noncontentious, academic material describing the emerging political groups in East Germany was reviewed by a CDU committee and was remitted on the Chancellor's instructions.[17]

3. Diplomacy. The imperatives of coalition government have obliged Chancellor Kohl to coexist with a Free Democrat foreign minister, Hans-Dietrich Genscher. This has sometimes led to tension between the foreign ministry and foreign policy advisers in the Chancellor's Office. During the months before German unification, there were repeated differences between the foreign ministry and Horst Teltschik, a senior adviser in the Chancellor's Office and a principal architect of Kohl's policy towards East Germany and Eastern Europe. In these circumstances, the Chancellor and his advisers have tended to use certain of the Adenauer Foundation's representatives in foreign capitals – particularly in Washington and in London – as alternative channels of high-level diplomacy.[18]

In summary, there is no evidence that political leaders continue to flout the laws requiring the separation of the party and of *Stiftung* funding. But even if the niceties of the legal distinctions between party organizations and political foundations are respected, their interlocking directorates and their complementary functions mean that the foundations continue to operate as adjuncts of the party organizations.

The foundations can save money for the party organizations by taking on tasks that these would otherwise have to carry out. The role of the *Stiftungen* in housing and administering party archives is an obvious example. The most important help given by the party foundations to the parties is in the areas of political education, research and polling. The "adult education" organized by the foundations, for instance, does not just consist of general discussions about citizenship, but serves as an instrument for building and consolidating party attachments.

POLICY IMPLICATIONS

Considering the extent of the German government's payments to parties and to the political foundations, it is hardly surprising that foreign observers and, occasionally, foreign governments should have become interested in the German experience and in the possibility of imitating aspects of the German system of political funding.

In the economically troubled 1970s, political scientists and politicians in Britain, especially those associated with the Labour and Liberal parties, argued for the introduction of public subsidies for political parties. The experience of political parties and party foundations in West Germany was repeatedly cited as an example. Dick Leonard, a former Labour member of Parliament and a distinguished journalist, based the case for public subsidies for British parties largely on what he saw as the successful results of foreign – particularly West German – experience (Leonard 1975, 1979).

In 1976, a high-level committee appointed by the Labour government (the Houghton Committee) issued a majority report that reflected the same views and recommendations (Seidle 1980, 81–82). Once again, a glowing report of the West German parties and of the party foundations was presented. Shortly afterwards, the Anglo-German Foundation published a study by the Liberal politician Alan Watson, which advocated the introduction of a system like that of the West German party foundations (Watson 1978).

More recently, some of the same arguments from European experience have been put forward by the scholar Keith Ewing (Ewing 1987).

A variety of aims has been cited for a system of regulation and subsidy of political parties on the West German model:[19]

- to encourage political participation and membership;
- to promote fairness, that is, to reduce the advantage that may be derived by certain groups or individuals because of their command of superior financial resources;
- to limit or, ideally, to eliminate corruption;
- to force parties to reveal their sources of income in order to clarify to the electorate what kind of interests their financial supporters represent;
- to reduce, limit or control the costs of politics generally; and
- to improve the effectiveness of party organization and of party research by assuring a sufficient income.

I shall summarize the evidence as to whether each of the above aims has been fulfilled by regulations that apply to the West German parties and, in particular, to the party foundations. I shall not reach a one-sided conclusion, however, and at the end shall set out the arguments both for and against the German system.

Participation and Membership

A major argument presented by opponents of public subsidies to parties and to party foundations has been that they may remove the incentive for them to recruit members. (For example, see Pinto-Duschinsky 1981, 292ff.) If there is an assured income from the public purse, why bother to look for money or for voluntary activity from a mass membership?

Advocates of the West German system point out that, to the contrary, the introduction of state subsidies has been followed by an *increase* in party membership. In particular, the CDU has apparently become less dependent upon contributions from big business and has concentrated on recruiting a mass membership instead.

When state payments to West German parties were first introduced in the late 1950s, CDU membership was about 250 000. When the subsidy system was extended in 1967 – the year that the global subsidy for the party foundations was introduced – the total was 286 000. Over the following 10 years, the growth of state aid to the parties and to the *Stiftungen* was accompanied by a dramatic growth in CDU membership, which reached 675 000 by 1978 (Haungs 1983, 27). The membership of the CSU also rose. From 43 500 in 1956–57 and 81 000 in 1967, it reached 166 000 in 1978. (See also Schönbohm 1985, part 2, II and III.)

The SPD's membership increased in the years following the introduction of state financial aid, albeit less dramatically. In contrast to the other established parties, the Free Democrats found it impossible to increase their modest membership. By the end of 1989, memberships of parties represented in the Bundestag were as follows: SPD 921 430, CDU 662 598, CSU 185 853, FDP 65 216, the Greens 37 956 (Drucksache 11/8130).

The causes of these trends are complex and uncertain. It is by no means clear that the regulations relating to political funding have been responsible to any significant degree. A reasonable interpretation is that a major reason for the CDU's efforts to increase membership after 1969 was the party's loss of power and the need to rebuild itself in opposition. Nevertheless, some proponents of state aid argue that public subsidies for improving facilities for party organization and for the educational activities of the *Stiftungen* have played a significant part in the rise in party membership in Germany. Moreover, as Ewing suggests, there has been buoyant party membership following the introduction of state subsidies in Sweden. By contrast, party membership in Britain, where there has been no direct state aid to political parties, has declined.

Besides the healthy number of West German party members, their political commitment may arguably be seen in the increasing subscriptions they are willing to pay, rates that far exceed those in Britain, for instance (see Haungs 1983, 91, 93; Nassmacher 1989, 250). In 1989, average membership subscriptions to the SPD were DM132 per annum, to the CDU DM127, to the CSU DM 81, to the FDP DM142 and to the Greens DM149 (Drucksache 11/8130). Total income from subscriptions received by all these parties amounted to no less than DM235.7 million.

A less favourable interpretation of these trends is possible, however. The decision to subscribe to a party need not indicate political commitment but may reflect more practical motives. Khayyam Paltiel pointed out that parties in a number of countries – particularly Israel and Austria – built powerful, non-political links with their members. In Israel party banks were maintained as well as party sports teams, housing projects, wholesale and retail cooperatives, hospitals and kibbutzim (Paltiel 1980a, 147). The dominance of the party is scarcely smaller in Austria where, as Hubert Sickinger and Rainer Nick (1990) have reported, political parties influence almost every job in the public and semi-public sector, where the allotment of semi-subsidized apartments actively involves the parties and where even services for vehicle breakdowns are organized on party lines.[20] Though the system of material incentives for party members is less developed in West Germany than in Austria, it is significant. In particular, party affiliation is frequently advantageous – even necessary – for those seeking jobs that depend on political patronage.

The growth in membership may thus be seen, at least in some part, as a reflection of the consolidation of the "party state." The "party ticket" is especially important for securing jobs in the state bureaucracies, where there has been a process characterized by Gordon Smith as "party infiltration" (Smith 1986, 71; see also Wildenmann 1987, 83–84).

In the early 1970s, the German political scientist Kurt Sontheimer had already expressed his concern about the pervasive system of patronage and the risk it posed of isolating the parties from ordinary German society: "The German political parties ... have tried harder than other western democracies to launch reliable people into important social and cultural organizations. The highest offices in German radio and television, in the educational system and generally the upper positions of the bureaucratic apparatus in Germany are usually given only to people who can show a membership card of a political party ... This tendency encourages career-conscious people to join parties for unpolitical motives, which hardly helps party politics ... This phenomenon ... harms the parties' image ... if the man in the street sees the party state as an 'alliance and a system of careers'" (Sontheimer 1972, 95–96).

Recently, a British scholar expressed this criticism even more strongly. Writing in 1989, Stephen Padgett condemned the "decline of party democracy" in Germany, "the sterilisation of party life" and the alienation from parties (*Parteienentfremdung*) resulting from the "top-down hierarchical character" of the German parties: "Intimate party-state relations and party patronage in the state bureaucracy meant that large numbers of civil servants joined parties for reasons of career opportunism" (Padgett 1989, 136ff.).

This was reflected in the assertion of a foundation official that "it is not possible to become a head teacher in Germany without a party card." According to this interpretation, enlarged membership need not signify voluntary adhesion or political conviction. Much party and party foundation activity may be interpreted as stemming from the efforts of party officials and employees. Following this reasoning, statistics of numbers attending residential meetings and conferences may therefore be seen not as evidence of participation but rather as a result of the efforts of well-subsidized, full-time organizers who are able to offer attractive facilities at little or no cost. "Political education" meetings of the party foundations may just be excuses for a cheap vacation or for absence from work. Alternatively, some of those attending may do so in order to advance their job prospects.

The system of party scholarships offered through the *Stiftungen* may be similarly viewed. The scholarships may be interpreted as a useful and legitimate means of encouraging participation in party activities and, in the words of the 1967 Parties Law, of "training talented people to assume public responsibilities" (Nicolls 1984, 198). Or they may be dismissed as an undesirable form of political patronage, likely to encourage careerists who may have little in common with most of their fellow students.

To critics, not only is the scale of party membership to be discounted as an indication of voluntary participation, but the existing German system of parties and associated foundations is condemned as giving too much influence to party bureaucrats. Whether measured by most transatlantic or by British standards, the main German party headquarters are impressive (Paltiel 1980b, 367). It is, however, not only the party offices, but also the political foundations that are the subject of this study. How can parties be an expression of genuine participation, it may be argued, if they are in the hands of such extensive, full-time staffs?[21]

The expansion of the political bureaucracies since the 1950s has resulted largely from the growth of public subsidies. The reliance of the German parties on the public purse is underestimated if the statistics are limited to those covering state aid to the extraparliamentary party organizations. As mentioned at the opening of this study, it is necessary to take account of state aid both to party caucuses in the legislatures and to the party foundations. In addition, some of the money funding the federal press and information office also functions as a form of political subsidy to the ruling party.

Between 1968 and 1978, for example, state aid to the extraparliamentary organizations of the parties represented in the Bundestag provided 26 percent of their combined national and local incomes. According to an internal SPD document, public funding reached 34.4 percent of total party income in the electoral cycle 1984–87. However, if public funds provided to the party foundations for domestic and for foreign purposes and to party organizations within the Bundestag and state legislatures are taken into account, as well as party contributions made by legislators from their public salaries, the proportion of the total provided by the state rises to about 60 percent for 1968–78 and to over two-thirds for the period 1984–87. If public payments for legislators' personal staffs and for the federal press and information office are included, the proportion of political money coming from the public treasury is even higher.[22]

Concern about the bureaucratic results of state aid to European parties was put forward in 1980 by Paltiel:

> The biggest immediate beneficiaries of direct cash subsidies tend to
> be the central party organizations and the party staff professionals

who serve them ... Public subventions in Austria, Canada, Finland,
Italy, Sweden, and West Germany have been accompanied by a vast
expansion in the apparatuses of the party organizations ... Increased
dependence on professional expertise has led to the relative decline
of middle-level party leaders and the restriction of party militants to
routine tasks. Austrian and West German party spokesmen have told
me that they are frequently embarrassed by the election activities of
their member-volunteers and prefer to use the professional staff of
the parties and their related foundations. (Paltiel 1980b, 367)

The party foundations play a significant part in this bureaucratization of political life and of election campaigning in Germany. The
Stiftungen have governing boards and large central staffs, but they do
not have subscribing members.

We should nevertheless guard against overestimating the consequences of public funding of the *Stiftungen* and of the party organizations. After all, reliance on pollsters and other campaign professionals
has increased in other countries, where there is little or no public funding of elections and parties. The lessening role of ordinary party members in election campaigns may be the result of technological
developments – particularly television – rather than the advent of state
subsidies.

In summary, the evidence on the participation in membership and
bureaucratization of party organizations leads to no clear conclusion.
Both supporters and opponents of the German system may use the
results to back their views.

Fairness

A basic aim of state regulation and subsidy is to produce fairness
between parties. According to this criterion, too, the West German system may initially appear to be vindicated. Not only have the budgets
of the SPD on the one hand and the CDU/CSU on the other been roughly
equal since the advent of state subsidies, but the two main parties also
receive equal amounts of aid for their party foundations. The advantages previously enjoyed by the CDU as a result of business donations
appear to have vanished. Moreover, a Constitutional Court decision of
2 March 1977 limited the use for political purposes of official advertising by government ministries. This had traditionally been a source of
indirect public subsidy for the election campaign of the ruling party.
(As already mentioned, this decision has not, in practice, eliminated
the political benefits derived by the government from the federal press
and information office.)

On closer examination, the situation is more complex than this account would suggest. This is partly because "fairness" and "equality of chances" (the term used in discussions of German constitutional law arising from the Basic Law) are open to a variety of interpretations:

Does "equality of chances" mean that all parties must be given the same amount of state financial aid? Or does it mean that the amount of money given to each party should correspond with the extent of their political support? The argument for giving all parties an equal share of subsidy is that they all require an equal opportunity to put their case to the electors. This is the principle followed in the allocation of free postal facilities to parliamentary candidates in Britain. Major and minor party candidates have equal entitlements. By contrast, it can be argued that equal treatment for major parties and for fringe groups is both impractical and would give unreasonable advantages to the latter.

If it is accepted that aid should be proportionate to a party's support in the electorate, should the amount of subsidy match the proportion of votes gained at the previous election? Alternatively, should it correspond to a party's existing support, possibly measured by opinion poll rating or by the results of recent local elections or parliamentary by-elections? During times of rapid political change these alternatives may produce significantly different patterns of subsidy. Basing subsidies on each party's performance at the last election may be criticized on the ground that it favours the status quo.

If state aid is designed to match the extent of political support, should it match the numbers of party members or small-scale subscriptions from members, rather than the number of votes obtained by the party? It can be argued that substantial inequalities of party funding are "fair" if they stem from one party's superior performance in raising money in small sums from a large number of members. Only if a party's financial advantages come from a small number of wealthy contributors should the situation be regarded as unfair. A variation of this argument is that state subsidy should not be given in proportion to a party's votes, but rather should match the amount raised by each party in small contributions from individual members.

Is it reasonable to argue that "equality of chances" demands that state aid should be directed disproportionately towards opposition parties, because ruling parties are able to use the governmental machine to project themselves?

Apart from the question of determining the nature of "fairness" between one party and another, there remains the problem of deciding what constitutes fairness between political parties on the one hand

and independent candidates on the other. (The German system of political subsidies discriminates severely against independents. There have been four independent candidates since 1950.)

Also, a system that aims to assure fairness between political parties may involve restrictions that, in effect, put parties at a disadvantage in comparison with interest groups or other organizations.

The conclusion that emerges is that the principle of "equality of chances" is riddled with ambiguity. But the problems do not end here. Even if there is agreement on what constitutes "fairness," this objective may sometimes conflict with other important goals such as political stability, avoidance of political extremism and the guarantee of free speech. There may be circumstances in which fairness needs to be abandoned in favour of these other principles.

It would seem to be impossible to devise an objective method of adjudicating these conflicts. In the real world, these difficult questions are not determined on bases of academic debate or objective reasonableness. Decisions are likely to reflect the interests of established political forces. In practice, lawmakers are likely to present lofty points of principle while consulting their pocket calculators to ensure that the implementation of the favoured principle is advantageous to their own party. As Paltiel asserted, "In every known instance, public subventions have been introduced by the parties in office. Given the nature of parliamentary regimes, this is inevitable ... It is scarcely to be expected ... that incumbents will adopt measures to their own detriment. Allied with the governmental parties are their smaller coalition parties, like the Free Democrats in Germany ... which, pressed for funds, are often the instigators of action in this field" (Paltiel 1980b, 366). Paltiel further warned that reforms of party funding thus "tend to freeze the status quo" (Paltiel 1980b, 367): "Subsidy systems and their accompanying regulations have made it difficult for new groups and individuals to enter the competitive electoral struggle and may be promoting the ossification of the party systems in certain states. To the extent that these schemes limit entry of new competitors and parties, they may well promote alienation from democratic methods of change and may stimulate recourse to extraparliamentary opposition tactics of violent confrontation by those who may feel themselves rightly or wrongly excluded from the electoral process" (Paltiel 1980b, 370).

How do these general arguments apply to Germany and to the party foundations? Do state grants to the *Stiftungen* promote an "equality of chances"? The distribution of subsidies between the foundations linked to the different parties does not correspond to their electoral support. The minor coalition parties – the FDP and the CSU – receive disproportionately large allocations, as shown in table 4.10. The disproportionately great benefits obtained by the Free Democrats from the system of state funding of party foundations is even clearer if grants are related to party membership. In this respect, as in so many others, the Free Democrats have been able to use their leverage as a coalition partner to extract the maximum of advantage from the two main parties. In the parliamentary cycle 1981–83, the "global subsidy" to the Naumann Foundation amounted to about DM500 for each member of the FDP, while total public payments to the foundation for domestic and foreign purposes totalled no less than DM2 000 per party member. This was about five times as much as the rate for the Social Democrats.[23]

While the small established parties, the FDP and the CSU, benefited disproportionately from state aid to their foundations, the Greens found themselves at a disadvantage. Parties are entitled to public subsidies for their federal campaign costs, provided that they gain 0.5 percent of the vote in federal elections. The Greens accordingly obtained these campaign subsidies from 1979 onward but remained excluded from the benefits of the *Stiftung* system. It took a challenge in the Constitutional Court to convince them to claim the same right to a publicly funded party foundation as those of the FDP and CSU. Even after this right was gained in 1986, the party faced a series of bureaucratic blockages that delayed their being able to take advantage of their new right. It was only in 1989 that the Greens started to receive any benefit from the global subsidy paid by the federal interior ministry.

It could be argued that the pattern of grants to the party foundations thus conformed to Paltiel's prediction that the status quo was being protected. Nassmacher (1989, 248) has, however, put forward a

Table 4.10

Percentage of federal subsidies to political foundations received by Naumann and Seidel foundations, compared with percentage of federal vote received by their parent parties, 1983–87

	Friedrich-Naumann-Stiftung	Hanns-Seidel-Stiftung
Percentage of federal subsidy to party foundations: 1983–86	15.4	14.3
	FDP	CSU
Percentage of votes received in Bundestag elections:		
1983	7.0	10.6
1987	9.1	9.8

Source: Based on data reported in table 4.1.

different interpretation. He points out that the German system of political funding did not block the emergence of the new party. This was partly because of the low threshold required for gaining campaign reimbursements (0.5 percent of the regional vote). This modest threshold had been set by the Constitutional Court. It was again the Constitutional Court that enabled the Greens to overcome the position taken by the established parties in 1986 and to gain the right to a publicly funded party foundation of their own.

There is nevertheless reason to believe that the new party's experience has conformed in some respects to Paltiel's interpretation. After all, the Greens did not break down the cartel of the *Stiftungen* but were co-opted into it. Their objective before the Constitutional Court in 1986 – to destroy the public funding of the party foundations – failed. Despite their apparent reluctance to accept state largesse, the Greens agreed to do so. In the period before their defeat in the 1990 Bundestag elections, the nature of the party was arguably being radically altered as a result of the professional staff it was able to employ.

Next, the crucial question of fairness between party organizations and non-party organizations. In view of the central political importance of elections and of the parties that contest them, it is hardly surprising that they are subject to special treatment in many countries. This often consists of benefits – state aid and subsidies in kind. On the other hand, it may also involve the subjection of parties to especially restrictive laws. Such regulations, frequently designed to assure fairness between candidates and parties, may have the side effect of creating inconsistencies with rules relating to other groups and individuals.

In Germany, companies are unable to claim tax exemptions for large donations to political parties, though the regulations introduced by the 1983 Parties Law are less severe than the constitutional judgement of 1958. There are special rules concerning the disclosure of payments to parties. A significant role of the party foundations in Germany has been to permit the parties to circumvent regulations and Constitutional Court rulings that apply to them but not to nonparty bodies, for the *Stiftungen* are able to escape party status. The party foundation device is the most significant method of evading the restrictions that apply to political parties but, as detailed later, it is not the only one. In practice, company donations to *Stiftungen* have generally been small.

It is open to question whether it is fair to subject parties to special restrictions. According to one view, the imposition of stringent regulations on parties alone is likely to lead to an undesirable increase in the influence of pressure groups. Whether this opinion is accepted or not, it is a simple reality that regulations that focus on candidates and parties alone are likely to lead to evasion. Just as offshore islands are used as tax havens, political foundations and similar organizations operating in the "forefield" of parties (to use a German term) are likely to be created in order to permit politicians to avoid the special limitations on parties.

The German *Stiftungen* are the prime example of such "parallel" organizations. Recent years have seen a mushrooming of politically motivated research institutes in a number of countries, including the United States and Britain. They frequently have the status of non-partisan charitable or educational bodies, even though their party connections are barely concealed. In Britain, one such organization appears to divide its activities and its funds into two parts. Whenever possible, projects are classified as "research" and are funded by a trust, donations to which are not considered "political." Only propaganda or activities directly related to it that cannot hope to escape the regulations for disclosure and tax applying to political donations are financed by payments that conform to these regulations.

The implication for policy is that special laws concerning the funding of electoral campaigns and political parties should be introduced sparingly, for they are likely to lead to inconsistencies and therefore to evasion. It was for this reason that the 1983 Parties Law created more generous tax exemptions for donations to parties. Following a 1986 Constitutional Court decision that adapted the provisions of the new law, payments to parties by individuals and by corporations became exempt from taxation, provided that they were no more than DM100 000 a year. In 1988 this exemption limit was lowered by the Bundestag to DM60 000 a year.

Another view is that consistency should be achieved by extending regulations and subsidies to non-party organizations. It has been argued, for instance, that it is of little value to limit campaign spending by candidates and parties if newspapers, often fiercely partisan, remain unregulated. Hence fairness, according to this view, requires subsidies to newspapers representing views other than those of the proprietors of the capitalist press. Alternatively, a statutory right should be given to candidates and parties to reply to attacks on them in the press.

The problem with this approach, in my opinion, is that it would require an all-embracing system of regulation and subsidy that would be inconsistent with the basic freedom of expression and probably would be unworkable in practice.

Eliminating Corruption

Germans have been particularly sensitive to the possibly corrupting influence of large payments to political parties. According to a common, though disputed, interpretation, donations from big business played a significant role in Hitler's rise to power. Removal of the taint surrounding such payments has been a major motive for Germany's regulations and subsidies relating to political funding. (See, for example, Kulitz 1983, 64.)

Foreign observers of the 1970s expressed confidence that the aims of the new funding system had been achieved. As the Houghton Committee asserted in 1976, following a visit to Germany, "it was clear that money provided from state funds was regarded as the only 'neutral' money received by the parties" (United Kingdom 1976, para. 8.32). By providing most of the parties' needs from the public purse and by giving tax incentives for small and medium-sized donations by individuals, it was intended to diminish the role of secret business contributions and thereby to eliminate the undue influence associated with them.

The revelations of the 1980s removed any previous illusions about the purity of the new system of German political finance. As Rudolf Wildenmann wrote (1987, 96), corruption relating to political donations was "blossoming" and German "practices of party finance are the dark spot of today's representative party government."

Public largesse had not provided a substitute for corporate payments. In their search for ever larger campaign budgets, the main parties had continued to solicit money from business sources. The press, in particular *Der Spiegel*, revealed an extraordinary pattern of sleaze and scandal relating to political donations. The failure to achieve a clean break from some of the funding practices associated with Hitler's rise to power was symbolized by the fact that some of the family names involved in the revelations were the same as those of leading figures of the Nazi era.

The revelations raise a number of significant points about German political finance. First, the scandals were notable not only for the large number of cases involved but also for the huge size of some of the payments that came to light and the political prominence of some of the subjects named. Scholars of comparative political finance would be hard pressed to find contributions in other Western nations on the scale of those of the Flick industrial concern's DM26 million. Second, some of the controversial political donations involved the party foundations. Third, the disclosures demonstrate that the huge public subsidies for German politics had clearly failed to eliminate corruption, at least until the mid-1980s. It may also be significant that Austria, another country that, like Germany, has a developed system of public political subsidies and political foundations, experienced serious corruption scandals relating to political payments.

The scandals of the 1980s triggered the 1983 Parties Law. The new regulations were designed to reduce the incentive for undercover political payments by introducing generous tax incentives. Since the law became effective in 1984 there has in fact been some reduction in the level of donations to the parties. This may not be a result of legal changes, however. The new law might have been expected to raise the level of donations. The apparent reluctance of some corporations to continue making political payments may be a cautious, and possibly temporary, reaction to the revelations and scandals that filled the press for much of the decade. It may also reflect a resentment by companies of the failure of attempts to introduce an amnesty for previous offences relating to political donations.

Disclosure of Political Donations

The Basic Law of the Federal German Republic laid down in Article 21 that "Political parties ... must publicly account for the sources of their funds." Until 1984, the history of the Federal German Republic was a chronicle of techniques for evading this constitutional obligation.

In the early years of the new republic, secret political funding was part and parcel of the cold war. For nearly a generation after the passage of the Basic Law in 1949, no law was enacted to give substance to its Article 21. Only with the passage of the Parties Law of 1967 (Article 25) did political parties become obliged to declare their sources of funding. Moreover, the new law – a *lex imperfecta* in the words of one scholar (Kulitz 1983, 104) – was almost totally ineffective. There was no shortage of loopholes. The motive for making secret donations was frequently tax evasion. The political will and the administrative capacity to enforce the law were both lacking, so that none of the parties represented in the Bundestag was in any position to throw stones at its opponents.

1. There was no penalty for contravening the law. It was hardly surprising that "without penalty clauses attached to the legislation, the [disclosure] rule proved hard to enforce" (Kolinsky 1984, 33).
2. The disclosure rule applied only to individual payments to a party in excess of DM20 000 per calendar year. Indeed, the legislators intended the law to exempt corporate donations up to DM200 000 a year. As Arnold Heidenheimer and Frank Langdon wrote in 1968, "this fantastically generous formula ... all but made a mockery of the disclosure provisions as a whole" (Heidenheimer and Langdon 1968, 87). It took a decision by the Constitutional Court in the same year to reduce the exception

from disclosure for corporate donations to the same DM20 000 as for individual donations (Kulitz 1983, 76).

By allowing confidential contributions up to DM20 000, the 1967 law made it possible for parties to conceal much larger payments, since they could be divided into separate donations of under DM20 000 (*Der Spiegel* 1976, 38, cited in Kulitz 1983, 91).

3. Even when donors were apparently identified, the names given were sometimes false, according to some reports. Eva Kolinsky (1984, 33) gives examples quoted by Jürgen Weber (1977) "of large amounts being given to the SPD by a Mr. Mayer, to the CDU by a Mr. Düren. The suspicion that these names are intended to conceal the financial sources rather than reveal them cannot easily be dispelled."

4. Names of donors could effectively be concealed by making political payments through intermediary organizations. Only the name of the donor body, not those of the corporations and individuals contributing to it, needed to be publicly identified by the party receiving payment.

As detailed by Duebber and Braunthal (1963, 777ff.), corporate sponsors' associations (*Förderergesellschaften*) and in particular the civic associations (*staatsbürgerliche Vereinigungen*) were already active in the 1950s and by 1963 had convinced "about half of all employers and more than 60 to 70 percent of the large corporations to support their efforts." Trade union organizations as well as employers' associations were popular as intermediaries. They provided a device for tax exemption for institutional political donations and offered the advantages of secrecy and political leverage.

Besides sponsors' associations, there were other types of intermediary bodies that could be used as funding channels. The party foundations provided one channel. Another was "political associations," namely, "party-related organizations such as the Wirtschaftsrat der CDU, the CDU Sozialausschüsse, the Heinemann-Initiative and the Fritz-Erler-Kreis of the SPD" (Schneider 1989, 223).

5. Institutional donations were sometimes laundered through foreign front organizations.

6. The political parties formed a variety of commercial enterprises from which corporations, unions, local governments and individuals could purchase services. In some cases, payments for these services could arguably be seen as disguised forms of political donations – donations that did not need to be declared as

such. Wewer (1988a) has detailed the ingenious ways in which political parties and occasionally the party foundations provided commercial cover for contributions. Costly advertisements purchased in party publications, and multiple subscriptions to economic newsletters produced by party organizations have been favourites.

Under the pressure of public criticism following the revelations of the 1980s, the committee of experts set up by the federal president, Professor Dr. Karl Carstens, produced recommendations in 1983 for a new system of regulations and subsidies that aimed to eliminate some of these loopholes and ensure a greater transparency of political funding. To make the new rules more acceptable to the established parties, the committee proposed increases in the level of public subsidies and increases in the levels of donations for which tax relief could be claimed.

The established parties in the Bundestag accepted the carrot offered by the presidential committee – namely, tax incentives for political contributions – but rejected some of the proposed sticks. For instance, the Bundestag greatly reduced the penalties proposed by the committee for illegal donations. Whereas the committee had proposed that parties caught receiving illegal donations should be subject to fines of up to 10 times the sums received, the Bundestag reduced the penalty to twice the sums received.

The new system introduced by the new Parties Law of 1983 had an unfortunate start. The publication of the very first set of party accounts under the provisions of the new law, which required all payments above DM20 000 to be listed by the name and address of the donor, had to be postponed when a press report revealed that the Free Democrats had failed to declare a donation of DM6 million (Schneider 1989, 232). The payment had been made just before the provisions of the law were due to come into force.

By 1989, when the 1983 Parties Law had been tested, Nassmacher was ready to draw a somewhat pessimistic conclusion about the declaration of the sources of political money in the Federal Republic: "The only legitimate claim to be made for the West German situation, based on the information available, is that more than half of all political money is covered by reporting. Any other estimate of how much of a party's 'combine' is revealed to the public would be premature" (Nassmacher 1989, 258).

The disclosure requirements under the terms of the 1983 Parties Law are somewhat more stringent than under the previous system, in particular because penalties, albeit modest ones, have at last been introduced for noncompliance. Also, tax concessions for political payments have been made conditional upon their publication. Nevertheless, loopholes remain.

First, donations need not be declared if they are given to the political foundations rather than to political parties. (Political foundations are, however, forbidden under the terms of the new law to transfer these donations to political parties.) Though this loophole could be enlarged in the future, the foundations' annual reports since the mid-1980s indicate low totals received as donations.

Second, a change in the law introduced in 1988 means that only payments to a party totalling over DM40 000 a year (rather than the previous DM20 000 a year) need be declared. A donor may make unpublished payments of up to DM40 000 to more than one party.

Third, a businessman may give separate nondeclarable payments to a party, not only in his own name but also in the name of a company he owns. Moreover, an industrialist who owns several subsidiary companies may give separate nondeclarable donations of up to DM40 000 for each of them. This provision, combined with the possibility of donations being made by different members of the same family, makes it possible for sizable totals to be shielded from public view.

Fourth, corporations may still disguise political contributions as commercial transactions, as before.

According to the published statistics for 1988, when the exemption from declaration was still DM20 000, only 11.9 percent of total contributions to the CDU were listed as being "large donations." For the other parties, the percentages of payments for which donor companies and individuals were publicly identified were as follows: CSU 6.3 percent, SPD 4.2 percent, FDP 9.6 percent and the Greens 20.2 percent (Drucksache 16/6885, 8).

Limiting the Costs of Politics

The costs of politics in Germany have increased sharply since the introduction of public subsidies in 1959.

In that nonelection year the national and local budgets of the three parties represented in the Bundestag totalled an estimated DM26.3 million (including public funding of some DM5 million). Donations to the party organizations (mainly to the CDU from the corporate sponsors' associations) amounted to about DM5 million (Duebber and Braunthal 1963, 779). The three main *Stiftungen* (KAS, FES, FNS) were still in their infancy, and the combined expenditures of the parties and party foundations probably did not exceed DM30–35 million.

In 1963, also a nonelection year, the combined budgets of the three party organizations more than doubled, reaching DM57 million. (Heidenheimer and Langdon 1968, 83–84).

By 1974, another nonelection year, the party budgets had reached DM230 million and those of the party foundations DM166 million, making some DM400 million in all. In 1988, the expenditures of the parties represented in the Bundestag totalled DM475 million, and in 1988–89 the four main party foundations spent an additional DM504 million. This represented a thirtyfold increase in the three decades since the introduction of public subsidies to the parties. Even when account is taken of inflation, this rise is notable.

Despite the growth of public subsidies to the parties and to the *Stiftungen*, shown in tables 4.1–4.3, the scramble for political donations has been unrelenting. Indeed, it is unrealistic to refer to the "needs" of parties as if they were finite requirements. An increased supply of funds has led to an even greater increase in parties' demands. As a result the totals raised by the parties from private sources have continued to grow, despite the advent of generous state aid.

In 1959, when state aid was still in its infancy, the Bundestag parties received private "donations," i.e., excluding membership subscriptions or payments from legislators, totalling DM6.4 million. In the election year 1961 donations totalled DM38.2 million. In the election year 1976 donations had reached DM100.2 million (Duebber and Braunthal 1963, 779; Kolinsky 1984, 34). Moreover, when account is taken of undeclared political donations in 1976, the total was probably considerably greater. The fact that the growing supply of state money failed to keep pace with party demands helps to account for the shady practices associated with the search for private donations in the 1970s mentioned previously, in the section titled "Funding and Organization."

Despite the scandals relating to political donations revealed from 1981 on, the pressure to collect donations has remained, especially as the CDU headquarters has accumulated a massive deficit. In 1989, a year when there was an election for the European Parliament but no Bundestag election and the most recent period for which statistics are available, donations to the political parties represented in the Bundestag totalled DM113.3 million (Drucksache 11/8130). This compares with DM44.6 million in the nonelection year 1977 (Kolinsky 1984, 34).

Effectiveness of Party Research and Organization

A prominent argument of those in Britain who argued in the 1970s for a German-style system of public funding of political parties was that parties could not be expected to play a proper role in public life unless they could afford to employ staffs that were sufficiently large and sufficiently well paid to provide a counterweight to the civil service. The fact that opposition parties could not afford to employ teams of researchers meant that they came into power with half-baked policies and were excessively vulnerable to the advice of their civil servants. Insufficiently staffed party headquarters were part of what Richard Rose (1975) identified as the "problem of party government."

Judgements about the quality of research and of organization produced by political staffs in different countries are difficult to make, not only because of a lack of comprehensive information but also because such judgements are inevitably subjective. The German party foundations – particularly the two largest (Ebert and Adenauer) – are certainly able to undertake projects on a scale that would be impossible for party organizations in most other countries. This applies to investigations related directly to campaigning (such as detailed voting analyses) as well as research into policy and the study of the history and organization of the political parties themselves. In the field of opinion polling, the Adenauer Foundation has the reputation of conducting some of the most advanced operations in the world.

The party foundations form a bridge between the worlds of politics and academic studies. In this respect, they resemble the functions of such bodies as the Ford and Rockefeller foundations, the Brookings Institution and the American Enterprise Institute in the United States. Indeed, the party foundations have active links with some of these organizations.

The party foundation attached to the governing party is in a good position to provide alternative advice to the chancellor when, as frequently occurs under the German system of coalitions, a particular ministry is in the hands of a minister from a different political party. The research units of the foundations are frequently in contact with the party caucuses in the Bundestag.

The main impression of those with firsthand knowledge of the foundations' research is that their influence at any time depends greatly on an interplay of personalities.[24] Whether the team responsible for opinion research at the party foundation has an important input into decision making depends on personal relationships with the equivalent unit at party headquarters and with the party leadership. The same applies to studies of domestic and foreign policy.

It is worth stressing that the influence of the party foundations' research departments is not related directly to their size or funding. The variability of influence of think-tanks in other countries also reflects access and personality. In Britain, for instance, some of the most influential political research institutes have been very small units that have relied on their close connections with the prime minister.

Despite the undoubted quality of many of their researchers, the departments do not generally appear to enjoy the prestige of some of the think-tanks in Washington. Policy makers within the German parties frequently seem to rely on research emanating from the universities, rather than from the *Stiftungen*.

CONCLUSION

The German system of political funding and, in particular, the system of party foundations can be defended and praised on several grounds:

- It has been accompanied by (and arguably has contributed to) a healthy growth in membership in three out of the four main parties.
- State aid has not led to a drop in financial contributions from ordinary party members.
- State aid did not block the emergence of a new party – the Greens.
- The two main parties in the Bundestag have broadly equal resources. Business contributions account for a far smaller proportion of the income of the parties and of the party foundations than before the introduction of state aid.
- The party foundations have played a role in fulfilling the stated aims of the Parties Law of 1967 to promote civic education, especially among students. They have provided a base for high-level policy research. In the field of foreign affairs, the projects undertaken by the party foundations have frequently been effective in promoting the cause of democracy as well as the German national interest.

There are contrary arguments. In contrast to the optimistic assessments of some foreigners, German scholars, commentators and many members of the general public have become cynical about aspects of the German "party state." Despite the escalation of public funding for various political purposes, including a current total of about DM500 million a year for the party foundations alone, the undesirable features traditionally associated with political funding in Germany have not disappeared. Political funding again emerged in the 1980s as a notable source of corruption and of undue influence, partly as a result of the fact that state aid had failed to act as a substitute for large private payments.

The German parties have excelled in devising ways to sidestep the regulation of political money, and because of their obstruction, there has been no serious effort to make political donations a matter of public record. The system of public funding of the domestic activities of the party foundations was itself a method for evading limitations on state aid to parties imposed in 1966 by the Constitutional Court.

Ever-expanding public subsidy has been associated with a system of party management that may be seen as top heavy and that left too small a role for the voluntary initiatives of members. The party foundations have possibly contributed to this process of bureaucratization. A related disadvantage is that the party system has relied excessively on job patronage. Moreover, the privileges enjoyed collectively by the party bureaucracies tended to make them into a club or cartel with greater common interests with each other than with their members.

The established system also may be criticized for allowing one of the parties – the Free Democratic Party – to retain advantages wholly disproportionate to its number of voters or its number of members. Without its access to job patronage, to state aid (including, notably, aid to its party foundation) and to corporate finance, it is open to question whether the party could have survived.

Finally, the system of public funding through party foundations raises questions about what Paltiel referred to as the danger of "neo-corporatism" (Paltiel 1979, 37). Paltiel expressed concern as early as 1979 about the wide-ranging activities of the German party foundations. According to this view, the state ought not to pay the parties or the churches to give scholarships to their adherents. It would be better to fund universities rather than party-linked institutes to carry out policy research. The "identification of party and state has, as we all know, serious implications for democracy" (ibid., 30).

Quite apart from the substantive merits and defects of its system of public financing for parties and party foundations, the German example is relevant to discussions about the regulation of political funding for another reason. The system of political foundations permits an evasion of the restrictions on the public funding of parties imposed by the Constitutional Court. It therefore serves as a warning for other countries that regulations directed towards electoral candidates and towards political parties may merely lead to an expansion of alternative channels for political money. This applies equally to the regulations relating to the publication of donations and to restrictions upon payments.

NOTES

1. As described later, parts of the Chancellor's Office and of the federal press and information office are additional political bureaucracies for the governing party.

2. "Political education" involved policies of the Allied occupying powers relating to schools and youth groups as well as adult organizations. See Turner (1984).

3. The Bundeszentrale für politische Bildung is a typical product of the German "party state" that will be described in later sections. Its funds come from the government (BMI). It has three directors, one drawn from each of the main parties represented in the Bundestag (CDU/CSU, SPD and FDP), and its board consists largely of members of the Bundestag from all parties. Its main current function is to produce publications and to finance seminars. Some of the publications are supplied free of cost and in large quantities to schools. They cover such topics as the foundation of the Federal German Republic, ethnic German populations in Central Europe, party democracy, Germans and Poles, and the history of the Jewish people. The Bundeszentrale also produces a newspaper, *Das Parlament*, and an academic politics journal, *Aus Politik und Zeitgeschichte*. The organization spent DM7.2 million in 1989 on subsidies for political education courses run by the political foundations, as well as by church and trade union organizations (Bundeszentrale für politische Bildung 1990, 62).

4. Information from an FES official.

5. In order to stress the legal boundary between the parties and their foundations, the *Stiftungen* are normally referred to in official publications as "political" foundations. In this study, the terms "political foundations" and "party foundations" will be used interchangeably.

6. An account of the financial transactions involved in the FNS's move to the Margarethenhof is given in Wewer (1988a).

7. Statistics of the staffing levels of the party foundations in 1975 are given in Vieregge (1975, 35). Vieregge's study gives the fullest available scholarly account of the party foundations in the mid-1970s and contains particular details about the Friedrich Naumann Foundation.

8. The memberships and roles of the Konrad Adenauer Foundation's governing boards are detailed in Deussen, chap. 4 and 6.

9. The Bundeszentrale für politische Bildung reports that it, too, has made no recent assessment of the effectiveness of political education. There is a detailed discussion of political education, including articles by officials of the party foundations and of religious organizations as well as by academics, in *Das Parlament*, 39/34, 18 August 1989.

10. Information supplied by the Konrad Adenauer Foundation.

11. Information from a senior member of the scholarship selection committee.

12. *Federal Education Promotion Act*, 1971.

13. This was reported by a Naumann official with reference to past practice.

14. The following examples of its influence on Free Democrat policy were suggested by the Friedrich Naumann Foundation: on constitutional reform arising from German unification and on the introduction of free market principles into environmental policy. Apart from policy making, the research department's work on Liberalism is intended, as with similar work by other party foundations, to foster the party's sense of historical identity and its image. The work of the *Stiftung* in the area of polling is also linked with that of the party. The party and the party foundation both use the same market research agency, and its work for both is frequently "closely coordinated." The foundation's poll analyses are circulated "to almost every important person in the party."

15. These activities are analysed in Pinto-Duschinsky (1991).

16. Information from a member of the Chancellor's Office.

17. In reply to a question as to whether a committee of the party rather than of the *Stiftung* had remitted the DDR task force's draft, I was informed that though it was apparently the party that had done so, it did not really make a great difference, since there was such an overlap of members on the boards of the two bodies.

18. This point was made by a member of the Chancellor's Office and by others.

19. Some of these objectives were set out in Andren (1970, 54).

20. For a detailed study of political funding within Austria, see Sickinger and Nick (1990).

21. It was suggested by Paltiel and especially by Leonard that the problem of bureaucratization may be minimized if state payments are directed to local and regional party organizations rather than to the centre. The Swedish model is frequently cited as an example. It is unclear whether the decentralization of state payments meets the problem.

22. The importance of state aid to the parliamentary caucuses and to the party foundations also emerges from Nassmacher's study (1989, 244). State aid to the party organizations between 1974 and 1985 totalled DM677 million. This was less than the subsidy for the parliamentary caucuses and to the *Stiftungen,* which amounted to DM1 019 million during the same period (including DM392.2 million to parliamentary groups and DM626.4 million in global subsidies to the party foundations). Moreover, the statistics include only the global subsidy to the party foundations. If other categories of federal government grants to the *Stiftungen* for domestic and overseas purposes are also included, the total granted to the parliamentary caucuses and to the *Stiftungen* during these years rises to no less than DM3 442.7 million.

It is arguable that public funding tied to foreign projects of the party foundations should be excluded from the calculation. What is beyond dispute is that state aid to the extraparliamentary party organizations is only the large tip of an even larger iceberg of state aid to party politics in Germany.

Apart from the categories of public funding included in the text, other forms of political subsidy would also need to be taken into account in order to give a comprehensive total. (a) Successive German governments have, according to some reports, continued to use ministerial information budgets for what may be seen as campaign uses. A CDU survey, cited by Eva Kolinsky (1984, 33), reported that DM122 million had been spent via the information funds of the federal ministries during the election year of 1972. In 1976 and 1980, too, "the SPD was accused of drawing on official resources and government facilities for its election campaigns" (Kolinsky 1984, 34). (b) Another form of public assistance to politics is the provision of facilities for free campaign broadcasts (Nassmacher 1989, 240). (c) The value of tax deductions for political donations would also need to be taken into account. According to Nassmacher (1989, 240), this totalled at least DM400 million between 1968 and 1983. (d) German parties and their elected representatives also receive a variety of payments from European Community sources.

23. The equivalent rates of subsidy per party member for the other party foundations were as follows: CSU (HSS) DM210 (global subsidy only) and DM620 (all domestic and foreign budget titles); CDU (KAS) DM120 and DM460; SPD DM100 and DM380.

24. Officials in one of the party foundations stated that they were ignored by one of the most important of the party's leaders. Another foundation clearly enjoyed intimate and influential relationships with the party leadership.

SOURCES AND REFERENCES

This study has been based mainly on unpublished and published documents of the political foundations, including their annual reports, and on interviews. These were carried out in 1989 and 1990, and the information used in the study is part of a larger project, which also included research into the foundations' international activities. Most of the interviews were with present and former officials of the Adenauer, Ebert and Naumann foundations. Additional interviews included officials of the Seidel Foundation, the SPD and CDU, the Chancellor's Office, the Bundeszentrale für politische Bildung and trustees of the *Stiftungen*. I alone am responsible for the opinions expressed and for any factual errors.

The following list of references does not include the annual reports of the political foundations cited in the text. The list also excludes Drucksachen (official publications of the Bundestag), which are cited in the text by their Drucksache numbers.

Alemann, Ulrich von. 1989. "Bureaucratic and Political Corruption Controls: Reassessing the German Record." In *Political Corruption: A Handbook*, ed. Arnold J. Heidenheimer, Michael Johnston and Victor T. LeVine. New Brunswick: Transaction Books.

Andren, Nils. 1970. "Partisan Motivations and Concern for System Legitimacy in the Scandinavian Deliberations on Public Subsidies." In *Comparative Political Finance: The Financing of Party Organizations and Election Campaigns*, ed. Arnold J. Heidenheimer. Lexington: D.C. Heath.

Blankenburg, Erhard, Rainer Standhammer and Heinz Steinert. 1989. "Political Scandals and Corruption Issues in West Germany." In *Political Corruption: A Handbook*, ed. Arnold J. Heidenheimer, Michael Johnston and Victor T. LeVine. New Brunswick: Transaction Books.

Bundeszentrale für politische Bildung. 1988, 1990. *Tätigkeitsbericht* 1987 and 1989. Bonn: Bundeszentrale für politische Bildung.

Deussen, Gigo. 1979. *Konrad-Adenauer-Stiftung*. Düsseldorf: Droste Verlag.

Duebber, Ulrich, and Gerard Braunthal. 1963. "West Germany." In *Comparative Political Finance: A Symposium*, ed. Richard Rose and Arnold J. Heidenheimer. *Journal of Politics* 25:774–89.

Ewing, Keith. 1987. *The Funding of Political Parties in Britain*. Cambridge: Cambridge University Press.

Fletcher, Raymond. 1978. "The Other Post-War German Miracle." *The Times*, 3 April.

Forrester, Veronica. 1985. "The German Political Foundations." In *EEC and the Third World: A Survey. Vol. 5, Pressure Groups, Politics and Development*, ed. Christopher Stevens and Joan Verloren van Themat. London: Hodder and Stoughton.

Friedrich-Ebert-Stiftung. 1989. *Friedrich-Ebert-Stiftung*. Bonn: Friedrich-Ebert-Stifung. (English-language booklet.)

Friedrich Naumann Foundation. 1988. *Friedrich Naumann Foundation*. Königswinter: Friedrich Naumann Foundation. (English-language brochure.)

———. 1989a. *Aims and Activities*. Königswinter: Friedrich Naumann Foundation. (English-language brochure.)

———. 1989b. *Themen und Termine: Veranstaltungsprogramm Juli-Dezember 1989*. Königswinter: Friedrich Naumann Stiftung.

Germany. *Basic Law for the Federal Republic of Germany* [Constitution], 1949, Article 21.

———. *Federal Education Promotion Act*, 1971.

———. *Parties Law*, 1967, Article 25.

————. *Parties Law*, 1983.

Haungs, Peter. 1983. "Die Christlich-Demokratische Union Deutschlands (CDU) und die Christlich-Soziale Union in Bayern (CSU)." In *Christlich-Demokratische und konservative Parteien in Westeuropa*, ed. Hans-Joachim Veen. Paderborn: Schöningh.

Heidenheimer, Arnold J. 1957. "German Party Finance: The CDU." *American Political Science Review* 51:369–85.

Heidenheimer, Arnold J., and Frank C. Langdon. 1968. *Business Associations and the Financing of Political Parties: A Comparative Study of the Evolution of Practices in Germany, Norway and Japan*. The Hague: Martinus Nijhoff.

Kitzinger, Uwe W. 1960. *German Electoral Politics: A Study of the 1957 Campaign*. Oxford: Oxford University Press.

Kolinsky, Eva. 1984. *Parties, Opposition and Society in West Germany*. London: Croom Helm.

Konrad-Adenauer-Stiftung. 1990a. "Geschäftsbericht, 1989." Sankt Augustin: Konrad-Adenauer-Stiftung.

————. Institut für politische Bildung. 1990b. Programm 1/91. Wesseling: Konrad-Adenauer-Stiftung.

Kress, Roland. 1985. *Die politischen Stiftungen in der Entwicklungspolitik: Eine Analyse der Kooperation von Friedrich-Ebert-Stiftung und Konrad-Adenauer-Stiftung mit politischen Partnern in Entwicklungsländern*. Bochum: Studienverlag Dr. N. Brockmeyer.

Kulitz, Peter. 1983. *Unternehmerspenden an politische Parteien*. Berlin: Duncker and Humblot.

Leonard, Dick. 1975. *Paying for Party Politics: The Case for Public Subsidies*. London: Political and Economic Planning.

————. 1979. "Contrasts in Selected Western Democracies: Germany, Sweden, Britain." In *Political Finance*, ed. Herbert E. Alexander. Beverly Hills: Sage Publications.

Nassmacher, Karl-Heinz. 1989. "Structure and Impact of Public Subsidies to Political Parties in Europe: The Examples of Austria, Italy, Sweden and West Germany." In *Comparative Political Finance in the 1980s*, ed. Herbert E. Alexander. Cambridge: Cambridge University Press.

Nicolls, Anthony. 1984. "Political Parties." In *Politics and Government in the Federal Republic of Germany: Basic Documents*, ed. Carl-Christoph Schweitzer et al. Leamington Spa: Berg.

Padgett, Stephen. 1989. "The Party System." In *Developments in German Politics*, ed. Gordon Smith, William E. Paterson and Peter H. Merkl. London: Macmillan.

Paltiel, Khayyam Z. 1979. "The Impact of Election Expenses Legislation in Canada, Western Europe, and Israel." In *Political Finance*, ed. Herbert E. Alexander. Beverly Hills: Sage Publications.

———. 1980a. "Campaign Finance: Contrasting Practices and Reforms." In *Democracy at the Polls: A Comparative Study of Competitive National Elections*, ed. David Butler, Howard R. Penniman and Austin Ranney. Washington, DC: American Enterprise Institute for Public Policy Research.

———. 1980b. "Public Financing Abroad: Contrasts and Effects." In *Parties, Interest Groups, and Campaign Finance Laws*, ed. Michael J. Malbin. Washington, DC: American Enterprise Institute for Public Policy Research.

Pinto-Duschinsky, Michael. 1981. *British Political Finance, 1830–1980*. Washington, DC: American Enterprise Institute for Public Policy Research.

———. 1991. "Foreign Political Aid: The German Political Foundations and their U.S. Counterparts." *International Affairs* 67:33–63.

Rose, Richard. 1975. *The Problem of Party Government*. New York: Free Press.

Schleth, Uwe, and Michael Pinto-Duschinsky. 1970. "Why Public Subsidies Have Become the Major Sources of Party Funding in West Germany but Not in Great Britain." In *Comparative Political Finance: The Financing of Party Organizations and Election Campaigns*, ed. Arnold J. Heidenheimer. Lexington: D.C. Heath.

Schneider, Hans-Peter. 1989. "The New German System of Party Funding: The Presidential Committee Report of 1983 and its Realization." In *Comparative Political Finance in the 1980s*, ed. Herbert E. Alexander. Cambridge: Cambridge University Press.

Schönbohm, Wulf. 1985. *Die CDU wird moderne Volkspartei: Selbstverständnis, Mitglieder, Organization und Apparat 1950–1980*. Stuttgart: Klett-Cotta.

Schürmann, Maximilian. 1989. *Zwischen Partnerschaft und politischem Auftrag: Fallstudie zur entwicklungpolitischen Tätigeit der Konrad-Adenauer-Stiftung*. Saarbrücken: Verlag Breitenbach.

Seidle, F. Leslie. 1980. "State Aid for Political Parties." *The Parliamentarian* 61:79–86.

Sickinger, Hubert, and Rainer Nick. 1990. *Politisches Geld: Parteienfinanzierung in Österreich*. Thaur, Tirol: Kulturverlag.

Smith, Gordon. 1986. *Democracy in Western Germany: Parties and Politics in the Federal Republic*. Aldershot: Gower.

Sontheimer, Kurt. 1972. *The Government and Politics of West Germany*. London: Hutchinson.

Tsatsos, Dimitros Th., and Martin Morlok. 1982. *Parteienrecht: Eine verfassungsrechtliche Einführung*. Heidelberg: C.F. Müller Juristischer Verlag.

Turner, I.D. 1984. "British Occupation Policy and Its Effects on the Town of Wolfsburg and the Volkswagenwerk, 1945–1949." Ph.D. diss., University of Manchester, Institute of Science and Technology.

United Kingdom. Parliament. Committee on Financial Aid to Political Parties. 1976. *Report*. Cmnd. 6601. August 1976 (The Houghton Report).

Vieregge, Henning von. 1977. *Parteistiftungen: Zur Rolle der Konrad-Adenauer-, Friedrich-Ebert-, Friedrich-Naumann- und Hanns-Seidel-Stiftungen im politischen System der Bundesrepublik Deutschland*. Baden-Baden: Nomos Verlagsgesellschaft.

Watson, Alan. 1978. *The Political Foundations in West Germany*. London: Anglo-German Foundation.

Weber, Jürgen. 1977. *Interessengruppen im politischen System der Bundesrepublik Deutschland*. Stuttgart: Kohlhammer.

Wewer, Göttrik. 1988a. "Structure and Function of Party-owned Enterprises." Paper presented to the World Congress of the International Political Science Association, Washington, DC.

―――. 1988b. "Transnational and International Political Funding Illustrations." Paper presented to the World Congress of the International Political Science Association, Washington, DC.

Wildenmann, Rudolf. 1987. "The Party Government of the Federal Republic of Germany: Form and Experience." In *Party Governments: European and American Experiences*, ed. Richard S. Katz. Berlin: Walter de Gruyter.

CONTRIBUTORS TO VOLUME 4

Herbert E. Alexander University of Southern California
Jane Jenson Carleton University
Robert E. Mutch Washington, DC
Michael Pinto-Duschinsky Brunel College, The University
  of West London, UK

ACKNOWLEDGEMENTS

The Royal Commission on Electoral Reform and Party Financing and the publishers wish to acknowledge with gratitude the permission of the following publisher to reprint and translate material from its works:

D.C. Heath and Company.

Care has been taken to trace the ownership of copyright material used in the text, including the tables and figures. The authors and publishers welcome any information enabling them to rectify any reference or credit in subsequent editions.

Consistent with the Commission's objective of promoting full participation in the electoral system by all segments of Canadian society, gender neutrality has been used wherever possible in the editing of the research studies.

THE COLLECTED RESEARCH STUDIES*

---

* The titles of studies may not be final in all cases.

VOLUME 9
Aboriginal Peoples and Electoral Reform in Canada
Robert A. Milen, Editor

ROBERT A. MILEN	Aboriginal Constitutional and Electoral Reform
AUGIE FLERAS	Aboriginal Electoral Districts for Canada: Lessons from New Zealand
VALERIE ALIA	Aboriginal Peoples and Campaign Coverage in the North
ROGER GIBBINS	Electoral Reform and Canada's Aboriginal Population: An Assessment of Aboriginal Electoral Districts

VOLUME 10
Democratic Rights and Electoral Reform in Canada
Michael Cassidy, Editor

JENNIFER SMITH	The Franchise and Theories of Representative Government
PIERRE LANDREVILLE AND LUCIE LEMONDE	Voting Rights for Inmates
YVES DENONCOURT	Reflections concerning Criteria for the Vote for Persons with Mental Disorders
PATRICE GARANT	Political Rights of Public Servants in the Political Process
KENNETH KERNAGHAN	The Political Rights of Canada's Federal Public Servants
PETER MCCORMICK	Provision for the Recall of Elected Officials: Parameters and Prospects
DAVID MAC DONALD	Referendums and Federal General Elections
JOHN C. COURTNEY AND DAVID E. SMITH	Registering Voters: Canada in a Comparative Context
CÉCILE BOUCHER	Administration and Enforcement of the Elections Act in Canada

VOLUME 11

Drawing the Map: Equality and Efficacy of the Vote in Canadian Electoral Boundary Reform
David Small, Editor

KENT ROACH	One Person, One Vote? Canadian Constitutional Standards for Electoral Distribution and Districting
HOWARD A. SCARROW	Apportionment, Districting and Representation in the United States
ALAN STEWART	Community of Interest in Redistricting
MUNROE EAGLES	Enhancing Relative Vote Equality in Canada: The Role of Electors in Boundary Adjustment
DOUG MACDONALD	Ecological Communities and Constituency Districting
ALAN FRIZZELL	In the Public Service: Representation in Modern Canada
DAVID SMALL	Enhancing Aboriginal Representation within the Existing System of Redistricting

VOLUME 12

Political Ethics: A Canadian Perspective
Janet Hiebert, Editor

PIERRE FORTIN	Ethical Issues in the Debate on Reform of the *Canada Elections Act:* An Ethicological Analysis
VINCENT LEMIEUX	Public Sector Ethics
IAN GREENE	Allegations of Undue Influence in Canadian Politics
WALTER I. ROMANOW, WALTER C. SODERLUND AND RICHARD G. PRICE	Negative Political Advertising: An Analysis of Research Findings in Light of Canadian Practice
JANE JENSON	Citizenship and Equity: Variations across Time and in Space
KATHY L. BROCK	Fairness, Equity and Rights
JANET HIEBERT	A Code of Ethics for Political Parties

VOLUME 13

Canadian Political Parties: Leaders, Candidates and Organization
   Herman Bakvis, Editor

KEITH A. ARCHER	Leadership Selection in the New Democratic Party
GEORGE PERLIN	Attitudes of Liberal Convention Delegates toward Proposals for Reform of the Process of Leadership Selection
R. KENNETH CARTY AND LYNDA ERICKSON	Candidate Nomination in Canada's National Political Parties
WILLIAM M. CHANDLER AND ALAN SIAROFF	Parties and Party Government in Advanced Democracies
RÉJEAN PELLETIER	The Structures of Canadian Political Parties: How They Operate
KEITH A. ARCHER	The New Democrats, Organized Labour and the Prospects of Electoral Reform

VOLUME 14

Representation, Integration and Political Parties in Canada
   Herman Bakvis, Editor

DAVID J. ELKINS	Parties as National Institutions: A Comparative Study
MAUREEN COVELL	Parties as Institutions of National Governance
RAND DYCK	Links between Federal and Provincial Parties and Party Systems
PAUL G. THOMAS	Parties and Regional Representation
DONALD E. BLAKE	Party Competition and Electoral Volatility: Canada in Comparative Perspective
JOHN FEREJOHN AND BRIAN GAINES	The Personal Vote in Canada
S.L. SUTHERLAND	The Consequences of Electoral Volatility: Inexperienced Ministers 1949–90
NEIL NEVITTE	New Politics, the Charter and Political Participation

VOLUME 19

Media, Elections and Democracy
  Frederick J. Fletcher, Editor

JACQUES GERSTLÉ	Election Communication in France
HOLLI A. SEMETKO	Broadcasting and Election Communication in Britain
KLAUS SCHOENBACH	Mass Media and Election Campaigns in Germany
KAREN SIUNE	Campaign Communication in Scandinavia
JOHN WARHURST	Campaign Communication in Australian Elections
DORIS A. GRABER	The Mass Media and Election Campaigns in the United States of America
FREDERICK J. FLETCHER AND ROBERT EVERETT	Mass Media and Elections in Canada

VOLUME 20

Reaching the Voter: Constituency Campaigning in Canada
  David V. J. Bell and Frederick J. Fletcher, Editors

DAVID V. J. BELL AND FREDERICK J. FLETCHER	Electoral Communication at the Constituency Level: A Framework for Analysis
ANTHONY M. SAYERS	Local Issue Space at National Elections: Kootenay West–Revelstoke and Vancouver Centre
ANDREW BEH AND ROGER GIBBINS	The Campaign–Media Interface in Local Constituencies: Two Alberta Case Studies from the 1988 Federal Election Campaign
DAVID V. J. BELL AND CATHERINE M. BOLAN	The Mass Media and Federal Election Campaigning at the Local Level: A Case Study of Two Ontario Constituencies
LUC BERNIER	Local Campaigns and the Media: The 1988 Election in Outremont and Frontenac
LEONARD PREYRA	Riding the Waves: Parties, the Media and the 1988 Federal Election in Nova Scotia

VOLUME 23
Canadian Political Parties in the Constituencies:
A Local Perspective

R. KENNETH CARTY   Canadian Political Parties in the
                                    Constituencies: A Local Perspective

COMMISSION ORGANIZATION

CHAIRMAN
Pierre Lortie

COMMISSIONERS
Pierre Fortier
Robert Gabor
William Knight
Lucie Pépin

SENIOR OFFICERS

Executive Director
Guy Goulard

Director of Research
Peter Aucoin

Special Adviser to the Chairman
Jean-Marc Hamel

Research
F. Leslie Seidle,
  Senior Research Coordinator

Coordinators
Herman Bakvis
Michael Cassidy
Frederick J. Fletcher
Janet Hiebert
Kathy Megyery
Robert A. Milen
David Small

Assistant Coordinators
David Mac Donald
Cheryl D. Mitchell

Legislation
Jules Brière, Senior Adviser
Gérard Bertrand
Patrick Orr

Communications and Publishing
Richard Rochefort, Director
Hélène Papineau, Assistant
  Director
Paul Morisset, Editor
Kathryn Randle, Editor

Finance and Administration
Maurice R. Lacasse, Director

Contracts and Personnel
Thérèse Lacasse, Chief

EDITORIAL, DESIGN AND PRODUCTION SERVICES

ROYAL COMMISSION ON ELECTORAL REFORM AND PARTY FINANCING

Editors   Denis Bastien, Susan Becker Davidson, Ginette Bertrand, Louis Bilodeau, Claude Brabant, Louis Chabot, Danielle Chaput, Norman Dahl, Carlos del Burgo, Julie Desgagners, Chantal Granger, Volker Junginger, Denis Landry, André LaRose, Paul Morisset, Christine O'Meara, Mario Pelletier, Marie-Noël Pichelin, Kathryn Randle, Georges Royer, Eve Valiquette, Dominique Vincent.

LE CENTRE DE DOCUMENTATION JURIDIQUE DU QUÉBEC INC.

Hubert Reid, *President*

Claire Grégoire, *Comptroller*

Lucie Poirier, *Production Manager*
Gisèle Gingras, *Special Project Assistant*

Translators   Pierre-Yves de la Garde, Richard Lapointe, Marie-Josée Turcotte.

Technical Editors   Stéphane Côté Coulombe, *Coordinator*;
Josée Chabot, Danielle Morin.

Copy Editors   Martine Germain, Lise Larochelle, Elisabeth Reid, Carole St-Louis, Isabelle Tousignant, Charles Tremblay, Sébastien Viau.

Word Processing   André Vallée.

Formatting   Typoform, Claude Audet; Linda Goudreau, *Formatting Coordinator.*

WILSON & LAFLEUR LTÉE

Claude Wilson, *President*

DUNDURN PRESS

J. Kirk Howard, *President*
Ian Low, *Comptroller*
Jeanne MacDonald, *Project Coordinator*

Avivah Wargon, *Managing and Production Editor*
Beth Ediger, *Managing Editor*
John St. James, *Managing Editor*
Karen Heese, *Special Project Assistant*

Ruth Chernia, *Tables Editor*
Victoria Grant, *Legal Editor*
Kathleen Harris, *Senior Proofreader*

Editorial Staff   Michèle Breton, Elliott Chapin, Peggy Foy, Elizabeth Mitchell, John Shoesmith, Nadine Stoikoff, Anne Vespry.

Copy Editors   Carol Anderson, Elizabeth d'Anjou, Jane Becker, Diane Brassolotto, Elizabeth Driver, Curtis Fahey, Tony Fairfield, Freya Godard, Frances Hanna, Andria Hourwich, Greg Ioannou, Carlotta Lemieux, Elsha Leventis, David McCorquodale, Virginia Smith, Gail Thorson, Louise Wood.

Formatting   Green Graphics; Joanne Green, *Formatting Coordinator;* *Formatters*   Linda Carroll, Mary Ann Cattral, Gail Nina, Eva Payne, Jacqueline Hope Raynor, Carla Vonn Worden, Laura Wilkins.

Printed and bound in Canada by
Best Gagné Book Manufacturers